Springer Proceedings in Business and Economics

Springer Proceedings in Business and Economics brings the most current research presented at conferences and workshops to a global readership. The series features volumes (in electronic and print formats) of selected contributions from conferences in all areas of economics, business, management, and finance. In addition to an overall evaluation by the publisher of the topical interest, scientific quality, and timeliness of each volume, each contribution is refereed to standards comparable to those of leading journals, resulting in authoritative contributions to the respective fields. Springer's production and distribution infrastructure ensures rapid publication and wide circulation of the latest developments in the most compelling and promising areas of research today.

The editorial development of volumes may be managed using Springer Nature's innovative EquinOCS, a proven online conference proceedings submission, management and review system. This system is designed to ensure an efficient timeline for your publication, making Springer Proceedings in Business and Economics the premier series to publish your workshop or conference volume.

This book series is indexed in SCOPUS.

Richard C. Geibel · Shalva Machavariani
Editors

Chances and Challenges of Digital Management

Proceedings of the International Scientific-Practical Conference (ISPC 2022)

Springer

Editors
Richard C. Geibel
E-Commerce Institute Cologne
Cologne, Germany

Shalva Machavariani
East European University
Tbilisi, Georgia

ISSN 2198-7246 ISSN 2198-7254 (electronic)
Springer Proceedings in Business and Economics
ISBN 978-3-031-45600-8 ISBN 978-3-031-45601-5 (eBook)
https://doi.org/10.1007/978-3-031-45601-5

This Springer imprint is published by the registered company Springer Nature Switzerland AG
The registered company address is: Gewerbestrasse 11, 6330 Cham, Switzerland

Paper in this product is recyclable.

Preface

The book is compiled from 22 scientific papers of the "International Scientific-Practical Conference (ISPC 2022)" held on November 4, 2022, of which 8 articles are from the session "Digitalization in Business", 7 articles from the session "Digitalization in Society", and 7 articles from the session "Digitalization in Education".

ISPC 2022 is the successful sequel to **ISPC 2021**, which focused on "Digital Management in COVID-19 Pandemic and Post-Pandemic Times". The conference proceedings have also been published in this series.

ISPC 2023 is scheduled for November 24–25, 2023, and will be dedicated to "Digital Management to Shape the Future". It is scheduled as a hybrid conference at the East European University and will be held in Tbilisi, Georgia.

The ISPC conference series is supported and facilitated by these partner institutions:

- E-Commerce Institute, Cologne, Germany
- East European University, Tbilisi, Georgia
- Adelphi University, New York, Garden City, USA
- Entrepreneurship Association FGF, Krefeld, Germany
- Friedrich Ebert Foundation, Tbilisi, Georgia

ISPC 2024 is planned for October 2024, and will focus on the important topic of "Digital Management and Artificial Intelligence". The conference is expected to take place at STARTPLATZ or at IU in Cologne, Germany.

Cologne, Germany
Tbilisi, Georgia

Richard C. Geibel
Professor at IU International University of Applied Sciences, Professor h.c. at East European University
Managing Director at E-Commerce Institute

Shalva Machavariani
Vice-Rector for Scientific Affairs at East European University

Contents

Contributors

Ulrich Arnold Gkv Informatik, Wuppertal, Germany

Nana Aslamazishvili National Bank of Georgia, Tbilisi, Georgia

Christin Barreira Klaas Management, Lingen, Germany

Stefan Gablowski gkv informatik GbR, Wuppertal, Germany

Richard C. Geibel E-Commerce Institute, Cologne, Germany; East European University, Tbilisi, Georgia

Tatia Gherkenashvili Department of Scientific Research and Development, East European University, Tbilisi, Georgia

Miranda Gogilashvili East European University, Tbilisi, Georgia

Giorgi Gulua Tbilisi State University, Tbilisi, Georgia

Vanessa Hering gkv informatik GbR, Wuppertal, Germany

Vasil Kikutadze East European University, Tbilisi, Georgia

Yeelen Knegtering CEO Klippa, Cologne, Germany

Tobias Oskar Lassmann E-Commerce Institut, Cologne, Germany

Tamta Lekishvili East European University, Tbilisi, Georgia

Shalva Machavariani Doctor of Technical Science, East European University, Tbilisi, Georgia

Temur Maisuradze Doctor of Science, Eats European University, Tbilisi, Georgia

Ana Medzmariashvili Faculty of Law and Social Sciences, East European University, Tbilisi, Georgia

Hendrik Müller University of Applied Sciences Fresenius, Idstein, Germany

Christoph Neu E-Commerce Institut, Cologne, Germany

Thaarun Palaniappan Airbus, Hamburg, Germany

Ana Palavandishvili Institute of Hydrometeorology, Georgian Technical University, Tbilisi, Georgia;
Vakhushti Bagrationi Institute of Geography of Tbilisi State University, Tbilisi, Georgia

Oliver Reinking Reinking Consulting, Lingen, Germany

Linus Roggenkamp Fresenius University of Applied Sciences, Hamburg, Germany

David Sikharulidze East European University, Tbilisi, Georgia;
International Black Sea University, Tbilisi, Georgia

Davit Sikharulidze East European University, Tbilisi, Georgia

Florian Studener E-Commerce Institute, Cologne, Germany

Nikoloz Suknidze Institute of Hydrometeorology, Georgian Technical University, Tbilisi, Georgia;
Vakhushti Bagrationi Institute of Geography of Tbilisi State University, Tbilisi, Georgia

Marika Tatishvili Institute of Hydrometeorology, Georgian Technical University, Tbilisi, Georgia

Antonia F. Terriuolo Dusseldorf, Germany

Mikheil Tokmazishvili Faculty of Engineering and Business, East European University, Tbilisi, Georgia

Gvantsa Tsikhiseli East European University, Tbilisi, Georgia;
International Black Sea University, Tbilisi, Georgia

Mariam Tsitsagi Institute of Hydrometeorology, Georgian Technical University, Tbilisi, Georgia;
Vakhushti Bagrationi Institute of Geography of Tbilisi State University, Tbilisi, Georgia

Mariam Tvaradze East European University, Tbilisi, Georgia

Markus Vom Scheidt gkv informatik GbR, Wuppertal, Germany

Digitalization in Business

The Potential of a Large IT Service Company for Digitization in the German Healthcare Market

Ulrich Arnold and Richard C. Geibel

Abstract The digitization of healthcare is advancing worldwide. The COVID19 pandemic has reinforced the trend while patients increasingly expect and use digital offerings, legislators and providers are scrambling to find solutions to promote and fund digital health solutions. Used correctly, digitization can help achieve four important goals: higher quality of care, greater cost efficiency, an improved patient experience, and an optimized work experience for healthcare staff. Germany has also embarked on the path of digitization: telemedicine, the billing of digital health applications (DiGA), online appointment bookings, electronic patient records (ePA) and e-prescriptions are just a few examples of the digital transformation in the German healthcare system. Nevertheless, not all the potential in this country has been tapped by a long shot. According to a study by McKinsey, the potential benefits of digitization in the German healthcare system have increased significantly in recent years and currently amount to around EUR 42 billion p.a. This is almost a quarter more than the EUR 34 billion in 2018. This noticeable increase is attributable to three influencing factors in total: In the realization of benefits, initial successes have been achieved in recent years, but not yet any drastic ones. The benefits realized are also offset by significantly stronger growth in healthcare spending. In addition, it has become apparent that some technologies promise significantly greater benefits than was assumed in 2018.This paper has examined, from the perspective of gkvi–a large IT service company–what contribution can be made and where the current limits of possible support lie.

Keywords Digitalization · Service provider · eHealth · Healthcare · Health insurance

U. Arnold (✉)
Gkv Informatik, Wuppertal, Germany
e-mail: ulrich.arnold@gkvi.de

R. C. Geibel
E-Commerce Institute, Cologne, Germany
e-mail: geibel@ecommerceinstitut.de

R. C. Geibel and S. Machavariani (eds.), *Chances and Challenges of Digital Management*, Springer Proceedings in Business and Economics,
https://doi.org/10.1007/978-3-031-45601-5_1

1 Introduction

Germany belongs to the eldest societies worldwide and the demographic change is progressing further. The German Federal Statistical Office forecasts an increase of up to 42% in the number of people over 67 in the population by 2040, which means that the need for medical treatment in the population is expected to rise (Bundesärztekammer, 2021). The German healthcare system is faced with the challenge of treating more and more older people with chronic diseases, which account for 80% of healthcare expenditure in Germany (German Trade and Invest, 2022). On the one hand, new medical innovations promote the range of health treatment options; on the other hand, they create new financial difficulties at the same time. According to a McKinsey study (Biesdorf et al., 2022, p. 5), it is estimated that the German healthcare market will spend 343 billion euros in 2021, with an expected annual increase of around 5%.

In fact, according to the German Federal Statistical Office (2022), health care spending is already over 440 billion euros in 2020 and is significantly higher than assumed. An expected growth rate of 5.8% is still expected as well. One main reason for the immense increase in healthcare spending is the containment of the Corona pandemic (Statistisches Bundesamt, 2022). Another burden on the healthcare system is the shortage of medical doctors, who are unable to cover the treatment needs of society. The shortage of doctors is already a current occurrence in many rural areas, and urban development is attracting more and more people to the city away from the countryside, making it increasingly difficult to provide medical care in rural areas (Bundesärztekammer, 2021).

2 Problem Definition

In addition to its existing influence on social life and the economy digitalization offers, regarding the current situation in the German healthcare system, a number of opportunities for healthcare. Since its beginning, the Corona pandemic has not only ensured a rise in healthcare expenditure, but also a drive for digitization in the healthcare system in Germany (Bundesministerium für Gesundheit, 2022). Increased user acceptance, more tangible benefits for the end user, and improved technologies ensure that, for example, online appointment booking, teleconsultations, or remote patient monitoring represent a greater advantage and create a greater readiness to utilize the technologies. Benefits are apparent in more efficient processes in the form of faster communication and exchange of data. In addition, reduced costs in medical, administrative or organizational expenses constitute a quantitative benefit in the area of digitization. In contrast, various qualitative benefits can be seen in the reduction or even elimination of print forms or fax messages. The provision of health-related data ensures that better and more effective treatment methods can be developed and implemented. It also forms the basis for new areas of research. The systematic analysis of medical data ensures functional improvement through the establishment of new healing methods and the prevention of diseases. Digitalization in healthcare also offers the end user the opportunity to open up a new self-determined role as a patient. The treatment processes open up the possibility of greater transparency and more flexible treatment methods, for example in the form of digital health applications. Overall, four overarching goals for the implementation of digitization in the healthcare sector are emerging: higher quality of care, improved cost efficiency, an optimized patient experience, and an optimized perception of work by healthcare workers. By implementing these potentials, the possibility of savings of 42 billion euros per year is formed, which in total cancels out 12% of the total costs of the healthcare system (Biesdorf et al., 2022, pp. 5–8.). The German Federal Ministry of Health (2022) sees digitization as a prerequisite for the further development of healthcare.

3 Governmental and Statutory Framework

"Data for Health" is an innovation initiative of three German federal ministries. The German Federal Ministry of Health, the German Federal Ministry for Economic Affairs and Energy, and the German Federal Ministry of Education and Research have collaborated to develop a roadmap for collecting, archiving, and analyzing digital health-related data in compliance with data protection regulations. The three core objectives of the initiative are to improve patient care, advance the medical process and support the development of healthcare innovations in Germany. One key aspect involves scientific analyses and studies of health-related data. These can ensure the effectiveness of pharmaceuticals and medical devices and identify medical risk groups, improving patient safety and individualized care. The progression of the medical process is ensured through the development of new diagnostic and therapeutic procedures based on the analyses of health-related data. The focus in the development of health innovations in Germany is on the general improvement of innovative strength with regard to securing jobs and expanding prosperity in the context of international competition. In order to generate the necessary foundations and framework conditions for the initiative, various laws and further initiatives have been passed by the federal ministries since March 2018. Further progress is defined by five operational fields of action:

- Establishment and expansion of structures for the digital networking of healthcare and healthcare research
- Improving the availability and quality of health-related data
- Improving data security and data interconnection through the development of innovative solutions
- Joint path to data-supported medicine
- Early identification of upcoming application opportunities

The above illustrate the priorities to be realized for the further course of action on the path to digitization in healthcare (Bundesministerium für Bildung und Forschung et al., 2020).

4 Stakeholders

Relating the potential to the stakeholders themselves, there are 71% in savings opportunities for all service providers. This includes mainly medical professions and hospitals. The other 29% relate to the remaining stakeholders in the healthcare system, which primarily includes health insurers. The main explanation is the reduction in demand due to, among other things, the avoidance of duplicate examinations as well as a slower progression or even a reduction in the development of chronic diseases. The result is improved patient care by avoiding extended hospital stays and financial savings.

5 Segmentation

The overall potential of digitalization can be divided into two different savings categories across all healthcare stakeholders (Fig. 1).

Within this, 61% of the potential savings in increased productivity are in the area of the healthcare providers. Administrative or other organizational tasks are facilitated by digital technologies, allowing staff to be more appropriately deployed for other processes. For example, online patient appointment bookings eliminate the need for staff to make phone calls to medical offices, allowing increased time resources to be utilized. The remaining 39% can be attributed among other things to a reduction in medical demand by avoiding unnecessary duplicate examinations (Biesdorf et al., 2022, p. 7).

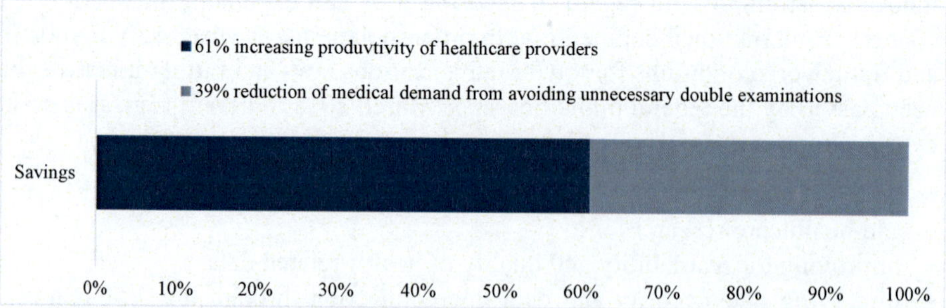

Fig. 1 Saving areas in the digital healthcare system (Biesdorf et. al., 2022, p. 7)

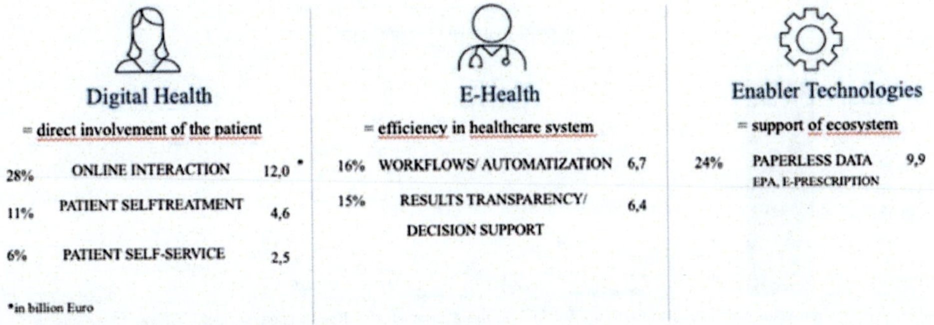

Fig. 2 Three areas of digitalization (own structure)

Digitalization can be generally divided into three areas in which digital solutions are applicable: Digital Health, e-Health and Enabler Technologies. All three areas together form six subcategories that include 26 digital health technologies in total. Digital health refers to direct patient engagement and forms the largest block of savings opportunities. Included are online interactions, which form the largest subcategory with 28% and €12 billion in potential benefits. Also included are the categories of patient self-care with a savings potential of 11% (4.6 billion euros) and patient self-service with 6% (2.5 billion euros). The e-health area relates to the healthcare system itself and the associated increased efficiency of workflows and automation (16%, 6.7 billion euros), as well as results transparency (15%, 6.4 billion euros). The third area includes all enabler technologies that are expected to support the overall ecosystem. That includes all digital health technologies that ensure paperless data exchange, such as the electronic patient record or the upcoming e-prescription. Overall, the area of enabler technologies comprises a potential of €9.9 billion, which accounts for 24% of the total realizable potential (Biesdorf et al., 2022, p. 3) (Fig. 2).

6 Development

The potential for digitalization in healthcare is constantly growing. Since 2018, the total realizable potential has increased by 24% from €34 billion to €42 billion. Improved technologies and greater consumer willingness to use them ensure that the area of "digital health" accounts for almost half of the total potential with a share of 45%. The annual average increase of 5% in healthcare spending increases the extent of potential cost savings. A key point for the continued increase in potential is the little progress that has been realized in the digitization of the healthcare sector. Since 2018, 1.4 billion euros of the then potential 34 billion euros have been realized, which corresponds to a percentage share of around 4% (Biesdorf et al., 2022, p. 5) (Fig. 3).

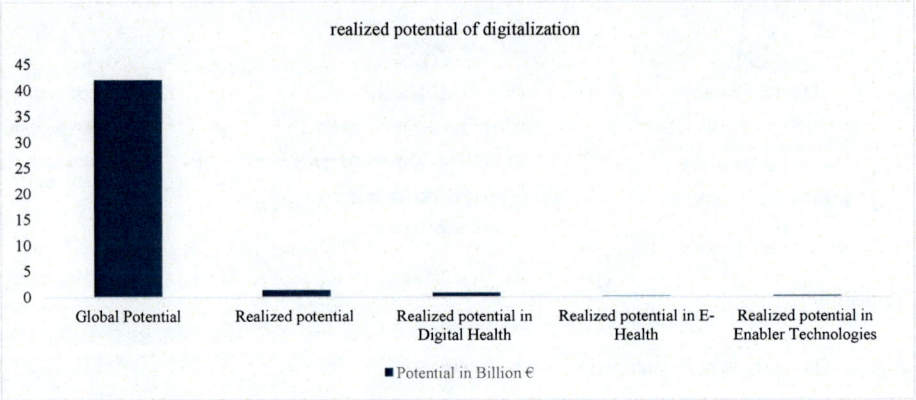

Fig. 3 Realized potential in billion Euro–different areas

7 Challenges

Although healthcare is one of the largest economic sectors in Germany and provides the opportunity for a lot of financial savings, digitization is making little progress. Reasons for this include the low use of digital solutions such as the electronic patient file, which has been on the market since the beginning of 2021. Other digital tools, such as the e-prescription, have not yet entered the market in Germany. The application is in the extended test phase and market entry is scheduled for the beginning of 2023 (Gematik, 2022). Despite the introduction of legal foundations and frameworks, bureaucratic hurdles for healthcare providers remain. Medical professionals are allowed to bill a maximum of 30% via teleconsultations, and all service rates above this are not reimbursed by health insurers (Kassenärztliche Bundesvereinigung, 2022). There is an uneven distribution of potential benefits among stakeholders. Payers have fewer opportunities for savings overall than service providers, which could result in a low drive to implement digital innovations (Biesdorf et al., 2022). Another problem is the use of different software systems by healthcare facilities, which means that no standardized IT solutions can be implemented. The consequence remains an increased workload. Even within most healthcare facilities and hospitals, software systems between the different departments differ from one another in terms of application. Without leveling up, Biesdorf et al. (2022, p. 11) see little potential for a breakthrough at national level.

8 Case Studies: Oscare Connect, Digital Health Applications and Cloud Services

Patient data, such as electronic health records, is scattered across a variety of systems in healthcare. In total, several dozen providers are involved. At the same time, data formats, interfaces and systems exist in a multitude of variants and standards, resulting in enormous heterogeneity. Out of this problem, gkvi created the oscare connect backbone infrastructure, which provides a network and seamless communication to all providers, systems and data.

Healthcare providers are increasingly supporting patients with apps on their smartphones. One example is the so-called digital health apps (DiGA). These are used to take the pressure off healthcare providers and give patients a more empowered role. Health apps continue to be prescribed by physicians after a diagnosis and are financially supported by health insurers. In addition to the DiGA, every patient also has the option of accessing and thus gaining an overview of their own medical data via the electronic patient record (ePa). The ePa thus forms an app for a digital health network. Here, too, gkvi has developed a backbone infrastructure through the "oscare connect" backend and the "oscare connect" streaming platforms to enable seamless communication. Data security and data protection pose a particular challenge.

Due to the strict data protection laws in Germany, the use of cloud services is also severely restricted–and currently even mostly prohibited for medical data. The gkvi's target model is a seamless multi-cloud environment that enables the use of applications from the on-premise infrastructure through national cloud solutions to hyperscalers. This is the prerequisite for a digitalization push that facilitates the use of data lakes and the use of tools from the operators of hyperscalers, e.g., data analytics or artificial intelligence on patient data. Thus, the gkvi creates the basis for the implementation of cloud applications, orchestration mechanisms or for data security and data protection mechanisms. In addition, discussions are being held with the legislator on how the future path can be shaped.

9 Perspective

The digitalization of healthcare in Germany is clearly taking high priority at the social, political and economic levels. The need for digital measures and technologies continues to be in high demand. At the political level, essential legal framework conditions have already been introduced and the expansion continues to progress. Fundamentally, investments in technological innovations create remedies for digital challenges and offer the greatest opportunity to further advance the areas of digital health, e-health and enabler technologies and make increasing adoption possible (Markets and Markets, 2021). Funding of outcome-based reimbursements is a conceivable way to further relieve the financial burden on health insurers or other payers. This can also help to equalize the disparity in the potential benefits between the players.

With the help of financial incentives, a balance of interests can be created. If there is a recognizable significant added value for payers through reimbursement of digital services, there is a possibility that further investments will be taken in hand by the payers themselves in order to promote them further. In the area of e-health, financial support ensures that automation processes and hurdles between different IT systems are overcome and enables a sustainable economic advantage (Biesdorf et al., 2022; International Trade Administration, 2022). According to the McKinsey analysis (Biesdorf et al., 2022), centralized identity and consensus management forms the second base for increased use of digital technologies. Entry and application aids and centralized consents for data uses increase user-friendliness and facilitate the transition and the entry into the use of digital innovations. Continued legislative support must support the further development of digital technologies such as the establishment of e-prescribing, as well as adapt framework conditions so as not to restrict the use of teleconsultations or other digital services (Gematik, 2022). Greater use of established technologies should be realized with end-to-end support for the end user. Simple operation or service assistance expedite the use of digital measures. With recognizable benefits in use, interest and awareness for digital changes increases among end users. Chronic patients can request long-term prescriptions from medical practices they have not consulted before. By placing them in their electronic medical file, patients' schedules and time spent repeating previously diagnosed medical histories are reduced. At the same time, the doctor's office saves on the organizational and time resources of a duplicate examination (Biesdorf et al., 2022, p. 11).

There is clear potential for more digitization in healthcare. To realize the full potential benefits, the end user needs to be at the center of the realization process. The focus of all stakeholders in healthcare should be on the benefits of digital solutions to remove existing and future barriers.

References

Biesdorf, S., Niedermann, F., Sickmüller, K., & Tuot, K. (2022). *Digitalisierung im Gesundheitswesen: die 42 Milliarden-Euro-Chance für Deutschland*. McKinsey & Company.

Bundesärztekammer. (2021). *Ergebnisse der Ärztestatistik zum 31.12.2021*. https://www.bundesaerztekammer.de/baek/ueber-uns/aerztestatistik/aerztestatistik-2021.

Bundesministerium für Bildung und Forschung, Bundesministerium für Gesundheit & Bundesministerium für Wirtschaft und Energie. (2020). *Daten helfen heilen. Innovationsinitiative "Daten für Gesundheit": Roadmap für eine bessere Patientenversorgung durch Gesundheitsforschung und Digitalisierung*. https://www.bundesgesundheitsministerium.de/fileadmin/Dateien/5_Publikationen/Gesundheit/Berichte/Roadmap_Innovationsinitiative_Daten_fuer_Gesundheit_barrierefrei.pdf (Accessed 11 Oct 2022).

Bundesministerium für Gesundheit. (2022). *Digitalisierung im Gesundheitswesen*. https://www.bundesgesundheitsministerium.de/themen/digitalisierung/digitalisierung-im-gesundheitswesen.html (Accessed 11 October 2022).

Gematik. (2022). *E-Rezept: Das e-Rezept für Deutschland*. https://www.das-e-rezept-fuer-deutschland.de.

German Trade and Invest. (2022). *HealthCare Market*. https://www.gtai.de/en/invest/industries/healthcare/healthcare-market-65626

ITA–International Trade Administration. (2022). *Germany–Country commercial guide*. Health-Care and medical technology. https://www.trade.gov/country-commercial-guides/germany-healthcare-and-medical-technology

Kassenärztliche Bundesvereinigung. (2022). *Telemedizin*. https://www.kbv.de/html/telemedizin.php.

Markets and Markets. (2021). *HealthCare IT market–Global forecast to 2026*. Report Broschure with sample pages. Report Code: Hit 2005. https://www.marketsandmarkets.com/Market-Reports/healthcare-it-252.html?gclid=Cj0KCQjw48OaBhDWARIsAMd966DmFMogsnJm4S1TWFOBTwGm9zOMOBMP5maA63JmF3BBvRnjgtqIjC4aAizqEALw_wcB.

Statistisches Bundesamt. (2022). *Gesundheitsausgaben 2020: Finanzierungsanteil der staatlichen Transfers und Zuschüsse auf 15,7 % gestiegen*. Pressemitteilung Nr. 255 vom 21. https://www.destatis.de/DE/Themen/Gesellschaft-Umwelt/Gesundheit/Gesundheitsausgaben/_inhalt.htm.

Development and Deployment of a Digital Customer Loyalty Program in Two Shopping-Centers

Christin Barreira and Richard C. Geibel

Abstract A significant amount of merchandise sales is conducted in large shopping centers. It is convenient and easy for customers to find many suppliers concentrated in one place an in this way they can cover a very large part of their needs at once. For the shopping center operators and for the individual stores, the shoppers are initially anonymous, because they go into the stores, buy the goods they want and leave again. This means that the centers and the stores cannot specifically address the respective customers an improve the shopping experience for them, because they do not know the customers and do not understand their shopping habits and personal preferences. This challenge can be solved by introducing an attractive digital loyalty program. In this program, customer receive points for their purchases and can then exchange the collected points for rewards. In this way, customers are incentivized to both visit the center and the stores more often, but also to buy more from these stores, as they are rewarded for doing so. This digital loyalty program is to be automated as far as possible, putting the customer at the center. This article describes the experience gained with custom software development and with the implementation of the program in two shopping centers. In the process, the lessons learned are evaluated and critically reflected with regards to the achievement of objectives.

Keywords Loyalty program · Digitalization · Digital transformation · Customer experience · OCR

C. Barreira (✉)
Klaas Management, Lingen, Germany
e-mail: c.barreira@klaas-management.de

R. C. Geibel
E-Commerce Institute, Cologne, Germany

East European University, Tbilisi, Georgia

R. C. Geibel
e-mail: geibel@ecommerceinstitut.de

R. C. Geibel and S. Machavariani (eds.), *Chances and Challenges of Digital Management*, Springer Proceedings in Business and Economics,
https://doi.org/10.1007/978-3-031-45601-5_2

1 Introduction and Theory

The competitive situation in retail stores has become much more intense due to the developments of the last few years, especially the increase in online retailing (Knoppe et al. 2022). Added to this, the Corona Pandemics accelerated the digital transformation (Gläß & Leukert, 2017a and 2017b). Both effects present the stationary trade and thus also the shopping center industry with challenges, but also opportunities (Commercetools, 2022). The customer no longer decides where to go shopping based on "hard facts"; softer factors are gaining more and more importance (Karner, 2022).

Customer data is the basis for successful customer retention; only those who know their customers can place them at the center of their trade. For this reason, bonus programs, especially multi-bonus programs such as the Payback program, are still popular means of acquiring data and simultaneously incentivizing customers (Chen, 2022).

On the part of the store operators, high expenses are paid annually in the form of membership fees to become partners of these multi-bonus programs (Davis, 2022).

Together with the University Fresenius of Applied Sciences and the E-Commerce Institute in Cologne, the shopping center operator has developed a loyalty program that is tailored to the needs of tenants and customers. In the run-up to this, a feasibility analysis was carried out to work out the opportunities and risks. However, the focus of the development was not only on the customer, but also on the store operators. The program was published at the end of September within the framework of a "soft launch" (Lookentor, 2023). This article describes the initial experiences, objectives, and problems in more detail.

2 Case Study—Development of a Loyalty Program

The focus of the developments was on customer loyalty and communication. As a shopping center operator, the main focus of all efforts is based on the store operators as well as on the end customer. The loyalty program to be developed was to create an incentive for both sides to use it, and the interests of the center management were also taken into account (see Fig. 1). Three stakeholder groups were defined for this purpose: Customer, store operator/store employees and center management. For each stakeholder group, an expectation and problem statement map were prepared, from which assumptions were identified and research questions developed. The importance of the statement was examined through a point evaluation to prioritize it. Against the background of conflicting expectations, the prioritization of the statements was necessary in order to reduce the conflicting goals of all stakeholder groups to a minimum, whereby compromises inevitably had to be found.

The loyalty program was designed to solve problems and potential challenges with the system. The most important challenges and proposed solutions are listed below, subdivided according to the respective stakeholder groups.

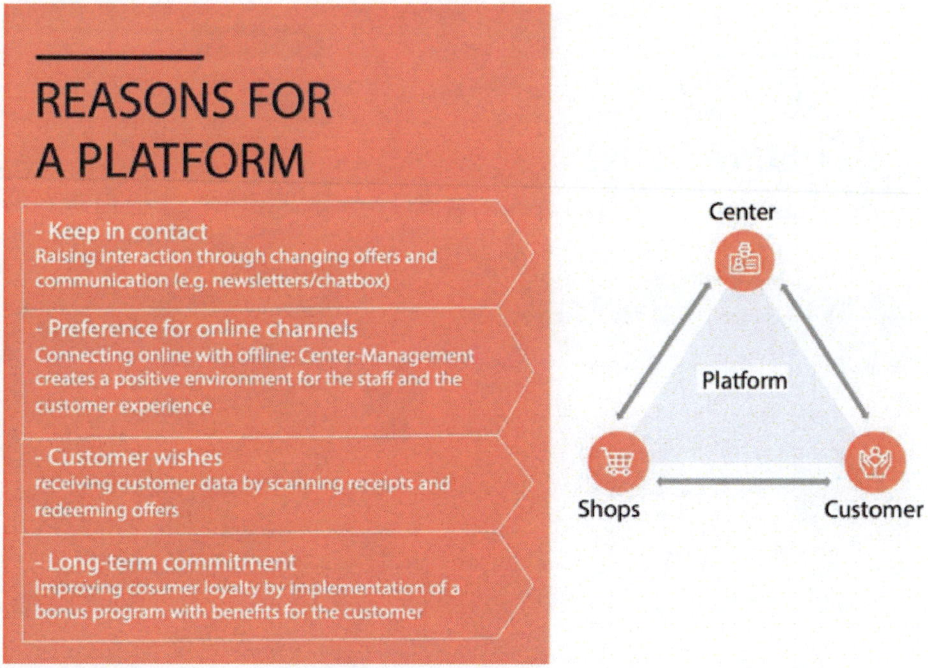

Fig. 1 Motivation for choosing a platform solution

3 Solution Approach via Loyalty Program

As a result of the various scoping exercises, a progressive web app, hereinafter referred to as PWA, was developed as a loyalty program, which is also used as a communication tool (see Fig. 2). As a consequence of the short distance of the two shopping centers (only 35 km), usage of one platform with separate databases was chosen. This offers independence for the customers: they can go shopping in both centers and use the system. Theoretically, they can collect points in both centers, but they can only redeem them in a center-specific arrangement.

The customer registers on the platform and selects the center they visit mostly. The selection of the center is used to personalize the cover page. The platform's setting enables the customer to switch between both centers, but the cover page remains the one fitting to the selected one at the beginning. If the customer agrees to receive a newsletter, the customer will receive the newsletter for the center which was chosen as preferred center.

To make the registration process user-friendly, the customer only has to enter the name and e-mail address. In this way, the customer is directly rewarded with points as soon as he/she enters further data.

On the cover page, the customer finds his/her current points balance, low-threshold offers (5–10%, consulting offers, etc.) that the customer can always redeem and exclusive rewards that can only be used by existing points (20–25%, goodies, etc.).

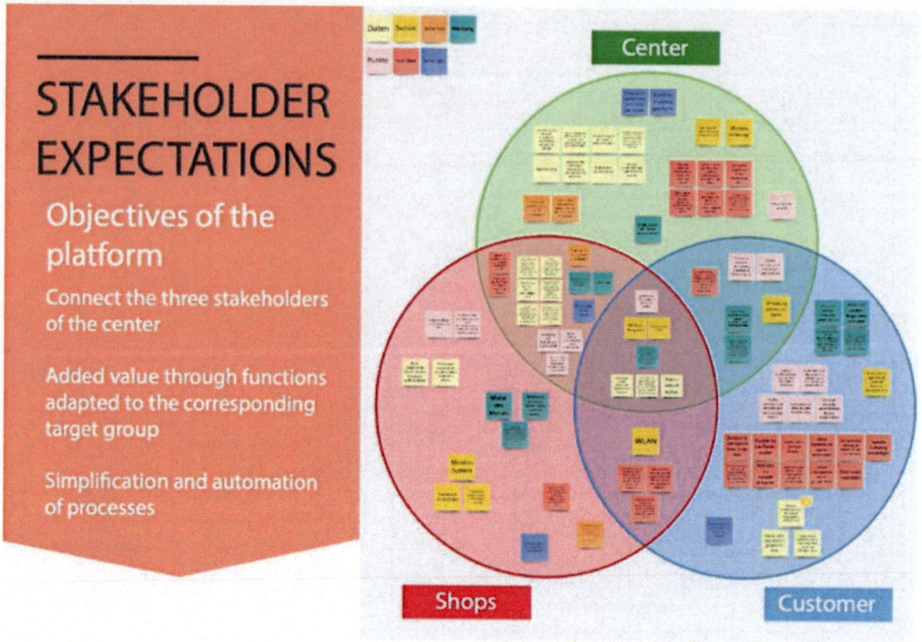

Fig. 2 Detailed analysis of expectations of the three stakeholder groups

To collect points, the customer can upload the receipts into the system via camera or select them as a file. Using OCR technology, the receipt is read and assigned to the respective shop and shopping center. The customer receives one point for every euro spent. The points are collected and redeemed on a shopping center-specific basis. The redemption of the reward takes place via time stamp. The customer selects his/her reward and activates it. The customer then has 15 min to show this reward at the checkout. When the time elapses, the points will automatically be deducted. The cashier does not need to scan or debit the reward, this is fully automated.

In addition to the rewards program, the customer can also contact the center management using a chat function.

In order to attract store employees to the program, the employees' staff discount card is stored in the system. The employees have the possibility to register as a customer in the system and to be assigned to the respective shop. Only then does the design change color allowing the stores to directly recognize a customer as employee. Through the assignment to the respective store, the employees can also receive messages from the center management. In the future, the center management would like to publish the information letters in a compact form, e.g. messages on the employees' phones. Basically, it is up to the employee whether he or she is assigned to the shop. Through the shorter communication channels, shop employees can make enquiries directly via chat system. As a result, both center management as well as the tenants save valuable time, as some stores do not have their own e-mail address.

Another advantage is the employee's possibility to share offers and rewards on their own mobile devices depending on their access rights.

Excerpt from the Store Operators and Store employee's Expectations and Problem Statement Map

Some stores participate in nationwide multi-partner programs or run their own single bonus program, which is why the willingness to participate is lower among branch-organized shops than among owner-operated shops. The effect of the programs is quite different. While nationwide multi-bonus programs primarily target the brands, the center loyalty program concentrates on the shopping center location. However, the attractiveness of the center loyalty program is related to the number of stores participating. In order to convince the shops of the benefits of the system, the conditions of participation for the stores should be low-threshold, user-friendly and resource-saving. The system should be usable by all employees. In addition, according to all store operators, the system must not be connected to the merchandise management systems of the cash registers. Another challenge is the implementation of the program.

Usually, shopping centers are home to different branches. However, the checkout processes at the individual branches are different. While in drugstores there is often a queue at the checkout, in restaurants the payment process usually takes place at the guest table. In the course of the project, the charging of points by the stores increasingly turned out to be a co-criterion.

Excerpt from the customer's and Visitors' Expectations and Problem Statement Map

Customers want benefits from a loyalty program in the shopping center. However, these benefits can vary. Discounts, offers or goodies are just a few examples. They require a simple system that offers the necessary security and enables easy exchange. In addition, the customer wants a simple registration process and to disclose as little data as possible. They look for relevant advertising to be displayed and expect moderate advertising penetration. The system should be able to function anywhere, even without WLAN, and provide an overview of the current points balance at any time. In order to actively use the loyalty program, it should offer a basic level of attractiveness and not only provide benefits in exchange for redeeming points.

Excerpt from the Center Managements Map of Expectations and Problem Statements

The center management would like all stores to participate and to be actively involved in setting the offers and rewards. For this purpose, there should be different authorization levels for the store employees. This implies the existence of individual accounts for each employee or at least different sub-accounts with authorization levels. A challenge that is seen in particular by the center management is the active use of the loyalty program by the store employees. In the past, center circulars that were printed out and sent to the stores often only reached a few store employees. A challenge which can also be seen as an opportunity for the development of the loyalty program. In addition to an incentive program for customers, the center management would like to have a simpler and faster means of communication with the store employees and customers.

Furthermore, the center management would like the loyalty program to provide the most valuable customer data possible from purchases made at the store operators. The dashboard should offer as many filter options as possible to provide targeted statements. The data is used to target marketing activities and to display relevant advertising.

4 Results and Discussion

The loyalty program is currently in use after a soft launch phase (see Fig. 3). The program seems to be well accepted with a CPC value of 1,24 €. At this point in time, all functions are in place, but the discussions with the store operators regarding offers and rewards are pooling extensive resources, which is why the advertising campaign will only start at the beginning of the season. Although it is possible for every store to post offers and rewards, this is currently done by the center management as a service. In addition, due to the past pandemic, the store operators are rather reluctant to offer discounts, which is why currently the offers cannot be rotated as first intended.

The entire course of the project has shown that the integration of a digital program entails very intensive communication work. Every innovation or technology holds opportunities and challenges, and from the employee's point of view, technologies

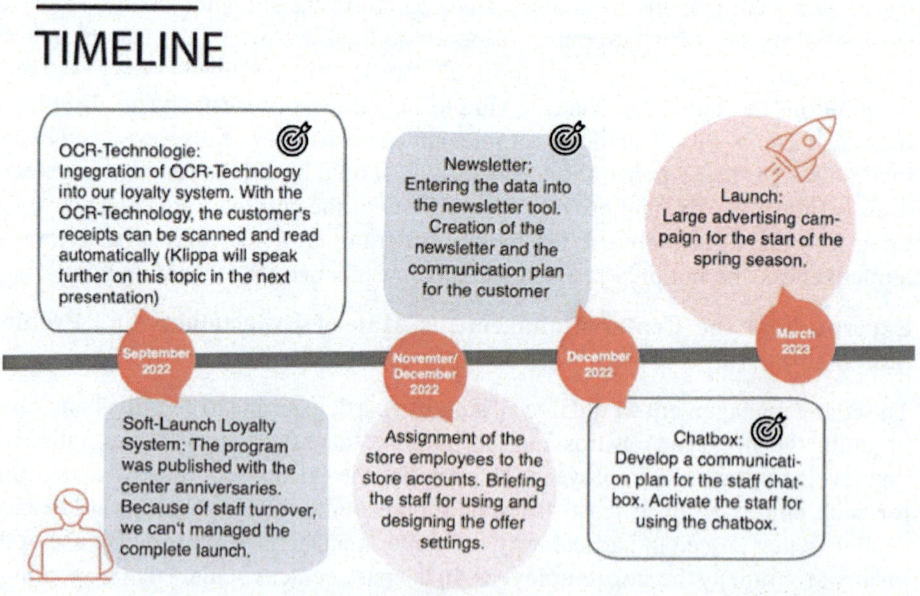

Fig. 3 The six phases of the implementation process

are often met with a certain skepticism. This skepticism can be overcome through targeted communication.

At the beginning of the program development, the points should be booked with the customer by means of a QR code or e-mail address. This idea was evolved after the scoping: As the branches have very different checkout processes and are partly not able to integrate further processes into their daily work in addition to their own processes. OCR technology offers an alternative here, as no further action is requirefrom the store (for more details regarding OCT see Studener 2023)). However, OCR Technology does not get by without manual checks. The center management has the possibility to define the values to be read out for each shop. These values are used for exact allocation to the shop (VAT number, postcode, etc.). These parameters must be entered into the system in advance, but the assignment to the respective shopping centers turned out to be more difficult than expected. Stores organized in branches mostly have stored the same VAT ID nationwide, sometimes even the addresses of the centers or the store were missing on the receipt, which made the allocation difficult. If the system cannot create the allocation to the shop or center, the center management has the option of subsequently entering the points.

For the communication tool, the initial idea was to open the communication channels to all stakeholders. Currently, communication is only possible between the center management and the stores or customers. Opening the communication channel from the stores to the customers is not being implemented. To use the communication channel, a communication strategy is still needed with the result that the store employees in particular will use this communication channel in the future.

5 Conclusion, Limitations and Further Research

The system represents the first digital transformation project for the shopping center operator. Based on this system, further digital touchpoints can be integrated, such as the integration of car parks or the restaurant ordering systems (Fig. 4).

Overall, the current version of the customer loyalty program in use is a promising starting point for gaining further important insights into customer behavior in order to both expand new customer acquisition and increase the loyalty of existing customers.

However, it should be noted that the present study is a concrete implementation of a customer loyalty program which, while providing many informative and valuable indications, cannot claim general validity in its statements.

The future experience of using the customer loyalty system described here, in terms of customer reactions and planned enhancements to the system, will be the subject of further research and publications.

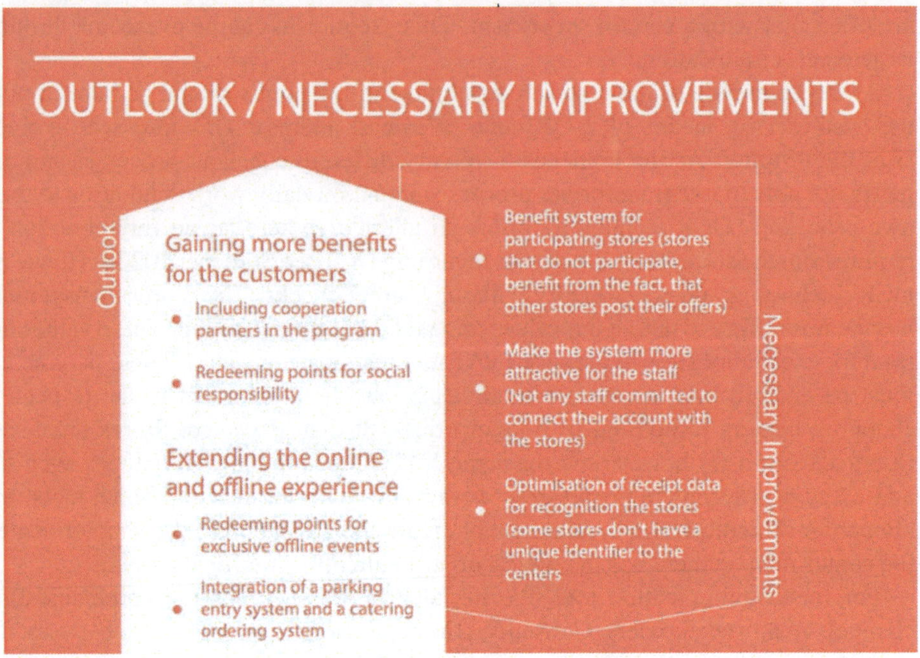

Fig. 4 The planned future enhancements to increase customer value

References

Boadum, L. (2023). *11 Gründe, warum Bestandskunden so wertvoll sind*. https://blog.hubspot.de/service/bestandskunden.

Chen, J. (2022). *Loyalty Program: Definition, Purposes, How it works, Example*. https://www.investopedia.com/terms/l/loyalty-program.asp.

Commercetools. (2022). *Reimagining retail commerce in a new normal world*. https://commercetools.com.

Davis, B. (2022). *8 Benefits of having a loyalty program in 2023*. https://www.stampme.com/blog/8-benefits-of-having-a-loyalty-program.

Gläß, R., Leukert, B. (2017a). *Handel 4.0: die Digitalisierung des Handels – Strategien, Technologien, Transformation, Springer Gabler, Heidelberg.*

Gläß, R., Leukert, B. (2017b). Herausforderungen und Chancen für die Digitalisierung von Handelsunternehmen. In: Gläß; Leukert (ed.), *Handel 4.0: die Digitalisierung des Handels*, pp.193–212. Springer Gabler, Heidelberg.

Karner, G. (2022). *Retail facts and figures*. https://www.shopreme.com/blog/retail-facts/.

Knoppe, M., Rock, S., & Wild, M. (2022). *Der zukunftsfähige Handel: Neue online und offline Konzepte sowie digitale und KI-basierte Lösungen*. Springer Nature.

Krcmar, H. (2018). Charakteristika digitaler Transformationen. In: Krcmar (ed.), *Informations management und digitale Transformation*, pp. 5–10. Springer Gabler, Wiesbaden.

Lookentor. (2023). *Rabatte im Treueprogramm*. https://www.lookentor.de/news-und-events/detail/jetzt-exklusive-rabatte-im-treueprogramm-sichern.

Studener, F., Knegtering, Y., Barreira, C., Reinking, O., Geibel, R. (2023). The importance of intelligent OCR software in a digital loyalty program. In: Geibel & Machavariani (ed.), *Chances and challenges of digital management—proceedings of the international scientific-practical conference (ISPC 2022)*. Springer Nature, Wiesbaden

The Transformation Process of an IT Service Provider in the Public Health Insurance Sector

Markus Vom Scheidt, Vanessa Hering, Stefan Gablowski, and Richard C. Geibel

Abstract The large health insurance market in Germany is divided into those with statutory insurance and those with private insurance. The vast majority of people with health insurance are insured through a statutory health insurance fund. These statutory health insurers are increasingly focusing on their core business of looking after their members and outsourcing service and support functions. The most important service functions include, in particular, IT technical support for all relevant IT processes and IT procedures. This study refers to the company "gkvi—Gesetzliche Krankenversicherung Informatik", which specializes in the planning, management, and control of IT processes for statutory health insurance companies. On the one hand, gkvi has to ensure the provision of services to its clients, and on the other hand, it has to outsource services that are not within its own competence focus to subordinate service providers. Two major changes were therefore implemented as part of the transformation. First, a service catalog was agreed with the five major health insurance customers and a service team was set up for each service. The gkvi organization was thus restructured in terms of the key service teams. One of the aims of this is to ensure end-to-end.

Keywords Transformation · Digitalization · Service provider · Service catalog · Outsourcing

M. Vom Scheidt (✉) · V. Hering · S. Gablowski
gkv informatik GbR, Wuppertal, Germany
e-mail: markus.vomscheidt@gkvi.de

V. Hering
e-mail: vanessa.hering@gkvi.de

S. Gablowski
e-mail: stefan.gablowski@gkvi.de

R. C. Geibel
E-Commerce Institute, Cologne, Germany

East European University, Tbilisi, Georgia

R. C. Geibel
e-mail: geibel@ecommerceinstitut.de

R. C. Geibel and S. Machavariani (eds.), *Chances and Challenges of Digital Management*, Springer Proceedings in Business and Economics,
https://doi.org/10.1007/978-3-031-45601-5_3

1 Introduction

The IT Service Provider gkv informatik GbR (gkvi), based in Germany, was formed as a joint venture of statutory health insurance in 2006. The shareholders, which are all health insurance public-law corporations, are AOK Nordost, AOK NordWest, AOK Rheinland/Hamburg, Barmer Ersatzkasse and HEK—Hanseatische Krankenkasse. Their customers represent approximately 25% of the German statutory health insurance market—this are around 17 million insured persons.

The statutory health insurance covers approximately 90% of the entire healthcare market in Germany (Döring and Paul, 2010; Simon, 2011). Gkvi supports the shareholders with their 41,000 users with various IT services such as provision and operation of a modern workplace including email, telephony, unified communication and software management. As another core business gkvi provides technological services such as infrastructure services, cloud-based or on-premise, for IaaS, PaaS, SaaS and network connections of (external) locations. In addition, gkvi operates the core application *oscare*. Basic services as for instance incident and problem management, data security and IT security as well as license management are also part of the range of services. Gkvi currently employs 663 people at 7 locations in Germany (01.11.2022).

The IT market and the expectations of IT users are developing rapidly on an ongoing basis. This is also increasingly affecting the area of statutory health insurance (Geiger & Geißler, 2021, p.8). As a result, the gkvi shareholders expect the gkvi to be able to continuously use new and more agile IT solutions to implement their business processes. In order to be able to meet the increasing demands of the market and the pressure on prices, the gkvi shareholders decided back in 2016 to specialize gkvi in its core competencies (Kern et al., 2002) and, in addition to revising the service portfolio, to outsource the operation of the data center and the hardware equipment for the workstation to sub-providers. Since the transformation process, gkvi's core competencies have included assuming end-to-end responsibility in the sense of coordinating and managing the participating sub-providers and shareholders with responsibility for the results.

Different requirements of the five shareholders for the gkvi, lack of resources and unclearly contractually defined interfaces and responsibilities in the supply chains—which cause additional effort in terms of coordination and have an impact that favors errors—as well as new technologies have a disruptive effect on the service concepts and organizational units established in the transformation process (Eberhart, 2021; Geiger & Geißler, 2021, p.15ff.; Berghold 2022, p.119ff.). After the operational implementation of the transformation project, the following three core deficits emerged in particular: Operational stability, cost efficiency and quality of the service portfolio (Heikkinen & Jantti, 2012).

2 Approach

In order to continue to position itself as a value-adding IT service provider for the shareholders, to be considered a competitive company in the health insurance sector in the future and to become more attractive to non-shareholders as well, a sustainable concept has been developed and implemented within a year in the form of *gkviNOW*—the follow-up project to the transformation project—which is intended to lead to the holistic further development of gkvi with high priority in all the objectives of the previous transformation that have not been fully completed. The aim is to establish a trusting service partnership with shareholders and sub-providers on an equal footing, accompanied by the optimization of organizational interfaces, a change in culture and end-to-end competence and responsibility for each established service, in order to increase shareholder satisfaction as a result. The success factors here are, on the one hand, the type of collaboration between gkvi and the shareholders and, on the other, the project framework defined at the start of the project. The former is achieved by each shareholder delegating persons with decision-making authority to the project. The latter is determined by a formal resolution of the boards of the shareholders. No individual cases or escalations are handled beyond the defined action lines—the focus of the *gkviNOW* project is exclusively on holistic process and workflow improvements. The establishment of gkvi's role as a service integrator for the shareholders is realized through the following seven fields of action and the corresponding measures.

2.1 ITt Service Catalog

The implementation of the *gkviNOW* project is based on a standardized IT service portfolio agreed with all shareholders. The IT service catalog represents the IT service portfolio and is the result of the transfer of previously agreed individual solutions to standard solutions. With the help of the IT service catalog, not only technical systems and corresponding processes are represented, but also all associated actions and communicative coordination, which are conducive to a low failure-prone functioning of the organization, its further development, and a high-quality service perception of the shareholders. The aim of this line of action is to reduce complexity and reduce costs through standardization (Brich, 2014; Schmidt, Brenner & Schaaf, 2019).

2.2 Service Request Management

Among other things, this project will be implemented by introducing a new ordering tool. The software to be used is Service Request Management (SRM) from USU Software AG. The new tool will be used to map all standard services in the IT service catalog. The introduction of a singular ordering tool pursues various goals: On the one hand, the minimization of ordering errors by the shareholders themselves, or when passing them on to the sub-providers, and on the other hand, the minimization of orders that need to be clarified through data validation (Ludwig et al., 2007). This is accompanied by a reduction of effort and complexity in the maintenance and expansion of the service offering. Validation rules and interfaces are uniformly specified by the ordering tool. In addition to automation, these goals are also achieved through complete coverage and permanent synchronization of the IT service catalog in the ordering tool, as well as integration with and synchronization of the necessary ordering tools of the sub-providers. The expected overall results include shorter ordering times, cost reductions and improved performance for the shareholders (Floerecke, 2021; Ludwig et al., 2007).

2.3 Service Teams

The introduction of a new ordering tool is accompanied by the establishment of end-to-end responsibility for the respective services, covering the process from ordering by the shareholders to delivery by the sub-provider, including maintenance and possible troubleshooting. This project requires an organizational change so that services can be managed holistically within one organizational unit. In this context, a service team with a service owner represents a service. The desired result is a measurable improvement for the shareholders in terms of defined key figures for the respective service. This requires regular further development in the fundamentals of IT service management and the service-centric way of working. One measure is the introduction of centralized management of both internal and external services. To this end, key performance indicators must be understood and used to design and live control and regulation systems (Carter-Steel et al. 2006). Another measure is the transparent presentation of contract knowledge to enable control at sub-provider level (Buchhorn & Shannon, 2014).

2.4 IT Service Management Processes

The goals of establishing and optimizing processes in accordance with the "Information Technology Infrastructure libary" (ITIL) standard across all service teams are to increase operational stability and service quality while at the same time reducing costs. These goals are to be realized by consolidating and simplifying processes (Jantti, 2011; Punyateera et al., 2014). The aim is to introduce a standardized and clear line of responsibility of the service teams for their service components in all ITIL processes. Ensuring security and compliance standards in change and release management as well as the perception of end-to-end responsibility are considered essential core competencies of gkvi. In order to reduce the core deficit of operational stability, a particular focus is placed on optimizing the processes of incident, problem, change and service level management (Böhlke, 2022; Cusick & Ma, 2010).

2.5 Configuration Management Database

The objectives of introducing and operating a configuration management database (CMDB) for managing IT assets (hardware and software, incl. licenses) are to link incident, problem, and configuration events, to log IT asset changes and to store IT asset details. In this way, the aim is to ensure the most complete and holistic process view possible in terms of end-to-end responsibility. Professional Service Asset and Configuration Management (SACM) should provide transparent relationships between services and configuration items (CI). The integration of CI relationships into knowledge management enables secure change management as well as efficient incident and demand management (Whyte, Stasis & Lindkvist, 2016; Ying, Lijun & Wei, 2009). Transparency in IT asset management allows compliance with relevant security requirements. Relevant gkvi processes are adapted to the necessary integration of the CMDB, including an examination of possible automation potentials (e.g. an automatic comparison of change tool and CMDB). If possible, there will also be a connection to the sub-provider CMDB to support synchronization.

2.6 Provider Management

Provider management is divided into strategic and operational provider management. As part of the implementation of strategic provider management, the sourcing strategy must be defined, the provider portfolio must be managed, and strategic provider management must be implemented and continuously reviewed. The definition of interfaces to related departments or service teams (e.g., interfaces to central purchasing) must be described to make a distinction between operational and strategic provider management. Outsourcing contracts should be designed with a win–win relationship. For both parties, there should be contractual terms with fair pricing and long-term, sustainable benefits, minimizing service quality issues (Young et al., 2008). The establishment of a strategic provider management further serves to support the service teams in the integration and in their operational end-to-end responsibility of the respective provider services in the service organization. Contractual issues or necessary escalations are also assigned to strategic provider management. The operational subarea of provider management, in contrast, focuses on the introduction of contract lifecycle management: The aim here is to ensure that work versions are always up to date and legally compliant, and to proactively initiate measures in the case of expiring contracts (especially in the case of contract renewals and legally required tenders). Furthermore, the development of contract knowledge is established at the service team level (Goldberg et al., 2014; Urbach & Würz, 2012). An integration of the gkvi sourcing contracts into the gkvi knowledge management takes place. The above measures are necessary to be able to control sub-providers to a sufficient degree. Also, the service teams—the operative provider management, the provider controllers—need contract knowledge to be able to efficiently, effectively, and responsibly control as well as also improve the individual provider services in day-to-day business. The link between the service teams and the provider management area covers the part of the day-to-day business that cannot be mapped via standard processes (ITSM and ITIL).

2.7 Cost Excellence

The objective of this work stream is to gain knowledge of standard market prices for services and personnel expenses. This is implemented by using price and personnel benchmarks. Another objective is to optimize contractual sub-provider volumes. An inventory of the contractual sub-provider quantities and an optimization of these through the evaluation of existing physical and virtual servers with the associated licenses are carried out within the *gkviNOW* project. The establishment of efficient cost management is expected to have a positive effect on the budget of the current and subsequent business plans in short and long term. This should strengthen the perception of gkvi as a reliable provider with regarding to the use of the IT budget (Rouse, 2005).

3 Results

3.1 IT Service Catalog

An agreement was reached with the shareholders on a service catalog. The service catalog describes what gkvi offers its shareholders as a standard. The following service groups were defined: GKV business transactions, telematics, application consulting, digital documents, supporting applications, workplace, consulting and project services, technological services, basic services operation, and basic services processes. Under each service group, individual services can be found in different versions. The product managers at gkvi are responsible for the service portfolio management. They make sure that the services exist. They also check the requirements of the shareholders against the portfolio of sub-providers, design service cuts and prices, and coordinate this in committees.

3.2 Service Request Management

The introduction of a singular ordering tool creates a one-stop shopping experience and increases the satisfaction of the gkvi shareholders. On the one hand, the introduction of the tool enables the shareholders to order, change and cancel all services independently and to monitor the order progress. On the other hand, it also minimizes order errors by the customers themselves or when transferring them to sub-providers. Another result of the introduction of the tool is the reduction of order processing times, cost reduction and an improved performance.

3.3 Service Teams

A service team is set up for each service group on the bases of the service catalog. The personnel size is 15 to 80 employees per service team. The role of service owner was defined and filled by internal employees. In order to be able to take end-to-end responsibility for a service, the entire working method has been worked out across service teams, which also includes cost responsibility for a service. Various key performance indicators and service level agreements (SLAs) have been drawn up to ensure that service teams are in a constant process of improvement. Examples include ticket turnaround times, shareholder satisfaction, and the number of highest priority tickets. Top-down training was provided for services, tools, contracts, provider management, processes, mindset, and communication. In order to be able to take responsibility for the services end-to-end in a team and to be able to follow the defined company wide ITIL processes. During the project, it appeared that some of the employees were missing the necessary management skills.

3.4 IT Service Management Processes

The closure of process gaps and the increase in speed, e.g. in the processing of incident tickets and orders, will have a significant effect on ensuring operational stability and service quality while reducing costs after the completion of the *gkviNOW* project. With the help of a stringent control of processes within gkvi and an adaptation to the processes of the sub-providers, which enables a higher level of standardization, the shareholders' expectations are also increased, as ticket throughput times can be shortened as a result. Within the project, the value of ticket throughput times has fallen by around 53% and has returned to a value range from before the transition (Fig. 1).

The number of ticket issues to be resolved also declined during the project. At certain times, the work reserve is around 1,000 cases and can be kept at a constant level of less than 25%. Another indicator is the reopening rate of tickets, which

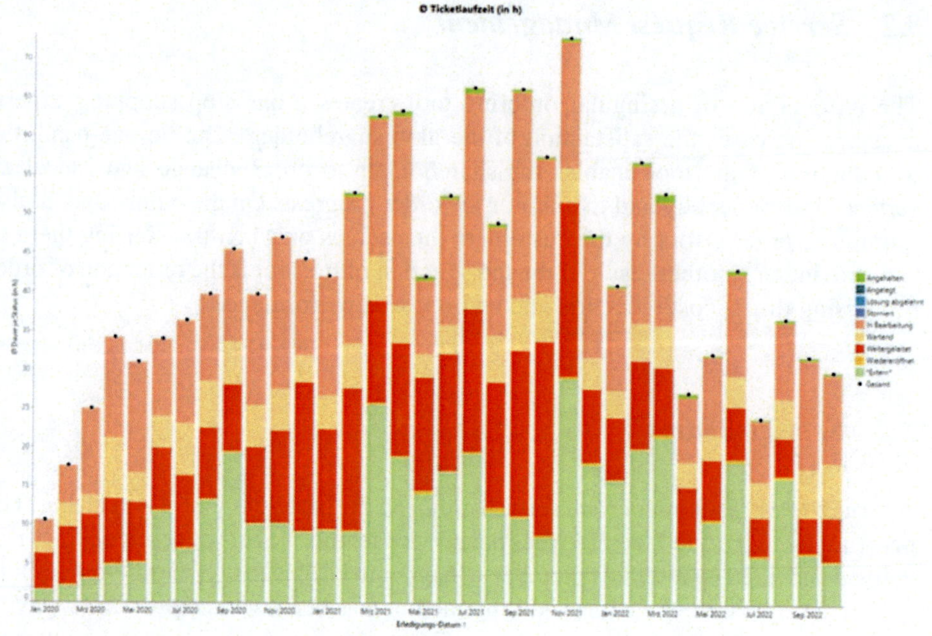

Fig. 1 Ticket running times in hours

shows whether tickets have been processed in a sufficiently good quality or have been complained about by end users (Fig. 2). Due to the *gkviNOW* project, the reopening rate can be reduced by 5 percentage points within a period of nine months—it has been consistently below 6% within the last six months.

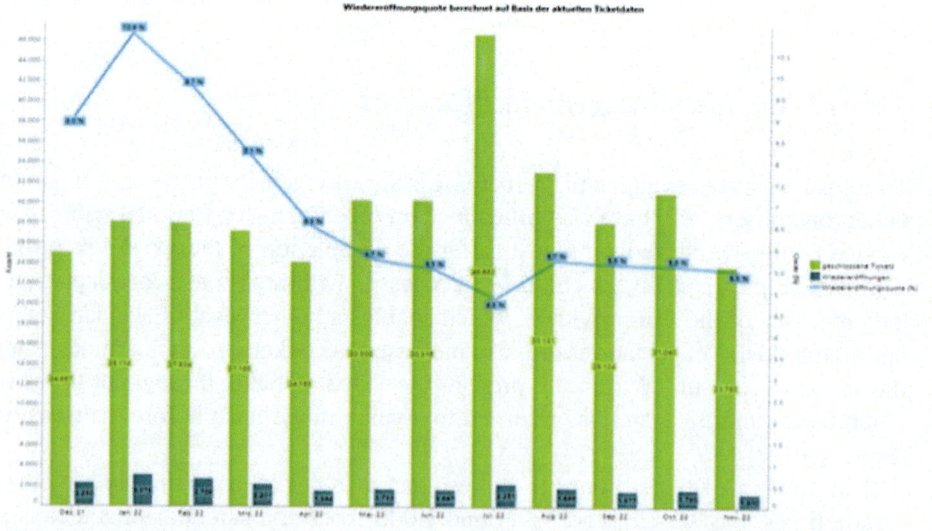

Fig. 2 Reopening rate

3.5 Configuration Management Database

Complete transparency of all relevant IT assets and their links—including infrastructure, operating system, middleware, and application—now allows faster responses to incidents. The introduction of a CMDB has resulted in the complete consideration of impact during changes, the optimization of the used IT infrastructure as well as the implementation of "what-if" scenarios. After project completion, the invoices issued by the sub-providers can also be checked much more efficiently.

3.6 Provider Management

After completion of the *gkviNOW* project, the services of sub-providers are made objectively measurable using standard market performance indicators. The sub-provider portfolio is actively managed and coordinated with the gkvi service portfolio. The above clearly demonstrates the long-term importance of adequate operational and strategic management of the sub-providers by gkvi: Services must be provided by the sub-provider in a contractually defined quality and monitored by gkvi. Change requests and non-standard service requests are identified and qualified by gkvi after project implementation. Relevant stakeholders have knowledge of all relevant contract contents and can make appropriate assessments, enabling more economical action by gkvi. The selection of the best service provision for the shareholders in terms of the decision of an internal vs. external service provision is now possible. As an essential component of project management, there are milestones defined in advance by gkvi for each of the seven streams. In total, nine milestones were defined as examples for the successful implementation of provider management (Table 1).

3.7 Cost Excellence

Rationalization of software licenses, bundling and renegotiation of existing contracts resulted in significant cost savings. A review and rationalization of externally staffed positions within gkvi as well as renegotiations with regard to daily rates to be paid also have a short- and long-term impact on the available budget. In addition, excess server inventories were identified and further costs were saved by reducing them. Moreover, further savings potential was uncovered through the optimization and standardization of ordering and invoice verification processes. The realization of further potential savings extends to the areas of telecommunications (consolidation of sub-providers and services), human resources (process optimization, skills, and staffing plan) and hardware (optimization of terminal equipment management).

Table 1 Milestones provider management

	Milestone description	Goal	Realization
1	Concept for contract document storage → Start of an active contract and knowledge management in the gkvi organization	29.04.2022	18.05.2022
2	Definition of SSO target vision	15.05.2022	27.04.2022
3	Interface definition to operational provider management (service teams)	30.06.2022	30.06.2022
4	Establishment of the committees with shareholders for the provider management	30.06.2022	30.06.2022
5	Target image of the active lifecycle management of contracts incl. contract document storage (Prio. 1 + 2 contracts = outsourcing & communication) completed	31.07.2022	11.08.2022
6	Target vision of active lifecycle management of contracts incl. contract document repository (priority 1 + 2 contracts = outsourcing & communication) completed	30.11.2022	Outstanding
7	Implementation regular assessment of sub-providers	30.09.2022	24.09.2022
8	Finalize provider development-organization/ staffing	31.12.2022	20.10.2022
9	Overview and cross-provider standardization of KPI and SLT with the development of contract standards	31.12.2022	Outstanding

4 Conclusion

The *gkviNOW* project is scheduled to end in December 2022. Not all sub-steps of the individual action lines could be realized to the planned extent. It is planned, therefore, to implement them in the following year. The open sub-steps will be continued on a project basis or as a linear activity. However, at the end of the project, all implemented activities will also be transferred to the organization line. The CIO Office, whose team members already manage the *gkviNOW* project, will be responsible for monitoring and controlling.

4.1 IT Service Catalog

There is continuous development in the organization line in consultation with the shareholders.

4.2 Service Request Management

The introduction of the singular ordering tool is associated with the most open sub-steps. Requirements management will be completed on schedule in 2022, whereas the actual implementation of the tool cannot yet be fully realized—this is scheduled for June 2023. Until the tool is fully implemented, the legacy system will continue to be operated at the same time.

4.3 Service Teams

The service owners will continue to be supported by trained consultants in the further development of the service teams. Furthermore, the service sections between gkvi and sub-providers have been chosen to be too complex and not very manageable in some cases, which is why the service sections must be adapted with the help of a further reduction in complexity. This also affects the SRM, CMDB and ITSM processes. For this reason, the above action streams are integrated into the same unit of the organization line, with the aim of ensuring end-to-end responsibility and being able to prioritize the resources required by the developers. After six months, there will be another self-reflection with an assessment of the situation within the organization.

4.4 IT Service Management Processes

In the future, the process from ordering to delivery must be considered in the individual service teams. The focus of this action stream has been so far on incident, change and release management. Among other things, the SLA key figures are analyzed in a four-week cycle to ensure the sustainability of the measures. Parallel to this tracking measure, the further mode of cooperation with the shareholders must be defined based on a reflection.

4.5 Configuration Management Database

The targeted scope of the action line will be realized in total in 2022. Identified dependencies on the SRM action stream will result in ongoing adjustments.

4.6 Provider Management

There will be a focus on operational provider management (service teams), as the greatest deficits have currently been identified in this area. In addition, employees are being continuously developed for the new area of responsibility.

4.7 Cost Excellence

The implementation of the savings potential in the area of provider quantities (server and workstation) was successfully started. Savings were realized through the rededication of physical servers and through higher-quality billing. Further potentials result from the migration of various virtual servers to physical servers, as these are more cost-effective, but have a longer contract commitment. By establishing a capacity management system at provider level, further optimization can be identified via utilization reports.

Overall, the comprehensive *gkviNOW* project was successfully structured, planned and implemented within the gkvi. It can be seen that the expected savings potentials were achieved or exceeded in terms of both throughput times and estimated costs. In addition, there have been significant improvements in the performance of the systems and the flexibility of the application with regard to the tasks to be supported.

References

Berghold, A. et al. (2022). *Tech-Giganten im Gesundheitswesen*. https://doi.org/10.11586/2022042.

Böhlke, L. (2022). Wie Sie Ihr IT Service Management mithilfe des ITIL Continual Improvements verbessern können. *Mind Square–IT-Beratung und Entwicklung*. https://mindsquare.de/fachartikel/itsm-durch-itil-continual-improvement-verbessern/.

Brich, S (ed.). (2014). *Gabler Wirtschaftslexikon. A–B*. 18., aktualisierte und erw. Aufl. Springer Gabler Verlag (Gabler Wirtschaftslexikon).

Buchhorn, H., & Shannon, E. (2014). From service provider to service manager: Exploring the transition experience. *Asia Pacific journal of health management*, 9(3), 4–30.

Carter-Steel, A., Toleman, M., & Tan, W.-G. (2006). Transforming IT service management–the ITIL impact. In: *ACIS 2006: 17th Australasian conference on information systems: thought, leadership in IS, 6–8 Dec 2006, Adelaide, South Australia*.

Cusick, J. J., & Ma, G. (2010). Creating an ITIL inspired incident management approach: Roots, response, and results. In *2010 IEEE/IFIP Network operations and management symposium workshops* (pp. 142–148). IEEE, Osaka, Japan. https://doi.org/10.1109/NOMSW.2010.5486589.

Döring, A. & Paul, F. (2010). The German healthcare system EPMA. *Journal, 1*(4), 535–547. https://doi.org/10.1007/s13167-010-0060-z

Eberhart, M. (2021). HIMSS Studie: Public cloud in deutschen Krankenhäusern. *What's next: Der Thought Leadership Blog mit Einblicken in neueste Technologien und Innovationen*. https://whatsnext.nuance.com/de-de/gesundheitswesen/himss-studie-public-cloud-in-deutschen-krankenhaeusern/.

Floerecke, S. (2021). 'Self-Service-Portale für das IT-Service-Request-Management: Identifikation relevanter Use-Cases', *HMD Praxis der Wirtschaftsinformatik* [Preprint]. *Available at:* https://doi.org/10.1365/s40702-021-00804-1

Geiger, I., & Geißler, J. (2021). *Digitale Transformation der gesetzlichen Krankenversicherung IT-Strategie, Steuerung und Sourcing als strategische und operative Herausforderungen.* MA, Akademie Verlags- und Druck- Gesellschaft mbH.

Goldberg, M. et al. (2014). Transition and delivery challenges of retained organizations in IT Outsourcing. In M. Snene & M. Leonard (eds.) *Exploring services science* (pp. 56–71). Springer International Publishing (Lecture Notes in Business Information Processing). https://doi.org/10.1007/978-3-319-04810-9_5.

Heikkinen, S., & Jantti, M. (2012). Identifying IT service management challenges: A case study in two IT service provider companies. In *2012 23rd International Workshop on Database and Expert Systems Applications (DEXA)* (pp. 55–59). IEEE. https://doi.org/10.1109/DEXA.2012.32.

Jantti, M. (2011). Improving incident management processes in two IT service provider companies. In *2011 22nd International Workshop on Database and Expert Systems Applications (DEXA)* (pp. 26–30). IEEE. https://doi.org/10.1109/DEXA.2011.42.

Kern, T., Willcocks, L.P. & van Heck, E. (2002). The winner's curse in IT Outsourcing: Strategies for avoiding relational trauma. *California Management Review*, *44*(2), 47–69. https://doi.org/10.2307/41166122.

Ludwig, H. et al. (2007). Catalog-based service request management. *IBM Systems Journal*, *46*(3), 1–18. https://doi.org/10.1147/sj.463.0531.

Punyateera, J. et al. (2014). Study of service desk for NEdNet using incident management (Service Operation) of ITIL V.3. In *Signal and Information Processing Association Annual Summit and Conference (APSIPA), 2014 Asia-Pacific. 2014 Asia-Pacific Signal and Information Processing Association Annual Summit and Conference (APSIPA)* (pp. 1–6). IEEE. https://doi.org/10.1109/APSIPA.2014.7041752.

Rouse, A. (2005). *The role of benchmarking and service level agreement (SLA) practices in IT outsourcing success.* Association for Information Systems AIS Electronic Library (AISeL)–PACIS. https://aisel.aisnet.org/cgi/viewcontent.cgi?article=1167&context=pacis2005.

Schmidt, M., Brenner, M. and Schaaf, T. (2019) 'IT Service Management Frameworks Compared–Simplifying Service Portfolio Management. In *FIP/IEEE Symposium on Integrated Network and Service Management (IM)* (pp. 421–427).

Simon, M. (2011). Das Gesundheitssystem in Deutschland: eine Einführung in Struktur und Funktionsweise (3., überarb. und aktualisierte Aufl.,1. Nachdr). Huber.

Urbach, N., & Würz, T. (2012). How to Steer the IT outsourcing provider: Development and validation of a reference framework of IT outsourcing steering processes. *Business & Information Systems Engineering*, *4*(5), 247–259. https://doi.org/10.1007/s12599-012-0231-7.

Whyte, J., Stasis, A., & Lindkvist, C. (2016). Managing change in the delivery of complex projects: Configuration management, asset information and "big data"'. *International Journal of Project Management*, 34(2), 339–351. https://doi.org/10.1016/j.ijproman.2015.02.006.

Ying, L., Lijun, X., & Wei, S. (2009). Configuration management process design and implementation. In *2009 ISECS International Colloquium on Computing, Communication, Control, and Management (CCCM)* (pp. 4–7). IEEE. https://doi.org/10.1109/CCCM.2009.5268166.

Young, A. et al. (2008). *Gartner on Outsourcing, 2008–2009*. Gartner. https://brazilexportati.files.wordpress.com/2008/11/gartner-on-outsourcing-2008-9.pdf.

Digital Transformation of Small and Medium-Sized Businesses

Mariam Tvaradze

Abstract The modern era and especially the pandemic period has caused the need to make certain changes in all areas, especially in the business sector. The purpose of our research is to determine the stages of digital transformation of small and medium-sized businesses, identify given opportunities, highlight inevitable changes and transformations, and develop a transformation action plan based on the example of a specific business unit. 30 Georgian small and medium companies participated in our research. With the received information, we will be able to determine the need for their digital transformation, the possibilities of transformation and the sequence of changes, and we can generalize the obtained results to the sector. In the current period, it has become clear that digital transformation is of crucial importance: to accelerate changes, ensure stability and better understand the needs of clients. All this adds more relevance to the issue. The study will also discuss studies, practices and guidelines to demonstrate that digital transformation is today's priority, which involves transforming awareness, skills and tools.

Keywords Digital transformation · Changes during the pandemic · Transformation plan

1 The Importance of Digital Transformation

In the modern era, we can say that if any enterprise, company or organization does not come in line with the technological development and digital media innovations, they will not be able to meet even the minimum requirements of the market. Therefore, digital transformation is one of the urgent issues, as well as an important and inevitable stage in doing business. In general, digital transformation is an approach where, using technology and information in a secure environment, key business

M. Tvaradze (✉)
East European University, Tbilisi, Georgia
e-mail: mariammtvaradze@gmail.com

R. C. Geibel and S. Machavariani (eds.), *Chances and Challenges of Digital Management*, Springer Proceedings in Business and Economics,
https://doi.org/10.1007/978-3-031-45601-5_4

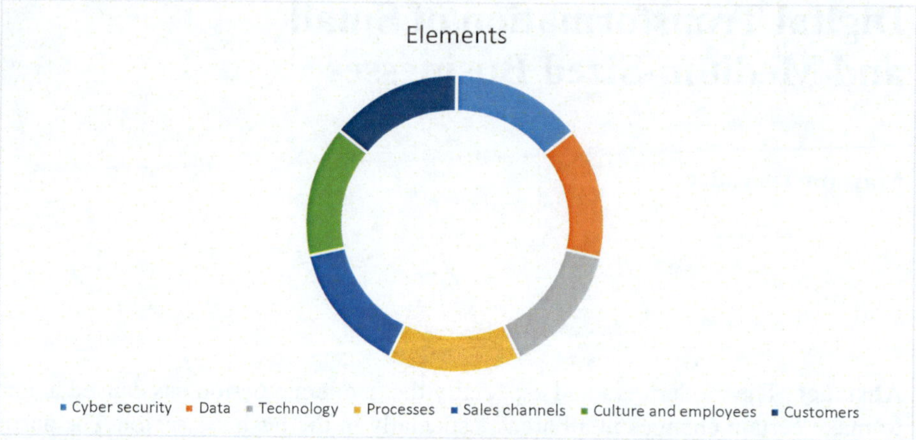

Fig. 1 Main business elements

elements are transformed so that your company is aligned with the challenges of the modern market and gains a competitive advantage.

Digital transformation is used to improve processes and productivity, improve employee skills, manage business risk and control costs. Digital transformation involves a variety of tools, solutions and continuous processes.

Analytical portal spaceo.ca defines that the process of digital transformation takes place in a chain and connects with it three main processes and terms:

- Digitization–digitization of data
- Digitization–digitization of processes
- Digital adaptation–digitization of the organization.

7 main business elements are also distinguished, which are important parts of the digital transformation of the business. These elements are: data, processes, customers, technology, culture and employees, sales channels and cyber security (Fig. 1).

Digital transformation essentially involves the adoption of new technologies and the creation of new opportunities and services of this method. This is beneficial for all parties involved in the business.

They are actively considering several stages that the company must go through before digital transformation and in its process:

- Stage 1 Comprehension Stage
- 2 Preparation Stage
- 3 Start of the process
- Stage 4 Active phase Stage
- 5 Sustainable development.

It should be noted here that the human factor plays an important role in all the mentioned processes.

From the main directions of digital transformation, we can single out some of them:

- **Activities and functions of the organization** means HR management, operations, marketing, etc.
- **Organizational processes**–project management, planning activities using various new technologies and services.
- **Organizational culture**–it is important to have a common goal in organizations that each employee shares.
- **A human-centered approach** implies the importance of customers, partners, employees and beneficiaries in identifying and improving their needs, as well as their active involvement in the processes.
- **The business model** implies a complete business cycle and its transformation.

Here we can note that digital transformation is not the only solution to possible situations. Modern technology is only a tool that can be used correctly to bring great success.

However, we must note that digital transformation can update and significantly improve business processes. Also, the processes become more flexible, the amount of manual work is reduced, which helps to prioritize different issues and spend resources on them.

2 Research and Research Results

Up to 30 small and medium enterprises participated in the research. Which are located in Georgia, exactly in Tbilisi region, in Kakheti region, in Imereti region, in Adjara and in Samegrelo region. The surveyed companies are distributed in different sectors, for example, wine production, nut processing, trading, manufacturing, tourism and services. The period of their existence on the market is limited to 10–20 years.

Information was obtained through direct communication and questionnaire survey method. The aim of the research was to find out (Figs. 2 and 3)

- How much companies were informed about digital transformation;
- How much they need digital transformation;
- Are they planning digital transformation;
- Are they ready for transformations and changes;
- What changes are they planning in the organization;
- At what stage are they in digital transformation;
- Do they need additional consultations to implement all stages of digital transformation, etc.

When asked whether companies need digital transformation, the results are as follows:

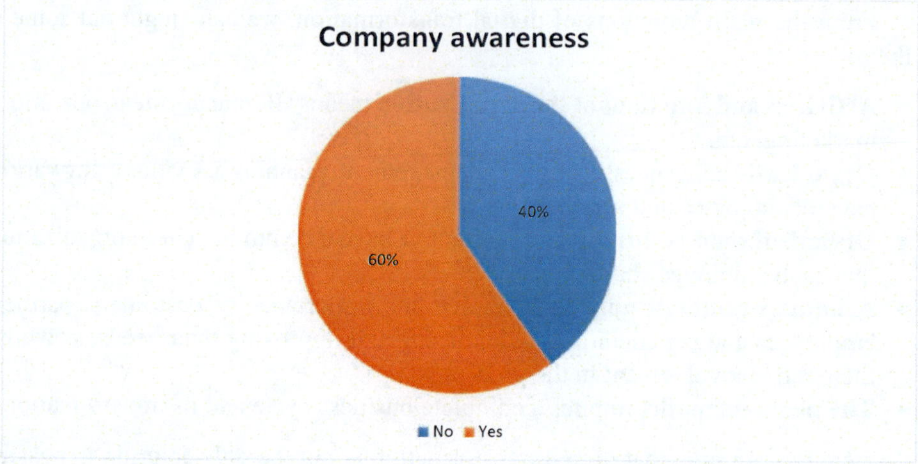

Fig. 2 Company Awareness

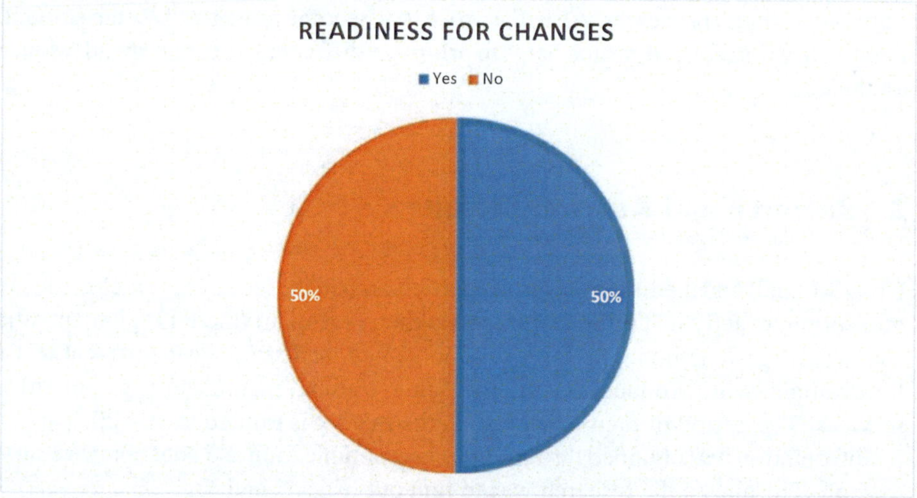

Fig. 3 Company's willingness

We can also say that it is difficult for companies to plan changes in advance, however, the Covid pandemic has clearly shown the entire business that changes are necessary, inevitable, and that immediate adaptation to the environment and adequate reaction to exogenous factors are important.

80% of companies cannot state at what stage they are in the process of digital transformation, which is caused by doubting the need for transformation, lack of information and unreliable attitude to processes.

90% of the surveyed companies have not planned changes in advance, therefore they do not have an action plan necessary for the transformation. Most companies would not refuse to receive information, consultations, and training.

To summarize, we can say that small and medium-sized enterprises in Georgia are not ready for radical changes, although they express their readiness and try to adapt to modernity. Some of them also suffer from information deficit, they do not have complete information to manage the processes required for digital transformation. Although few companies successfully implement transformations, they have gone through several stages and successfully manage the processes required for transformation. Also, some of them cooperate with a company that helps them in a number of processes (eg B2C company). We also discussed the steps taken for digital transformation of one of the companies. In particular, what processes have been planned and at what stage of digitization is the medium-sized Georgian wine-producing company. The company first determined:

- What did the digital transformation mean for his company?

  The company defined what is meant by digital transformation.

- Determining the existing capabilities, which means evaluating the existing resources, technologies and capabilities.

  Specifically, the mentioned wine producing company chose to digitize the product and service and introduce new technologies in the wine production process.

- Priority was given to the mentioned issue and appropriate support was obtained, both financial and human

  And then the company created a team that was tasked with implementing the mentioned changes and the selected confirmed project. The company announced that the changes are being successfully implemented, new technologies are being tested and further used, and they are also monitoring the results frequently. According to them, the mentioned processes and results will be the key to the company's success.

3 Conclusion

Digital transformation concerns not only small and medium-sized businesses, but the entire industry and business. We can say that this is the future and inevitable process of business. Georgian companies will gradually be able to adapt to the environment, with the support of IT programming, "building a foothold" for technological progress will be easier, and companies will be able to undergo digital transformation more easily.

On the one hand, the Covid pandemic has made it clear to companies how much changes are needed, and global market trends have made it clear that strategic communications and digital transformation in general are vital for business existence and development.

Digital transformation is beneficial for both suppliers and customers. This has a global aspect and it causes massive changes.

It is possible to single out some of the digital transformation trends:

- Quick adaptation

It is important for companies to be able to quickly adapt to the environment, accept world challenges and update technologies.

- Rapid innovation

Rapid innovation enables rapid development, creates new opportunities. As mentioned above, the pandemic has highlighted both problems and opportunities that can be addressed and exploited in this way.

It is important for companies to pay attention to:

- Introduction of technical innovations
- raising the qualification of human resources.

Despite the fact that digital transformation is a complex process, it creates a lot of new opportunities that will improve and develop Georgian business. By analyzing the information obtained as a result of the research of Georgian small and medium companies, we can make several recommendations:

- It is important for companies to determine the need for changes
- to get to know modern trends
- to adopt new technologies
- to determine in what direction transformations are needed
- to plan digital transformation processes
- to receive information and consultations in this direction.

to take advantage of all the opportunities created by the environment and thus the main goal of digital business transformation Adoption of new technologies, introduction of electronic services, development of human resources and raising of qualifications, reduction of manual work, reduction of administrative work, saving of time and financial resources, simplification of communication and management of a number of processes easily and quickly. It is the mentioned issues that ensure the development and competitiveness of companies.

References

EU4Digital (eufordigital.eu).

Kanchaveli, G.(2011). *E-Book: Digital Transformation.* Creative Development Center.

Bouza, A.(2018). *What is digital transformation, digitalization, and digitization.*

Wade, M. R. (2019). *What-is-digital-transformation.*

Javakhadze D. (2019). *Global trends in the digital transformation of business.* Ivane Javakhishvili Tbilisi State University Press. Global trends in the digital transformation of business.pdf.

Shengelia, T. (2011). *International Business, Universal.*

What is Digital Transformation? Why Is It Important–Salesforce.com.

Telemedicine During Pandemic in Georgia

Miranda Gogilashvili and Giorgi Gulua

Abstract The subject of the present paper is the use and the importance of the telemedicine in Georgia during pandemic (2020–2022). During the pandemic, the use of telemedicine has increased in different countries, Including USA and the members of the European Union. In Georgia, the implementation of the telemedicine is still at the early stage. There are different reasons for the underdeveloped telemedicine. Problem is that most of the healthcare providers are the private organizations. Most of these organizations have no telemedicine services. No public institutions can effect on the implementation of the telemedicine services in those organizations, if the owners of the healthcare providers have no interest to use telemedicine. Meanwhile, the ministry of the healthcare of Georgia had some interesting initiatives linked with the implementation of the telemedicine services in those organizations. Thus, the representatives of the healthcare sector did not welcome the initiatives of the ministry. On the other side, the providers of the healthcare services had no need for telemedicine before pandemic. After the pandemic started, the need for the telemedicine increased. Patients were not able to get to the healthcare providers for the services. Only few healthcare providers offer telemedicine in Georgia, including the Giorgi Eliava Pago therapy center. Those organizations who has no telemedicine services risk losing the clients and the income if the pandemic starts again. The present conference topic focuses on the benefits of the telemedicine services during pandemic and on the reasons for the aggravation of the implementation of those services in the healthcare sector of Georgia.

Keywords Telemedicine · Healthcare provider · Pandemic · Healthcare services

M. Gogilashvili (✉)
East European University, Tbilisi, Georgia
e-mail: mirandagogilashvili@yahoo.com

G. Gulua
Tbilisi State University, Tbilisi, Georgia

R. C. Geibel and S. Machavariani (eds.), *Chances and Challenges of Digital Management*, Springer Proceedings in Business and Economics,
https://doi.org/10.1007/978-3-031-45601-5_5

1 Introduction

During Covid19 pandemic from 2019 to 2021, the need for the telemedicine increased in the member states of the European Union and in USA. Telemedicine was an opportunity for the prevention of the pandemic. Digital healthcare was useful for the economy of time and human resources of the healthcare system. Telemedicine became an opportunity for the treatment and the monitoring of the patients.

Meanwhile, in Georgia telemedicine was not properly implemented in the healthcare system. It is underdeveloped for the several reasons: the absence of the guidelines for telemedicine, lack of the technological knowledge of the medical staff, privatization of the healthcare services.[1]

Because of the low level of the development of telemedicine, it was not properly used for the prevention of the Covid19 pandemic. Therefor the need for that type of service did not increase.[2] Opportunities linked with the telemedicine, those for the prevention of the pandemic and for the economy of the human resources not used properly. Considering the fact that pandemic risks will exist for the next few years and the world may face new pandemic treats during the next decades, the development and the implementation of telemedicine is a must in Georgia. Problem is that the development and the implementation of telemedicine does not depend on the policy of the government. State institutions cannot force the healthcare providers to implement the telemedicine services, as most clinics are a part of a private property.[3] Still there is no unified digital healthcare platform were the information on the treatment of the patients was uploaded. The reason for the absence of such platform is that part of the owners of the clinics and hospitals consider the platform will be risky for the security of the personal data of the patients. Others simply refuse to upload the data on the digital platform, because they do not want to deliver the information about the treatment of the patients.[4] Government can only partly effect on the implementation of the telemedicine services by creating the digital platforms for those who are involved in the universal healthcare program. They also can develop the applications and launch the web sites during the pandemic, as it happened in 2020. These digital services are not enough for the prevention but they are helpful. On the other side, the above-mentioned digital services did not work properly during the pandemic, as

[1] Verulava, T., Navrozashvili, N., Telemedicine - the health care challenge of the twenty-first century,,,Forbes" Georgia, 2020, retrieved from https://dspace.tsu.ge/bitstream/handle/123456789/707/%E1%83%A2%E1%83%94%E1%83%9A%E1%83%94%E1%83%9B%E1%83%94%E1%83%93%E1%83%98%E1%83%AA%E1%83%98%E1%83%9C%E1%83%90.pdf?sequence=1&isAllowed=y.

[2] Mezvrishvili, K., the specifics of the strategic management, University,,Geomed", Tbilisi, 2022, p. 33.

[3] The healthcare policy during pandemic, an interview with Nino Khelaia, a center of the social justice, 2020.

[4] Jafaridze, Z., availability of the healthcare services during the pandemic period on the example of Georgia, Tbilisi State University, Tbilisi, 2022, p. 36.

mentioned by one of the respondents during the research of 2021 on telemedicine in Georgia.[5]

2 The Essence of the Telemedicine

Telemedicine is a service delivered to the patients by the providers. According to some literature sources on telemedicine, it is one of the fields of medicine, which is not correct.[6] Telemedicine emerged because of the technological development and is not related to some specific fields of medicine. For example, telemedicine can be useful in cardiology as well as in traumatology and Oncology. Telemedicine is used for the diagnosis and treatment of a patient using digital communication technologies. It simplifies the communication between the doctor and a patient.[7] Therefor, telemedicine is more a service than a field of medicine. During the research conducted by Mezvrishvili in 2022 doctors employed at the "Aversi clinic" were asked to explain the essence of telemedicine. During the interview one of the respondents mentioned that in some cases there is no need for special technologies to deliver the service of telemedicine. Doctors can use laptops or personal computers for the communication with their patients. In other cases, medical staff may need high-resolution screens to check the body of the patient. Standard internet packages are not useful for these cases. High-speed internet is necessary for the permanent communication with the patient.[8] Another function of the telemedicine is a communication between the doctors. Medics can organize consiliums on the issues of treatment or exchange the information about the different issues.[9] In some cases, even trainings for the students are organized using telemedicine. Another function of the telemedicine can be the collection of the information about the patient (or about the patients). Later this information is sent to the doctor and used for treatment of for the diagnosis of the patient.[10] As mentioned by the respondent of the research conducted by Mezvrishvili in 2020, doctors in Georgia do not work only on telemedicine. As it is a service, medics use telemedicine in practice to communicate with their patients for different purposes. Mostly telemedicine is used for the consultation rather than for the diagnosis. The respondent noted that telemedicine is limited in some cases. For example, surgical operations, childbirth, neurosurgery, proctology and bariatric surgery are services

[5] Ratishvili, N., "New economic reality and medical services, on the example of the Eliava Phage Therapy Center" Gipa, Tbilisi, 2022, p. 26.

[6] Kldiashvili, E., Telemedicine, 2007, retrieved from http://www.modernpublishing.ge/view_post.php?id=4&pub=1&year=2007.

[7] Ibid.

[8] Mezvrishvili, K., the specifics of the strategic management, University, Geomed", Tbilisi, 2022, p. 33.

[9] Ashugashvili, M., Doctor remotely–telemedicine has eliminated the distance, Journal, Aversi" # 183, retrieved from https://www.aversi.ge/ka/cnobari/2272/eqimi-distanciurad-telemedicinam-mandzili-gaaqro.

[10] Ibid.

that require direct contact with the patient to perform medical manipulations on his (or her) body. Telemedicine can be used Where these manipulations are not necessary. These fields are gastroenterology, dermatology, endocrinology, gynecology, and endoscopy. In such cases, the patient has to visit the doctor only for analysis. Patients can do the analysis on their own and send them to the doctor who does a treatment.[11]

3 The Development of the Telemedicine in Georgia

The first attempt for the development of the telemedicine in Georgia was made in 1999, when a draft on the telemedicine development strategy was presented to the council of the president of Georgia. Later, in 2003 another strategy plane was offered to the council. Both strategy plans were developed by National Information Learning Center. None of those planes were adopted.[12] Before the pandemic, the development of the telemedicine was a necessity for Georgia, because of the unequal distribution of the human resources in medicine. Most part of the human resources are concentrated in urban areas. In rural areas, there was a need for the medics. To deal with the lack of doctors telemedicine had to be implemented in the clinics in the rural areas. Still in those regions of Georgia, there is a problem of the healthcare accessibility. The problem of the healthcare services is especially sharp in the high mountain regions of the country. The development of the telemedicine, reflected in the implementation of the digital technologies for the delivery of the healthcare services, may be useful to deal with that problem.[13]

The active phase of the development of the Telemedicine started in 2014 when the unified medical base was formed for the universal healthcare program. Since 2015, national register of cancer is in action. In 2016 birth register started operating. Next year electronic prescriptions were putted into the action. Since 2019, the unified digital informational platform is used for the universal healthcare program of Georgia. On the platform, the information of the patients is uploaded. In 2019 the ambulatories and networks of clinics launched their own platforms were the information of the patients was uploaded.[14] Still there use no unified platform in Georgia on which the medical histories of all of the patients is uploaded. Meanwhile, there are some separate digital platforms with the information on the particular groups of patients. For example, programs used for the mobile tele monitoring of arrhythmias, electronic tele monitoring of arterial hypertension, mobile screening of a skin cancer.

[11] Mezvrishvili, K., the specifics of the strategic management, University "Geomed", Tbilisi, 2022, p. 33.

[12] Kirtava, Z., Study on the Harmonization of the Digital Markets (HDM) in the Eastern Partnership (EaP) Topic: eHealth questioner 1–fact based questions, 2017, 13.

[13] Kirtava, Z., the four packet recommendations of "Geocase", Electronic healthcare, telemedicine–possibilities and challenges, 2021, 26.

[14] Ibid, 26.

4 The Factors Which Aggravated the Development of the Telemedicine in Georgia

There are several factors, which aggravated the development of the telemedicine in Georgia. Among those factors, there is a problem of the internet in the high mountain regions of Georgia. Because of the absence of the high-speed internet, people cannot connect with the doctors or with the other providers of the healthcare services.

Another problematic aspect, which aggravated the development of the telemedicine in Georgia, is the absence of the guidelines. Still there are no guidelines for telemedicine in Georgia. Therefor it is unclear which documents should be used for the treatment using the above-mentioned service.

The third problematic aspect, which limits the implementation of the service, is a risk for the personal data of the patients. In one of the researches conducted on telemedicine in 2022 a respondent who has worked at the ministry of the healthcare of Georgia mentioned, that one of the initiatives of the ministry was not accepted by the providers of the healthcare services for the high risks for the personal data.[15] According to the initiative, a unified platform for the medical data had to be created. On the platform, data on the history of the illness of the patients had to be uploaded. According to the data, doctors would easily get access to the medical history of the patients. The platform would have been useful in the cases when the patients change the doctor and new doctor continues the treatment. On the other side, the use of the electronic platform simplifies the data collection on the patients. There is no need to visit the previous healthcare provider for getting the documentation on the treatment. Patients can easily give access to the medics on the documentation uploaded on the platform.[16] Along with the risks for the privacy, the realization of such initiative needed the unified approach toward the systematization of the personal data. There was no agreement among the providers of the healthcare services on the use of the unified digital platform. Here comes another problematic aspect of the implementation of the telemedicine in Georgia. Problem is that the healthcare sector was privatized. Government owns a small part of the clinics. As the owners are the individuals, they make decision on the systematization of the personal data of the patients. In this case uploading the data on the digital platform for the telemedicine thought to be a risky action. The privatization of the healthcare system of Georgia not only complicated the implementation of the telemedicine but also the delivery of the healthcare services during pandemic. The state institutions were not able to use

---

15 Verulava, T., Navrozashvili, N., Telemedicine–the health care challenge of the twenty-first century, Forbes" Georgia, 2020, retrieved from https://dspace.tsu.ge/bitstream/handle/123456789/707/%E1%83%A2%E1%83%94%E1%83%9A%E1%83%94%E1%83%9B%E1%83%94%E1%83%93%E1%83%98%E1%83%AA%E1%83%98%E1%83%9C%E1%83%90.pdf?sequence=1&isAllowed=y.

16 Jafaridze, Z., availability of the healthcare services during the pandemic period on the example of Georgia, Tbilisi State University, Tbilisi, 2022, p.36.

the resources of the private owners during the pandemic: beds, the instruments for the artificial respiration.[17]

During the research conducted by Ratishvili in 2021, one of the respondents mentioned that Telemedicine not properly implemented in the healthcare system of Georgia, because there was no need for such service. On the other side, the medical personal is not experienced in using the digital technologies. Simply they do not know how to use the tools for the telemedicine.[18]

Several factors, which also aggravated the development of the telemedicine, were revealed during the research conducted by Mezvrishvili in 2022. One of the respondents, a doctor employed at "Aversi", who uses telemedicine for the treatment admitted, that telemedicine like any other service can be delivered only if there is a need on the market. In Georgia 17,5% of the population lives in an absolute poverty.[19] People have no money to pay for the healthcare services. On the other side, Georgia is not that big. According to the statistics service of Georgia (hereinafter Geostat) most part of the population lives in the urban areas. 33% of the population of the state lives in the capital of Georgia.[20] As supposed by the respondent, the unequal distribution of the human resources leads to the concentration of the population in few cities. Therefor there is no need for the telemedicine in Georgia. People can visit the providers of the healthcare services. They do not need digital communication for the treatment.[21]

5 Telemedicine During the Pandemic in Georgia

During the pandemic, the need for the telemedicine services increased in the world. Since 2019 in the member states of the European Union only 11% of the patients used telemedicine for the treatment. In 2020, the share of those patients consisted 76%. The need for the telemedicine services also increased in USA. In 2020 180.000 Americans used this service, while in 2018 the number of the treatments using telemedicine consisted 2,6 million.[22]

The use of the telemedicine services was found to be effective during the pandemic not only in Georgia but all around the world. Using telemedicine, it was possible to avoid the long ques of the patients and it was helpful for the prevention of the spread of

[17] Ratishvili, N., "New economic reality and medical services, on the example of the Eliava Phage Therapy Center" Gipa, Tbilisi, 2022, p. 26.

[18] Ibid, P.28.

[19] Rate of the absolute poverty in Georgia, Geostat, 2021, retrieved from https://www.geostat.ge/ka/modules/categories/192/tskhovrebis-done.

[20] The population of Georgia in the towns and cities, Geostat, 2022, retrieved from https://www.geostat.ge/ka/modules/categories/41/mosakhleoba.

[21] Mezvrishvili, K., the specifics of the strategic management, University "Geomed", Tbilisi, 2022, p. 42.

[22] Interview with professor Tengiz Verulava, 2021, retrieved from https://euronewsgeorgia.com/2021/05/13/tengiz-verulava-meditsinis-doktori-profesori/

the pandemic.[23] Along with the prevention of the pandemic telemedicine was found to be useful for the treatment and for the permanent monitoring on the patients. According to one of the researches conducted on the treatment using telemedicine, during the pandemic patients in USA who used the service for different purposes were satisfied by the quality of the service as well as with the results of the treatment. Among the patients were those who had a kidney transplant, suffered from diabetes or needed a prenatal care. Some of the patients had been treated for ophthalmological disorders or for cancer treatment.[24]

Telemedicine was effective for the simplification of the access to the healthcare services. Using the video chat and SMS patients were able to get the consultation about the treatment or about the symptoms of the infection. The medical staff had an opportunity to diagnose the patients quickly. Less time was needed to make decisions on the treatment of the patients. Using the healthcare applications patients were able to find the healthcare providers and get the services quickly.[25]

In Georgia, telemedicine played the same role as in the world. Namely, the service was found to be effective for the delivery of the healthcare services during the pandemic. The restrictions on the public transport in Georgia complicated the treatment of the illnesses. Telemedicine was especially important for those patients who suffer from the chronical diseases. As mentioned in the research conducted by Shport in 2021 the pandemic restrictions limited the access to the healthcare services and worsened the conditions of the socially unsecured people. Pandemic especially negatively affected on the healthcare of people with disabilities.[26] Because of the absence of the healthcare services, telemedicine was found useful during the pandemic in Georgia, like in the several countries of the west.

While discussing the effects of the telemedicine in Georgia, we have to separate two groups of the results of the use of the telemedicine in Georgia. the first one includes the results of the use of the telemedicine by the public bodies for the prevention of the pandemic, including the ministry of the healthcare of Georgia and the second one is the national center for the disease control and public health (hereinafter NCDC). Another group of the results of the use of the telemedicine during the pandemic includes those outcomes for the providers of the healthcare services of the use of the service. For example, two different researches conducted on the use of the services revealed that using telemedicine the management of the clinic reduced the

---

[23] Nunez, A., Sreeganga, S., D., Ramaprasad, A., Access to Healthcare during COVID-19, international Journal of Environmental Research and Public Health, 18(6), 2021, p. 32.

[24] Mezvrishvili, K., the specifics of the strategic management, University "Geomed", Tbilisi, 2022, p. 26.

[25] Maintaining essential health services: operational guidance for the COVID-19 context, WHO, 2020.

[26] Shport, M., Provision of social services to vulnerable groups by the municipality under pandemic conditions.

on the example of Zugdidi and Bolnisi municipalities, Gipa, Tbilisi, 2021, p. 16.

financial damage of the company.[27] In one case, the company was able to maintain the patients by offering them the digital healthcare services. Further, I will analyze both of these effects of the telemedicine during the pandemic.

During the research conducted by Ratishvili on telemedicine in Giorgi Eliava Pago therapy center one of the respondents admitted the strength and the weaknesses of the delivery of the healthcare services during pandemic by the ministry of the healthcare of Georgia. The respondent mentioned that organizing the call centers during pandemic was useful for the Covid19 prevention. Meanwhile, the level of the professionalism of the staff at those call centers was low as only students were employed. In some cases, the students were giving incorrect information to the citizens. Because of these citizens found hard to get the healthcare services.[28] As mentioned by the respondent, the ministry of the healthcare organized few measures for the prevention of the pandemic, which was not enough. The first measure was the web-page-stopcovid.ge and the second one the online application. The web page was operating badly and stopped working few times for the registration of the huge number of the citizens in the same time.[29] During the research conducted by Jafaridze in 2022 one of the respondents who worked at the ministry of the healthcare of Georgia listed few weaknesses of the application developed for the prevention of the pandemic. According to the respondent, the application was useless without the internet and Bluetooth. Few consumers use internet on their cell phones. In the most cases, Bluetooth is switched off. Therefore, most of the citizens did not use the application. The program itself was useful for the informing the citizens about the contacts with those people who had or has had Covid19 symptoms. Even though the program was useful with WIFI and Bluetooth connection, 14.000 citizens were informed about the contacts with those who had Covid19 symptoms.[30] Therefor we can say that the application was useful for the prevention of the Covid19 pandemic.

As I already mentioned above, telemedicine was effective for those clinics, which implemented this service and offered it to the clients during the pandemic. According to the research conducted by Ratishvili in September of 2021 Giorgi Eliava Pago therapy center gradually amended the methods of the face-to-face treatment of the patients to the telemedicine. Because of the changed methods of treatment, the clinic avoided the financial loses during the pandemic. As mentioned by one of the surveyed respondents, who works at the center, those clinics that did not offer telemedicine to their clients faced financial loses. As revealed by the research, the center mostly worked on the clients who live abroad and are not the citizens of Georgia. Once again, this fact shows that on the local market there is no need for the telemedicine. According to the results of the above-mentioned research during the pandemic, the

---

[27] Mezvrishvili, K., the specifics of the strategic management, University "Geomed", Tbilisi, 2022., Ratishvili, N., "New economic reality and medical services, on the example of the Eliava Phage Therapy Center" Gipa, Tbilisi, 2022.

[28] Ratishvili, N., "New economic reality and medical services, on the example of the Eliava Phage Therapy Center" Gipa, Tbilisi, 2022, p. 25.

[29] Ibid, p. 26.

[30] Jafaridze, Z., availability of the healthcare services during the pandemic period on the example of Georgia, Tbilisi State University, Tbilisi, 2022, p. 35.

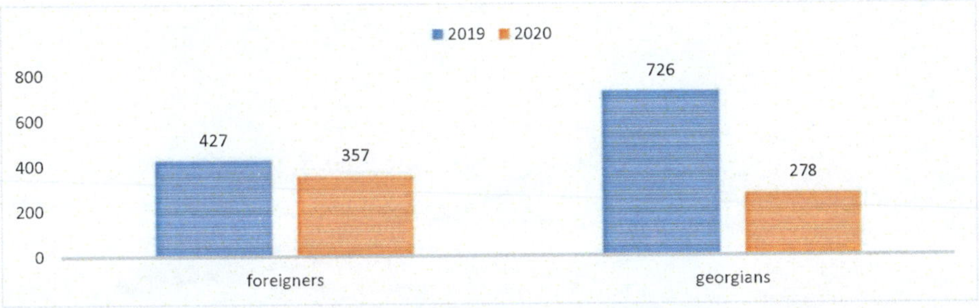

Fig. 1 The consumers of Giorgi Eliava Pago therapy center. 2022 *Source* Ratishvili,

share of those patients, who are not the residents of Georgia increased and the share of the Georgian patients decreased, which means that foreign consumers replaced the Georgian consumers (Fig. 1).

In 2019, a year before the pandemic Giorgi Eliava Pago therapy center had 726 Georgian clients and 278 foreigners. In 2020 after the outbreak of the pandemic, the number of the Georgian consumers decreased down to 427 and the number of the foreign clients increased up to 357. 57% of the foreign patients. In 2019 57% of the foreigners used telemedicine for treatment. In 2020 the share of this consumers increased. 321 patients who were not the citizens of Georgia used telemedicine for the treatment. Only 36 foreigners did the same with face-to-face treatment. The number of the citizens of Georgia who were the clients of Giorgi Eliava Pago therapy center decreased down to 38%. 62% less Georgian consumers used the services of the clinic in 2020 than in 2019. What can be concluded according to the data mentioned above is that telemedicine is mostly used for the treatment of those patients who live abroad. Georgian citizens use telemedicine in few cases. The statistical data shows that even during the Covid19 pandemic in Georgia the need for the digital healthcare did not increase. During another research on telemedicine conducted by Mezvrishvili in 2022, respondents confirmed that in Georgia the increment of the use of the telemedicine was not observed during the pandemic. Telemedicine was more an opportunity for the prevention of Covid19 pandemic than an opportunity for the treatment of the patients. Even the focus on the international market was not a prevention for the financial loses of the organization. Both: the revenue and the profit of Giorgi Eliava Pago therapy center decreased from 2019 to 2020. In 2019, the profit of the organization was 2.733.000 GEL, while in 2020 the revenue of the clinic decreased down to 1,943,000 GEL. In 2019, the revenue of the center consisted 5,161,000 GEL and decreased down to 4,199,000 in 2020.[31]

Mezvrishvili conducted another research, which revealed the effectivity of the telemedicine during the pandemic, in 2022. According to the results of the research, the revenue and the profit of the clinic decreased from 2018 to 2021. Thus, the revenue and the profit accumulated by the telemedicine increased during the same period. The

[31] Ratishvili, N., "New economic reality and medical services, on the example of the Eliava Phage Therapy Center" Gipa, Tbilisi, 2022, p. 20.

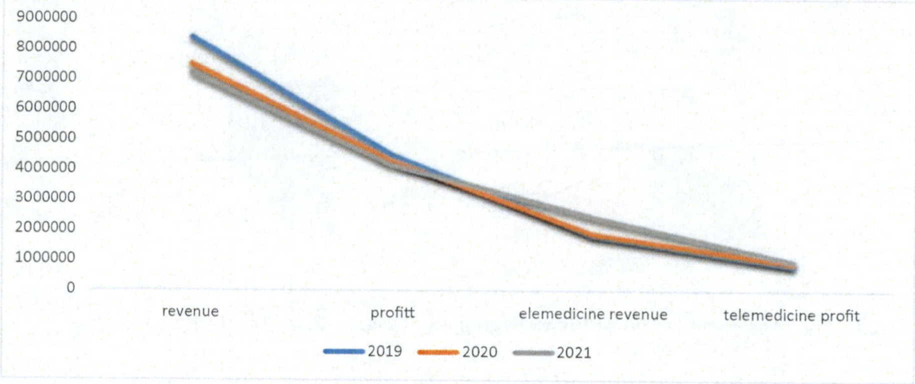

Fig. 2 Aversi" clinic revenue and profit during the pandemic. 2022 *Source* Mezvrishvili,

statistics show that telemedicine was useful to avoid the financial loses. Logically, more the company would have been focused on telemedicine during pandemic, less the financial damage would have been[32] (Fig. 2).

The results of the research revealed that even the revenue and the income of the telemedicine decreased after the outbreak of the pandemic. From March to May of 2020, the revenue and the profit of the telemedicine decreased slightly but then it went back to the previous parameters in November of 2020.[33] According to the results of the research, the number of the patients who used telemedicine did not decrease during the pandemic. Contrary more patients used telemedicine for the treatment during the pandemic from 2020 to 2021. The number of the patients who use telemedicine was regularly increasing from time to time. In 2015 when the services were first implemented at "Aversi" clinic 644 patients applied to this service. In 2019, number of the patients was 742 and in 2020 it consisted 749. It is notable that during the pandemic from 2019 to 2020 the number of the patients only slightly increased. The progress slowed down in comparison with the previous periods. Still it remained even during the pandemic. What the statistics show is that like in Ratishvili's research, pandemic did not increase the need for the telemedicine in Georgia.[34] Like Ratishvili's research of 2021 the study of 2022 uncovered that mostly telemedicine is used for the treatment abroad. For example, in 2021 93% of the consumers were those, who lives abroad. According to the results of the research in most cases, telemedicine was used for consultation. 16% of the total number of the cases goes to the heart diseases. 13% goes to the post stroke cases or to the stroke prevention. In 17% of the total cases, telemedicine was used for the prevention of the Covid19 pandemic. According to the statistical data delivered in the research, telemedicine

[32] Mezvrishvili, K., the specifics of the strategic management, University "Geomed", Tbilisi, 2022., p. 27.

[33] Ibis, p.32.

[34] Mezvrishvili, K., the specifics of the strategic management, University "Geomed", Tbilisi, 2022., p. 33.

was rarely used in dermatology, gerontology, diet ology, like for the prevention of the infections and heart dieses.[35]

6 Conclusions

The results of the researches on the use of telemedicine during the pandemic in Georgia show, that the implementation of the digital healthcare services significantly depends on the owners of the healthcare providers. There is a need for a consensus between the government and the private sector on the digitalization of the healthcare services. What the research has uncovered is that the privatization of the healthcare system of Georgia not only aggravated the implementation of the telemedicine but also complicated the process of the mobilization of the material and technical resources of the government, for the prevention of Covid19 pandemic in Georgia. The research shows that the implementation of the methods of the digital healthcare, namely telemedicine was limited for the several reasons. Part of those factors can be eliminated, while others need cooperation between the government and the providers of the healthcare services. For example, high-speed internet and the equipment for the ambulatories for the telemedicine may be useful for the implementation of the methods for the digital healthcare, while the emergence of the digital platforms is not possible without the agreement between the government and the business sector. According to the results of the research, telemedicine is useful for the effective treatment and for the monitoring on the patients during the pandemic. It is helpful to maintain the clients, the revenue and the profit during the pandemic and avoid the financial loss for the providers of the healthcare services. The research also revealed that those clinics, which offer digital healthcare services in Georgia mostly work for the foreigners. The local Georgian market is not enough to gain a profit on telemedicine. We can also conclude that the implementation of the digital services, including telemedicine depends on the demand on the market.

7 Recommendations

1. The ministry of the healthcare of Georgia has to continue equipping the ambulatories in the regions of Georgia with the equipment for telemedicine
2. The guidelines for telemedicine has to be developed by the ministry of the healthcare of Georgia
3. All regions of the country have to be supported with a high-speed internet
4. The ministry of the healthcare of Georgia has to conduct a platform. On the platform the medical records of the beneficiaries of the universal healthcare program should be uploaded

[35] Ibid. p. 36.

5. According to the guidelines on telemedicine, the issues of the personal data of the patients should be regulated.

References

Ashugashvili, M. Doctor remotely–telemedicine has eliminated the distance. *Journal Aversi 183*

Interview with Professor Tengiz Verulava. (2021). https://euronewsgeorgia.com/2021/05/13/tengiz-verulava-meditsinis-doktori-profesori/

Jafaridze, Z. (2022). *Availability of the healthcare services during the pandemic period on the example of Georgia.* Tbilisi State University.

Kirtava, Z. (2017). *Study on the Harmonization of the Digital Markets (HDM) in the Eastern Partnership (EaP) Topic: eHealth questioner 1–fact based questions*

Kirtava, Z. (2021). The four packet recommendations of "Geocase". *Electronic healthcare, telemedicine–possibilities and challenges*, 20–25.

Kldiashvili, E. (2007), *Telemedicine*. http://www.modernpublishing.ge/view_post.php?id=4&pub=1&year=2007.

Maintaining essential health services: operational guidance for the COVID-19 context. WHO

Mezvrishvili, K. (2022). The specifics of the strategic management. University Geomed, Tbilisi

Nunez, A., Sreeganga, S. D., Ramaprasad, A. (2021). Access to Healthcare during COVID-19. *International Journal of Environmental Research and Public Health, 18*(6).

Ratishvili, N. (2022). *New economic reality and medical services, on the example of the Eliava Phage Therapy Center Gipa, Tbilisi.*

Shport, M. (2021). *Provision of social services to vulnerable groups by the municipality under pandemic conditions on the example of Zugdidi and Bolnisi municipalities, Gipa, Tbilisi.*

The healthcare policy during pandemic, an interview with Nino Khelaia, a center of the social justice, 2020

The population of Georgia in the towns and cities, Geostat. (2022). https://www.geostat.ge/ka/modules/categories/41/mosakhleoba.

Verulava, T., & Navrozashvili, N. (2020). Telemedicine—the health care challenge of the 21st century, Forbes Georgia.

Rate of the absolute poverty in Georgia, Geostat. (2021). https://www.geostat.ge/ka/modules/categories/192/tskhovrebis-done.

Digitization to Increase Efficiency of SMEs in Georgia

Shalva Machavariani

Abstract The development of Small and Medium-sized Enterprises (SMEs) in Georgia can bring enormous economic as well as social benefits. One of the necessary conditions for improving the current situation is the purposeful implementation of digitization in SMEs. The article provides an in-depth analysis of the situation of small and medium-sized enterprises in Georgia and the European Union (EU) in the pandemic and post-pandemic period caused by Covid-19 and presents the results of the implemented digitization process in SMEs in Georgia and the European Union. The experience acquired as a through the implementation of targeted digitization of small and medium-sized businesses in EU countries serves a good case for enterprises operating in Georgia in terms of enhancing their competitiveness. It is recommended to draw out complex measures mainly: elaboration of an enterprise development strategy, legal and financial support, wide spread of digital technologies, implementation of systematic changes, wide utilization of innovations, establishment of regional centers, formation of University-Clusters and businesses, and creation of relevant portals for timely resolution of problems/challenges. As an example, the activities planned within the framework of the project "**Business Problems Interactive Web Portal**" approved by the International Visegrad Fund, aimes at solving the problems faced by small and medium enterprises by interactive web portal and integrated information network, which links research institutions and businesses in close cooperation. Project is funded by the Visegrad Fund and focuses on gaining SME competitiveness in Georgia and Visegrad countries. On the basis of all above mentioned, relevant proposals are presented in the paper, which should contribute to the development of small and medium-sized enterprises.

Keywords SMEs · Digitization · Business efficiency · Research · Business Problems Web Portal

S. Machavariani (✉)
Doctor of Technical Science, East European University, Tbilisi, Georgia
e-mail: s.machavariani@eeu.edu.ge

R. C. Geibel and S. Machavariani (eds.), *Chances and Challenges of Digital Management*, Springer Proceedings in Business and Economics,
https://doi.org/10.1007/978-3-031-45601-5_6

Table 1 Indicators of enterprises registered in Georgia (*Source Geostat, business sector in Georgia*)

N	Main indicators of activity	2016	2017	2018	2019	2020
1	Number of registered enterprises, unit	595,782	638,488	680,936	722,695	758,478
2	Turnover, mln. GEL	64,081.8	71,740.1	86,625.1	109,024.3	114,348.5
3	Output, mln. GEL	34,156.9	38,206.8	41,649.2	47,494.7	46,227.3
4	Value added, mln. GEL	16,772.4	19,036.3	20,726.9	23,296.0	22,263.0
5	Number of employees, person	666,790	708,165	734,215	756,852	703,874

1 Introduction

Small and medium-sized enterprises (SME) represent the backbone of the country's economy, since:

- they employ a significant part of the population and create new jobs;
- they produce a certain part of the gross domestic product (GDP);
- have the ability to quickly adapt to external influences;
- have high development potential.

Before the pandemic, in 2016–2019, business in Georgia was developing quite intensively (Table 1). The share of small and medium enterprises was: 99.7% of operating enterprises, 65% of employees and 59% of total added value. It should be noted that 66.4% of the total turnover was generated from large businesses, 15.1% from medium, and 18.5% from small businesses. The situation was slightly different in the case of manufacturing products: large businesses produced 49.1% of all products, medium—23.4%, and small businesses- 27.5%.[1]

Before the pandemic, there were approximately 26 million small and medium-sized enterprises operating in the EU, employing 109 million people and contributing to 2/3 of the European GDP.[2] Table 2 shows the general indicators of small, medium and large businesses in EU countries. It is worth noting the higher labor productivity of EU enterprises of different sizes compared to Georgian enterprises. One of the reasons for this is the wider and earlier implementation of digitization processes in EU countries (Radostina Emilova Yuleva—Chuchulayna, 2021). Notably, the sectors most affected by public health measures during the pandemic, in terms of employment and reduced working hours, were commerce, hospitality, financial and other services. More than a third of the establishments have changed their main business activities—shifting their main production lines to the production of protective equipment, respirators, disinfection tools and other means. Many organizations have switched to remote work to respond to public health demands.

[1] Business sector In Georgia. https://www.geostat.ge/media/41841/Business-sector-in-Georgia-2021.pdf.

[2] Eurostat. 2019. Statistics on SMEs. https://ec.europa.eu/eurostat/statistics-explained/index.php/Statistics_on_small_and_medium-sized_enterprises.

Table 2 EU small and medium-sized enterprises: an overview

N	Main indicators of activity	Large enterprises (249 and more) %	Medium enterprises (50–249) %	Micro and Small enterprises (1–49)
1	Number of enterprises	0.2	0,9	99,0
2	Number of persons employed	35,7	15,7	48,5
3	Value added	47,5	17,1	35,4

source: World Economic Forum (Non Financial business economy) https://www.weforum.org/agenda/2023/01/europe-smes-business-resilience-covid-19/.

More than a third of the establishments have changed their main business activities—shifting their main production lines to the production of protective equipment, respirators, disinfection tools and other means. Many organizations have switched to remote work to respond to public health demands. In 2019, this trend was not common in most companies, but they saw the benefits of remote work and quickly adapted to the situation.

According to Eurofound, Companies across the EU have had to make significant adjustments to their business models, processes and jobs in order to stay in business. The health and safety of customers and staff was a priority. The sweeping changes that organizations and their employees have experienced have reshaped the world of work: workplaces have been reorganized to allow for social distancing, teleworking has become popular, and the pandemic has accelerated digital transformation.[3]

2 The Impact of the Covid-19 Pandemic on Small and Medium-Sized Businesses in Georgia

In Georgia, the pandemic led to a decrease in the number of employees (Fig. 1), and had an impact on turnover and employee share indicators depending on the size of enterprises (Fig. 2).

The pandemic process has particularly affected small and medium-sized enterprises (SMEs) in such areas as wholesale and retail trade, real estate activities, construction, tourism and financial and insurance business.[4]

Depending on the size of enterprises, the share of added value and sales expenses has changed (Fig. 3).

[3] Business not as usual: How EU companies adapted to the COVID-19 pandemic, https://www.eurofound.europa.eu/sites/default/files/ef_publication/field_ef_document/ef21033en.pdf.

[4] The Impact of COVID-19 on trade and structural transformation in Georgia https://unece.org/fileadmin/DAM/trade/StudiesRegulatoryProceduralBarriersTrade/ThematicPublications/Impact_COVID-19_Georgia.pdf.

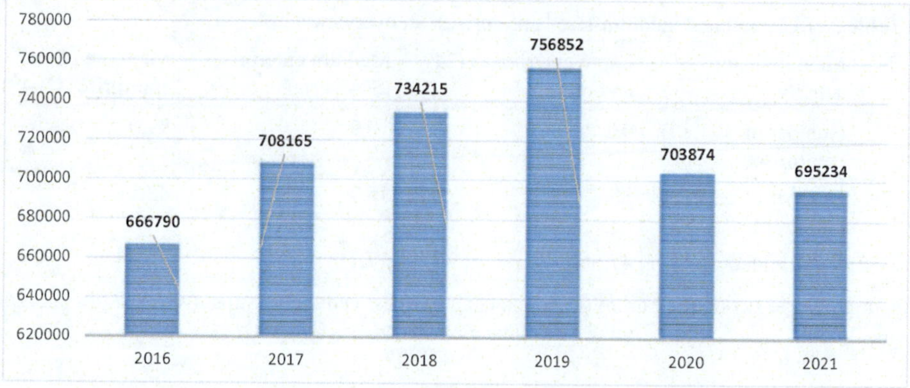

Fig. 1 Number of Employees (*Source Geostat, business sector in Georgia)*

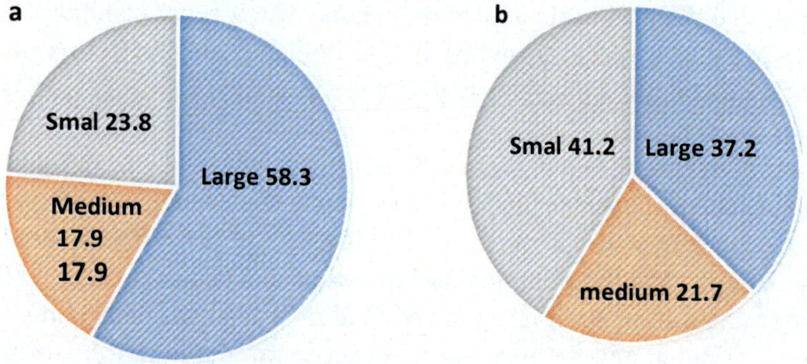

Fig. 2 **a** Share of turnover by size of enterprises in 2020, %, **b.** Share of employed persons in by size of enterprises in 2020, %. (*Source Geostat, business sector in Georgia)*

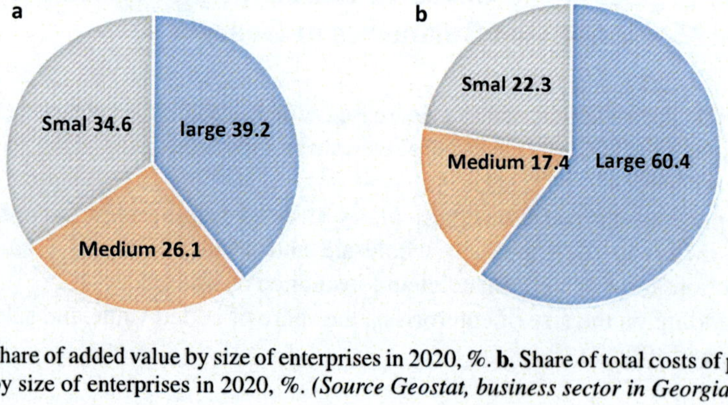

Fig. 3 **a** Share of added value by size of enterprises in 2020, %. **b.** Share of total costs of production and sales by size of enterprises in 2020, %. *(Source Geostat, business sector in Georgia)*

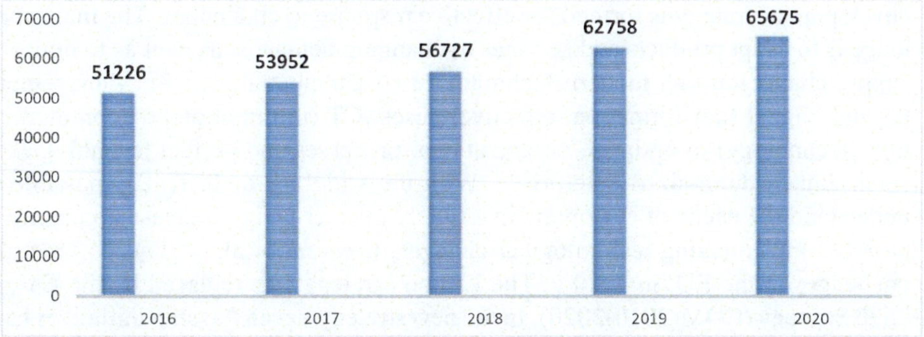

Fig. 4 Labor productivity per employed person, Gel (*Source Geostat, business sector in Georgia)*

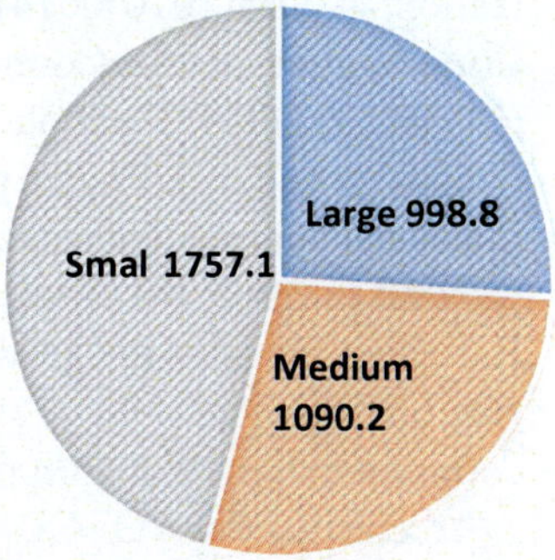

Fig. 5 Capital Productivity, Gel. Output per 1000 Gel of Fixed Capital, (*Source Geostat, business sector in Georgia)*

Digitization processes supported SMEs operating throughout the pandemic to increase labor productivity by 4.4% (Fig. 4) compared to the pre-pandemic period.

In addition to the above, the introduction of digital technologies in Georgia led to an increase in capital productivity compared to the pre-pandemic period (Fig. 5).

3 Digital Transformation and Experience of EU Countries SMEs Increasing Competitiveness Using Digital Technologies

Digitization reduces transaction costs and improves communication between employees, suppliers and customers. In addition, digitalization increases the consumer value of products and the efficiency of services, stimulates the demand for innovation and, importantly, finds new opportunities for earning income. From the beginning, digital transformation in the EU has focused on the "processes of socio-technical structures," which have facilitated the development of small and medium entrepreneurship (Yoo et al, 2010). Digital transformation includes: technological, organizational (structural) and social processes (Reis et al., 2018). Enterprise development strategy is formed for effective response to challenges. The main challenge is to adapt products and services to changing demands, as well as to optimize supply chains through modern technologies (Biahmouet al., 2016). Management, through digital transformation, effectively uses ICT (information and communications technology) to optimize organizational processes and perfect technologies in small and medium-sized enterprises. With the wide use of ICT, it is possible to understand the needs of customers in a timely manner and to increase competitiveness by implementing technological changes. (Lederer et al., 2017). To meet the challenges in the EU, in 2010 г. The Lisbon Strategy was replaced by the Europe 2020 Strategy (COM(2010)2020). In the new strategy, seven flagship initiatives have been put forward, four of which are particularly important for increasing the competitiveness of EU industry: «Innovation Union» (COM(2010)0546), «Digital agenda for Europe» (COM(2010)0245), «Integrated industrial policy» in the era of globalization" (COM(2010)0614) and "New skills for new jobs" (COM(2008)0868). The Communiqué of the Commission «Industrial policy: increasing competitiveness» (COM(2011)0642), adopted in 2011, called for deep structural reforms, as well as consistent and coordinated policies in the member states to increase the economic and industrial competitiveness of the EU and promote long-term the term of sustainable growth. In 2012, the Commission issued a communication entitled "Strengthening European industry for growth and recovery of the economy—updated communication on industrial policy" (COM(2012)0582), in 2014, the Commission launched a communication "For European industrial renaissance" (COM(2014)0014).

According to the OECD, only 60% of SMEs have adopted new digital technologies during the COVID-19 crisis.[5] According to available data, the pandemic accelerated the widespread abandonment of digital technologies by 7 years,[6] and led to the implementation of appropriate changes in the strategy.

In its communication published in January 2020 on the first annual work program (COM(2020)0037), the Commission stressed that the EU's position as a digital leader will be underpinned by the European Data Strategy and White Paper on Artificial Intelligence. In March 2020, the Commission launched a New Industrial Strategy for Europe Communication (COM(2020)0102) to help European industry lead the dual transition towards climate neutrality and digital leadership, and strengthen Europe's competitiveness and strategic autonomy. In March 2021, the European Commission adopted a document entitled "Europe's Digital Compass" (European Commission, 2021c), updating the European Digital Strategy Shaping Europe's Digital Future (European Commission, 2020a),[7] In its communication published in January 2020 on the first annual work program (COM(2020)0037), the Commission stressed that the EU's position as a digital leader will be underpinned by the European Data

[5] Benefits of digitalization in SMEs https://cefe.net/2022/02/28/benefits-of-digitalization-in-smes/#:~:text=Among%20others%2C%20digitalization%20reduces%20transaction,new%20opportunities%20to%20generate%20income.

[6] The Digital Opportunity: COVID-19 Pandemic Impact on European SMEs https://publicpolicy.paypal-corp.com/sites/default/files/2021-09/EU_C19_SME_Research_Paper.pdf.

[7] Shaping Europe's Digital Future. https://commission.europa.eu/strategy-and-policy/priorities-2019-2024/europe-fit-digital-age/shaping-europes-digital-future_en.

Strategy and White Paper on Artificial Intelligence. In March 2020, the Commission launched a New Industrial Strategy for Europe Communication (COM(2020)0102) to help European industry lead the dual transition towards climate neutrality and digital leadership, and strengthen Europe's competitiveness and strategic autonomy.[8] In March 2021, the European Commission adopted a document entitled "Europe's Digital Compass" (European Commission, 2021c), updating the European Digital Strategy Shaping Europe's Digital Future (European Commission, 2020),[9] whose functions are:

- funds many initiatives that help small businesses access new markets.
- Programming, monitoring and evaluation,
- Supporting entrepreneurs
- Improving conditions for competitiveness

To manage digital processes in front of small and medium production it is recommended by the OECD to solve the existing problems[10]:

- Internal capacity building of SMEs
- Improving SMEs access to strategic resources
- Creating the right business environment for SMEs transformation
- Getting effective support from the government.

In the European Union, digital technologies have been implemented for the development of small and medium-sized businesses, it encompasses[11]:

- **Your European Business Portal**—is a practical guide to doing business in Europe. It provides entrepreneurs with information and interactive services that help them expand their business abroad.
- **The Enterprise Europe Network**—helps SMEs and entrepreneurs access market information, overcome legal obstacles, and find potential business partners across Europe.
- **SME Internationalization support**—page provides information on foreign markets and helps European business internationalize their activities.
- **The single Portal on Access to Finance**—helps SMEs find finance supported by the EU.
- **The European Cluster Collaboration Platform**—offers dynamic mapping of over 1000 profiled cluster organizations worldwide or supports the emergence of new value chains through cross-sectorial cooperation.

---

8 Small and medium-sized enterprises Small and medium-sized enterprises | Fact Sheets on the European Union | European Parliament (europa.eu).

9 COSME Europe's programme for small and medium-sized enterprises https://single-market-economy.ec.europa.eu/smes/cosme_en.

10 Stimulation of the digital development of SMEs by the state . https://www.oecd.org/industry/smes/PH-SME-Digitalisation-final.pdf.

11 Internal Market, Industry, Entrepreneurship and SMEs. https://single-market-economy.ec.europa.eu/smes_en.

- **Erasmus for Young Entrepreneurs**—is a cross-border exchange program that gives new or aspiring entrepreneurs the chance to learn from experienced entrepreneurs running small businesses in other participating countries.

As a result, in 2022, 84.6 million people were employed by SMEs in the EU,out of which 37.7 million were employed in micro-enterprises, 26.1 million in small businesses, and 20.8 million in medium-sized businesses, which is a significant improvement in the post-pandemic period.[12]

4 Digitization Processes to Increase Efficiency of SMEs in Georgia

According to the 2021–2024 Government Program of "Building a European State" of Georgia (Government Program, 2020) obtained by sharing the experience of the EU countries, the economic policy is focused on the development of the private sector, especially small and medium entrepreneurship, by creating favorable conditions for it. Georgia has adopted a new strategy for the development of small and medium-sized enterprises (Ministry of Economy & Sustainable Development of Georgia, 2021), which was implemented with the support of the European Union and the German government. The role of digital transformation for the development of small and medium-sized enterprises has been emphasized, which corresponds to the requirements of the DCFTA.

The strategy is based on the main principles of the European Small Business Act and the best practices of EU countries based on SME policy. In accordance with the priorities of the strategy, today, due to the events taking place in the world, digitization is given special importance for more accurate calculation of external influencing factors, which contributes to better adaptation of enterprises to the environment, perfect planning of activities, regulation of work processes, adoption of innovative decisions and rational distribution of resources. In general, the increase in production productivity and the increase in the competitiveness of the enterprise. The 5th priority of the strategy for the development of small and medium-sized enterprises in Georgia: "The promotion of electronic communications, information technologies, innovations, research aims to increase the use of information communication technologies (ICT), which has a great impact on the productivity of small and medium-sized enterprises and their innovative capabilities."

Organizations and associations supporting the strategy (Ministry of Economy & Sustainable Development of Georgia, 2021): a. Chamber of Commerce, b. Association of Small and Medium Enterprises of Georgia and c. Employers' Association. The European Union is the biggest supporter of private sector development in

[12] SMEs in Europa-Statistics & Facts, 2022. https://www.statista.com/topics/8231/smes-in-europe/#topicHeader__wrapper.

Georgia. Within the EU4Business program, access to finance and markets, introduction of innovations, and successful activities of small and medium-sized businesses are promoted.

The strategy for the development of small and medium-sized businesses requires the creation of regional entrepreneurship centers and close cooperation with universities. One of the interesting cases of digitalization process of small and medium-sized businesses in Georgia. is considered Project: *Business Problems Interactive Web Portal* funded by Vishegrad International Fund in 2022. Participants: University of Finance and Administration (Czechia), East European University (Project initiator, Georgia), Georgian Small & Medium Enterprise Association, University of Zilina (Slovakia), University of Lodz (Poland), Budapest Enterprise Agency (Hungary). The project aims at improving the competitiveness of SMEs through university research and businesses practical life. The project will focus on specific problems that arise when founding and managing startups and SMEs and, thanks to a large amount of input, will create a platform for sharing solutions and creative approaches to problems in an international context. In long term effect helps the businesses sustain the business over the long term and despite a highly competitive environment (Machavariani and Maisuradze. 2021).

The European experience shows that the competitiveness of small and medium-sized businesses is largely determined by the purposeful use of digital processes, which leads to:

- increase in operational efficiency;
- increasing customer satisfaction;
- reduction of operating costs;
- Growing needs for innovations.

5 Conclusion

Digitalization in the pandemic and post-pandemic periods had a significant impact on the development of small and medium-sized enterprises in Georgia. Taking into account the experience of the EU countries and with the direct support of the EU:

- "2021–2024 governmental program for the construction of the European state" was created;
- "Georgian Small and Medium Entrepreneurship Development Strategy 2021–2025" was approved;
- The legislation is being perfected;
- In order to obtain economic and social results, for the development of small and medium-sized businesses, the digitization process is being developed, in accordance with the Georgia-EU association agreement;

As modern trends in the development of small and medium-sized businesses show, the next stage of digitalization requires businesses to:

- Implementation of complex software and latest technologies.
- Adoption of new work processes.
- Timely response to the growing demands of customers.
- the use of innovative technologies and approaches to increase the competitiveness of small and medium-sized businesses;
- forming an adaptive organizational culture;
- Creating regional centers of business.

References

Biahmou, A., Emmer, C., Pfouga, A., & Stjepandić, J. (2016). Digital master as an enabler for industry 4.0. *Advances in Transdisciplinary Engineering, 4*, 672–681. https://doi.org/10.3233/978-1-61499-703-0-672

European Commission (2015). Fostering SMEs' growth through digital transformation. *European Commission*, Retrieved from http://s3platform.jrc.ec.europa.eu/-/fostering-smes-growth-through-digital-transformation (13 June 2018).

Government Program 2021—2024, "For the Construction of the European State", 2020 https://www.gov.ge/files/68_78117_645287_govprogramme2021-2024.pdf

Lederer, M., Knapp, J. & Schott, P. (2017). The digital future has many names—How business process management drives the digital transformation. In 2017 6th International Conference on Industrial Technology and Management (ICITM) (pp. 22–26), IEEE, Cambridge, UK, March 7–10, doi:https://doi.org/10.1109/ICITM.2017.7917889.

Machavariani, S., & Maisuradze, T. (2021). Vision for increasing university scientific potential under the modern conditions. In *Proceedings of the International Scientific-Practical Conference (ISPC 2021)*, (pp.159–168). Springer Proceedings in Business and Economics.

Ministry of Economy and Sustainable Development of Georgia, (2021), Development Strategy for the Development of Small and Medium Entrepreneurship of Georgia 2021–2025. http://www.economy.ge/uploads/files/2017/ek__politika/sme_strategy/sme_development_strategy_2021_2025_.pdf

Radostine Yuleva-Chuchulayna (2021), Digitalization and Innovation as a Factor in Increasing the Competitiveness of Small and Medium-Sized Enterprises, Knowledge-International Journal, Vol.44.1 https://www.researchgate.net/publication/351411520_DIGITALIZATION_AND_INNOVATION_AS_A_FACTOR_IN_INCREASING_THE_COMPETITIVENESS_OF_SMALL_AND_MEDIUM-SIZED_ENTERPRISES

Reis, J., Amorim, M., Melão, N., & Matos, P. (2018). Digital transformation: A literature review and guidelines for future research. *Trends and Advances in Information Systems and Technologies, 1*, 411–421. https://doi.org/10.1007/978-3-319-77703-0_41

Tarutė, A., Duobienė, J., Klovienė, L., Vitkauskaitė, E. & Varaniūtė V. (2018). Identifying Factors Affecting Digital Transformation of SMEs. In *Proceedings of The 18th International Conference on Electronic Business* (pp. 373–381). ICEB, Guilin, China, December 2–6.

Yoo, Y., Lyytinen, K.J., Boland, R.J. & Berente, N. (2010). The Next Wave of Digital Innovation: Opportunities and Challenges: A Report on the Research Workshop 'Digital Challenges in Innovation Research'.

Problems of e-commerce in the Field of Garments and an Increase in the Volume of Returns of Goods on This Basis

Temur Maisuradze

Abstract The work deals with the problem of managing and selling clothes through e-commerce systems and studying the main reason for returning goods, namely knitwear, hats, etc. The impossibility of remotely fitting the body and significantly reducing the return rate of goods. The objective of the study was to find out the details of the problems that caused the buyer to mistrust to make a choice in favor of e-commerce in clothing items, as well as the reasons for the increase in the volume of returned goods if such a choice had already been made. The study of these problems is seen as providing sufficient data for scientists interested in creating and managing digital platforms to solve these problems in favor of intensifying virtual trading networks as reliably as in the field of electronics, household appliances, etc. It is also a challenge to create opportunities for remote orders that correspond to the real characteristics of the customer's body with the specified ranges of deviations from the real dimensions in the body regions. Despite the many inventions created to create these types of services for the consumer, none have caught on that reduce garment return rates. For this purpose, the characteristic flaws of the virtual measurement platforms of clothing created for the solution of the problem were studied and the ways of their possible solution were outlined.

Keywords E-commerce · Digital · Platforms · Virtual · Trading

1 Introduction

E-commerce has become an indispensable part of global retail. Like many other industries, retailing has undergone a significant transformation since the introduction of the Internet, and thanks to the ongoing digitalization of modern life, consumers in virtually every country now profit from online transactions. The trend of rapid growth

T. Maisuradze (✉)
Doctor of Science, Eats European University, Tbilisi, Georgia
e-mail: T.maisuradze@eeu.edu.ge

R. C. Geibel and S. Machavariani (eds.), *Chances and Challenges of Digital Management*, Springer Proceedings in Business and Economics,
https://doi.org/10.1007/978-3-031-45601-5_7

of Internet users is obviously reflected in the dynamics of the growth of electronic sales and buyers.

At the same time, certain problems associated with this field represent a serious challenge for both manufacturers, suppliers and consumers. Accordingly, many scientific and research institutions are working in this direction. In addition to commercial, social and other pragmatic meanings, the issue is also related to hygienic problems. For example, if the buyer buys clothes electronically, he is deprived of the opportunity to fit the body, and if he takes advantage of the opportunity to fit the body in the retail network, he faces serious and considerable hygienic problems (the clothes may have been worn many times on different bodies and without any hygienic treatment). Many shoppers order multiple variations of the same item to increase fit (eg, multiple sizes) and return items that don't fit (Stock and Mulki, 2009). It turns out that too many consumers use their home as a fitting room (Fit for Commerce, 2016).

The challenge is for the consumer to take advantage of the flexibility of e-commerce and at the same time, the ability of the retailer to fit the body, i.e., to virtually fit the garment as it would be possible in a retail measuring booth, and in this way, significantly reduce garment return rates. He must be sure of the conformity of the choice to his wishes (with the possibility of a simulated fit as close as possible to the real one), which will make it compatible for the user, taking into account the variety of existing and other manufacturers, countries and size units, to fit the desired garment exactly and at the same time avoid possible hygiene problems and multiple dressings are tiring., not very pleasant procedures.

Although there are many inventions to solve this problem, the question arises why the problem cannot be solved? It is to be clarified whether the problem is technical, technological or other. In order to get answers to the questions, not to go only in the direction of theoretical discussions, not to be limited to literary studies in which there is already a shortage of studies in this direction, we considered it more appropriate to study only the quantitative and accurate statistics of the mentioned problems and meaningfully use the inventions created and already patented to solve the mentioned problems. In this way, it was determined what problems the authors are trying to solve in their inventions, what is the defect to be corrected and in what way? What remains unaddressed to make their implementation acceptable to the manufacturer, supplier and buyer, that is, what needs to be considered to create a one-size-fits-all platform that would significantly reduce garment return rates?

2 The Main Features of e-commerce in the Apparel Sector

According the statistical data, in 2021, retail e-commerce sales amounted to approximately 5.2 trillion U.S. dollars worldwide. This figure is forecast to grow by 56 percent over the next years, reaching about 8.1 trillion dollars by 2026.[1] According

[1] Global retail e-commerce sales 2014–2026, Global retail e-commerce sales 2026 | Statista.

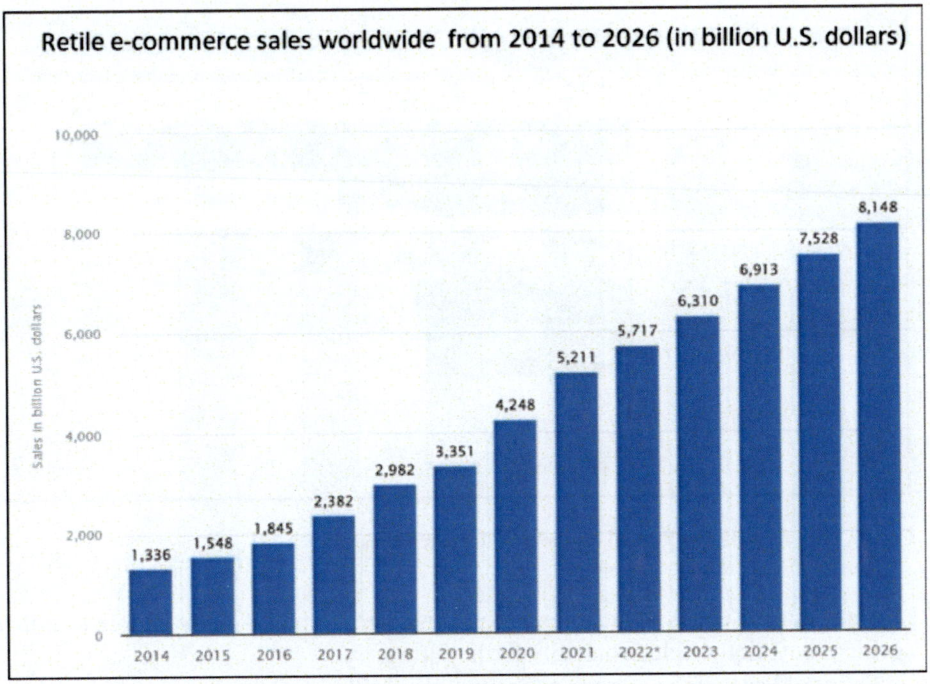

Fig. 1 Retail e-commerce sales worldwide from 2014 to 2026

to the forecast, by 2026, the share of electronic commerce will reach the mark of 8.5 trillion dollars (see Fig. 1).

Existing online trading platforms offer only a picture of the product and information about its size and fabric. Some suppliers will also post videos to provide more information, as the buyer needs much more information to make an informed choice. For example, how the item will feel to the touch, or how the texture will feel, and how the garment will fit when worn, is very important for decision-making. Are you starting to wonder how much of a risk it is that the garment will fit her? Statistics also confirm that in electronic purchases, the highest rate of returns comes from clothing.[2]

3 Goods Return Statistics

Figure 2 shows the highest return rate of 56% for clothing, which is unmatched by any other product type. The fact that some of the customers who are dissatisfied with the purchase prefer to sell the product themselves rather than start the unpleasant procedures of returning the goods, that is, the number of dissatisfied customers may be much higher than it appears in the results of the mentioned research, requires a

[2] Most Returned Product Categories, https://www.salecycle.com/blog/featured/ecommerce-returns-2018-stats-trends/.

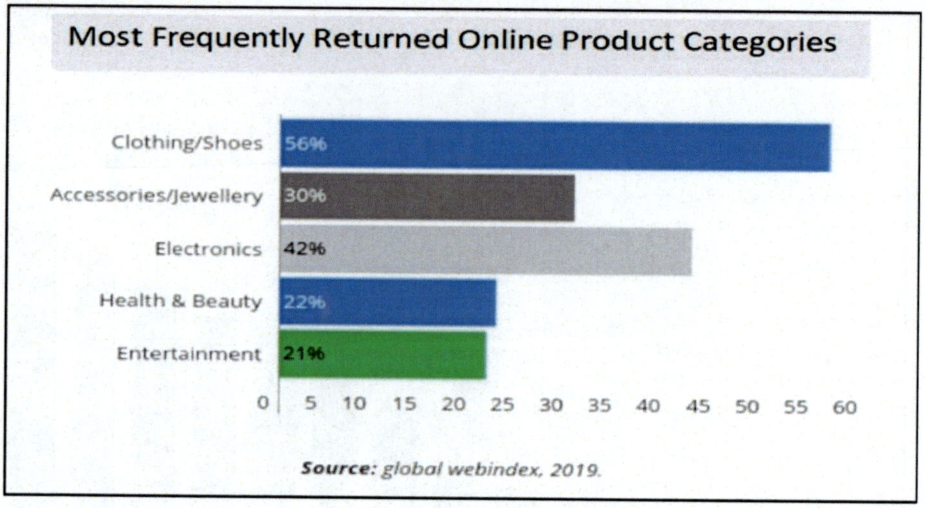

Fig. 2 Most frequently returned online product categories

separate study. Such a negative experience is likely to make many people lose their desire to buy clothes electronically in the future.

The world's leading e-commerce companies, with current and prospective forecast indicators, are presented in Fig. 3.[3] The very positive and growing dynamics of e-commerce is clearly visible, although in the garment part, consumer dissatisfaction is likely to increase further, which can have a very negative effect on this type of e-commerce products. It is clear that the problem of the garment's fit is the main motivation for returning.

The aim of the mentioned research is to reveal what caused the non-acceptance of the rational proposals, which are called to solve the mentioned problems, in the conditions of such high interests and needs?

The fact is that despite numerous attempts to solve the problem in some technical or technological way, the issue still remains unsolved. The proposed technical or technological solutions are somehow unacceptable to the manufacturing or supplying organizations.

It is likely that the approaches that guide the authors of the possibilities of virtual tailoring of the garment are focused more on the interests of the buyer and less or not at all take into account the diverse and in some cases very different specifications of manufacturers and suppliers. Along with this, the anonymity of personal information remains behind the scenes. Without the mentioned information, it is very difficult to imagine creating any new and acceptable possibility for remote customization.

It is clear that the solution to the mentioned problem should be in the interest of all participants, but the innovation that will create comfort for the buyer of the garment should be convenient and acceptable for manufacturers and e-commerce networks

[3] Leading e-commerce electronics, office, leisure, and entertainment retailers worldwide in 2022 and 2027, based on estimated sales Office & leisure top e-tailers by sales 2022-2027 | Statista.

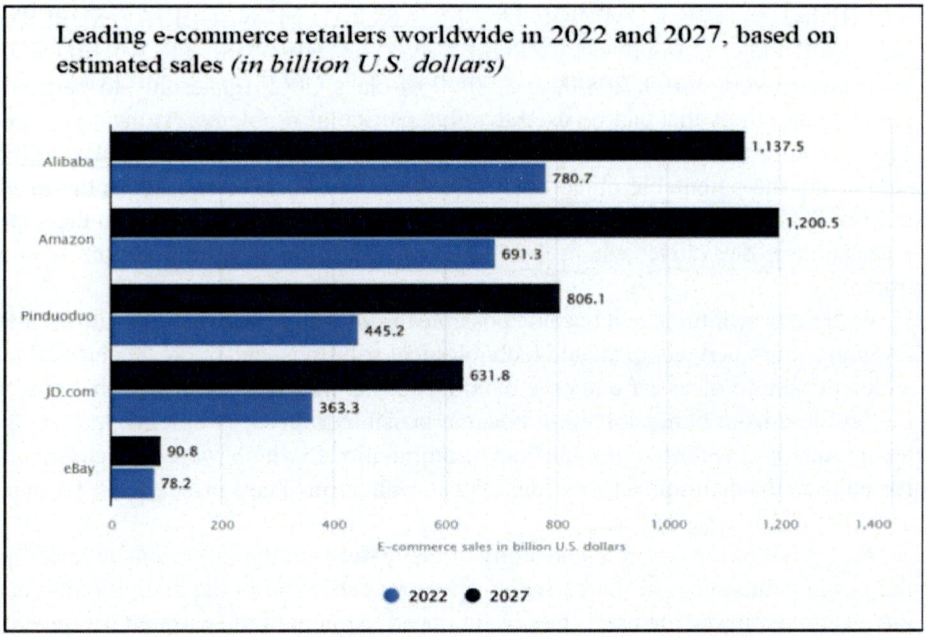

Fig. 3 Leading e-commerce retailer worldwide in 2022 and 2027, based on estimated sales

as well, it should be in harmony with the technical, technological and size system used by them. Especially if we take into account the fact that such innovations are always introduced by the manufacturers themselves, e-commerce networks or other third parties interested in new revenues, and not by the end users of the garment, who are directly affected by the problem.

4 Inventions for Remote Adjustment of Shrouds

As mentioned, for purchasing a garment through e-commerce, it is quite difficult to make a positive decision without a fitting. To solve the mentioned problem, the high level of science, digital techniques and technologies, human and institutional capabilities, are most closely concentrated and implemented, in specific inventions and not in individual scientific works or achievements, because it is logical that owning a patent to solve such a global problem is associated with a very large material and with receiving moral benefits. Accordingly, the international inventive classes (IPC) G06F and G06Q.[4] From here G06Q (DATA PROCESSING SYSTEMS OR METHODS, SPECIALLY ADAPTED FOR ADMINISTRATIVE, COMMERCIAL, FINANCIAL, MANAGERIAL, SUPERVISORY OR FORECASTING PURPOSES; SYSTEMS OR METHODS SPECIALLY ADAPTED FOR

[4] International Property Classification IPC Publication (wipo.int).

ADMINISTRATIVE, COMMERCIAL, FINANCIAL, MANAGERIAL, SUPERVISORY OR FORECASTING PURPOSES, NOT OTHERWISE PROVIDED FOR) subclasses 30/00, 10/00, 20/00, and 50/00 of class G06F relate only to particular methods and tools that can be used to solve particular problems. At the same time, 125 scientific works were studied, which were related to the technical solutions supporting the patentable object and reflected in one form or another in the inventions of the mentioned class. Therefore, there are no references to them in the paper, because their derivative, which is adapted to perform a specific function, is more important.

With such an approach, it became possible to study combined more result-oriented findings, combined technical and technological solutions, and to create and evaluate a clearer picture of target outcome data. Better identify the key details that prevent the problem from being solved. It became possible to group problems, knowledge, techniques and technologies into new combinations, which were reflected in the formulas of the mentioned inventions, as a combination of new principled approaches and functional combinations.

As a result of the research and study of the features of the inventions intended for the virtual adjustment of the garment, it was revealed that in the main directions of the patented objects, the user's interest in the adjustment of the garment is especially dominant, in the ways of realization of which, massively, other and different methods/ technologies of creating the exact avatar of the user are intersected everywhere, and in the next step, the conditions are met. Formation that must be met by the supplied products (conditions that must be met by manufacturers and e-commerce networks). The results are grouped below into 5 similar groups that share a typical set of similarities. For example, only one is presented, in which relatively comprehensive information is presented with a discussion of specifics, methods and tools used.

Among them, the fact that the vast majority of them offer, using different technologies, the creation of the most accurate avatars of the user or a set of actions based on it was clearly highlighted. Each of them offers its decision as a new fact that should be taken into account by all producers and sellers if they want to use the service. It is not considered how his method will adapt to the formats presented in the standards of manufacturers and e-commerce networks. Perhaps it would be much better if the proposed option, which is designed for the interests of the buyer, at the same time takes into account the existing bases and standards of manufacturers and electronic trade networks as much as possible or requires only minimal (acceptable) transformation of the system. On the other hand, it is also incredibly difficult to account for all the diversity that the participating entities rely on. It is because of this incompatibility that the issue still remains an unsolved problem. That is, it is necessary to create a method that, taking into account these requirements, will be able to provide the buyer with such a virtual format, where it will be possible to imagine a specific design on himself, so that he can see exactly which part of the body the clothes will fit exactly, where and by how many centimeters it will be wide or narrow. At the same time, his personal data was not made available to third parties and to avoid the hygienic problems characteristic of the retail network, which is characterized by the direct measurements of the garment.

In particular, one group of issued patents includes a set of inventions that, using different methods, provide the goal of remote ordering or measurement of clothing by the user, according to the dimensions of the user's body, which should also be accompanied by a three-dimensional image of the user's body.[5] It means a garment database based on a predefined library of three-dimensional patterns of the goods in it, and at the same time a kind of database of similar three-dimensional patterns of the user's body. It is clear that in order to create such a service system, the manufacturer must create three-dimensional models of all the garments, all sizes and all types of products produced by him, which we think is difficult to imagine entering into the interests of the manufacturers (related to the emergence of many new tasks and also requiring huge resources). At the same time, it should not be acceptable for the user to place personal data on the suppliers' databases and servers. On the one hand, the decision is precisely aimed at solving the problem, but the concomitants, i.e., the other features that accompany the innovation, show other, such new negative sides, which completely balance the positive result achieved.

The second group of inventions combines a concept built with the method of tailoring measurements, which are used to tailor clothing to the actual anatomical features of the user's body.[6] The technology is based on proposals for creating one's own avatars, when the user operates only by entering their own data in special applications created in Internet databases, that is, by entering their own anatomical parameters, an avatar of a specific subject is created, for example, according to the size of the pelvis, waist and chest, shoulder width and height. The next step is a virtual measurement by the manufacturers against the 3D models of the garment placed in the bases. With this approach, manufacturers face exactly the same problems as described in the first case. What makes it particularly difficult is that the system requires fabric patterns to be made with more and more variations. On the one hand, with good intentions, as if to provide more flexibility, the system becomes extremely complex. This group of inventions involves the involvement of many participants, who must adapt to these proposals by creating appropriate bases and tools, where the mechanical properties of the fabric, the ability to scan the garment details and fabrics must be taken into account. On the one hand, such an approach will make users more informed to make better choices, but such approaches make the system so complicated that the vast majority of users will no longer be able to use it. For full use, it will be necessary to master new skills. Most of them will no longer want to delve into such complicated processes, and even more so for one purchase that can be easily forgotten before making the next purchase.

The third group of inventions relates to methods and technologies for creating user avatars.[7] This group presents all possible methods and techniques for creating a 3D model (avatar) of a user. In this part, we consider not the method of creating the model itself as a problem, but the format and algorithm of its use. In order for the user to be able to choose the preferred method, there must be an agreed specific

[5] Patent, 2015 – US 0134496A1.

[6] Patent 2011 – US 0298897A1.

[7] Patent, 2015 - RU2551731C1.

standard to which the data will be digitized, although the protection of personal data after it is uploaded to trading networks will remain a problem.

In the fourth group of inventions, the technologies used in 3D models of the manufactured garment are considered. In particular, with what dimensions, with what tools and methods will it be possible to convert any garment from 2D format to 3D format.[8] In our opinion, this direction requires the most attention, because if it is possible for manufacturers to convert any sewn garment into a 3D model in the simplest way, the entire virtual fitting algorithm that all garment manufacturers will seize would be greatly simplified, because after the introduction of such a possibility, electronic sales can be expected through a sharp increase in sales and a sharp decrease in the current rate of return. In such a situation, only the issue of personal data will remain a challenge.

The fifth group of inventions is dedicated to the conversion of garment data for electronic devices, through which it will be possible to use virtual cabins to adjust the garment.[9] There is much less of a problem in this group, since coding systems are already widely used in sales. In particular, the QR coding system is the most common. All that needs to be considered is that everyone agrees to use any one particular encoding system, or that support applications are created that ensure that any encoding system can be adapted to the different electronic devices and applications used by users. Creating such applications or building new systems into them does not present any difficulties. If it becomes possible to agree on some universal system, that is, a kind of standardization, only the operating systems and, accordingly, the user's algorithm to simplify the use of the application will be simplified.

5 Conclusion

As a result of the conducted studies, the assumption was confirmed that the main reason for the return of the garment is due to its inability to fit the body.

It has also been proven that through the use of digital technologies, it is technically and technologically quite possible to virtually measure a garment, as well as to create accurate 3D avatars of customers, but how easy are the systems created for this purpose not only to generate the buyer and his avatar, but also for manufacturers and suppliers, tested and To integrate into existing systems in use?

As revealed, the tools and technologies developed and offered for the digital transformation of manufactured garments in 3D format have the most difficult and still insurmountable tasks to solve for garment manufacturing organizations. In the inventions made to date, all the proposed technical or technological proposals put manufacturers or representatives of e-commerce networks in front of such a choice, which obliges them to make the existing, even flawed, model of cooperation so complicated that they lose the desire to implement the proposed model, because

[8] Patent, 2006 - US7149665.

[9] Patent, 2017 - US9799064.

the assembled The large-scale system change and the risk factor of possible new problems creates more difficulties in the end than even a high 56% rate of return of the shroud. This means serious changes in the production process. Taking into account the established individual production specifics, it becomes necessary to come up with such a special and flexible technology that converts the 2D dimensions of fabrics of different sizes, different models, and different mechanical properties into accurate 3D dimensions. Converting the received data into one agreed format or developing such individual formats and creating converter applications that will adapt said data for users' devices, including some industrial machines, adapting the software taking into account all its specifics. In this case, it is the most difficult to get such a universal agreement. In the presence of such an agreement, everyone will have the need to mobilize individual resources, which each of them will find before a new task. In any case, the fact is that none of the inventions developed to solve the problem excites either manufacturers or representatives of electronic or retail chains.

It would probably be acceptable if such a platform was created, on which it would be possible to convert a flat image of all the details of the cut fabric into an accurate 3D model, by calculating and taking into account the geometric dimensions of the design and sewing fields. In this case too, in order to avoid errors, the input of geometrical dimensions should be done by automatic scanning or other similar precision device. Such devices do not exist yet and will be employed for this purpose.

We also consider the issue of personal information very important. It will be necessary to consider the creation of such technologies and, most importantly, the possibility of its use, in which the protection of the subject's personal data will be ensured. Reasoning leads to the conclusion that some kind of method should be employed, which will compare the data in the personal device, and not on the server of e-commerce networks or manufacturers. It is even more unacceptable to place personal data in open databases in the form of digital libraries. It is much easier to reach a common agreement on this matter, because the protection of personal data is in the interests of all users.

In the conditions of solving the problems listed above, it is quite real and possible to offer the user such desired applications that, using QR coding or any convertible coding system, will make a virtual adjustment of the garment inside his electronic device and without transferring personal data. Creating applications for this purpose and building new systems into them should not present any difficulty, because the varieties of such functions and their derivatives are already used in other and other techniques, and in combinations to perform completely different functions. If even in this case it will be possible to create a universal system or standard, the operation and consumption procedures will be simplified even more.

References

Fit for Commerce. (2016). May. Welcome to the new retail reality. Commerce Disrupted.

Stock, J. R., & Mulki, J. P. (2009). Product returns processing: An examination of practices of manufacturers, wholesalers/distributors, and retailers. *Journal of Business Logistics, 30*(1), 33–62.

Digitalization in Society

Potentials of Blockchain Technology for Developing Countries

Linus Roggenkamp

Abstract The spread of blockchain technology within industrialized countries has progressed increasingly in recent years, revealing numerous potentials. In consideration of the numerous challenges that developing countries are facing on a social, economic and environmental level, it is necessary to explore the opportunities of the new technology for these countries. The goal of this paper is to identify ways in which developing countries can benefit from the use of blockchain technology. For this purpose, the following research question is posed: What are the opportunities for societies in developing countries through blockchain technology? To answer the central question, an integrative review was conducted. Specifically, the work examined the opportunities and risks of three application areas: supply chains, the public sector, and cryptocurrencies. The focus is primarily on the area of supply chains. The results show that the use of blockchains in supply chains can increase transparency, reduce companies' running costs and make logistics processes more efficient. This is offset by high implementation costs. For the use of blockchains in politics and administration, opportunities for fighting corruption as well as increasing the efficiency of the systems could be shown. The research on the scope of cryptocurrencies found that the use of decentralized cryptocurrencies and central bank digital currencies can promote the financial inclusion of developing countries. Future research could concretize the evidence of cost savings from blockchains in supply chains using business metrics. An investigation of the cost-benefit ratio by means of ex-post analyses of existing projects could empirically consolidate the findings.

Keywords Blockchain technology · Developing countries · Supply chain · Cryptocurrencies

L. Roggenkamp (✉)
Fresenius University of Applied Sciences, Hamburg, Germany
e-mail: linus.roggenkamp@rundetrends.com

R. C. Geibel and S. Machavariani (eds.), *Chances and Challenges of Digital Management*, Springer Proceedings in Business and Economics,
https://doi.org/10.1007/978-3-031-45601-5_8

1 Introduction

Current studies continuously underline the potential of blockchain technology for the economy and society. In an analysis, the *German Development Institute* forecasts fundamental changes in global trade because of blockchain technology. Developing countries, which offer ideal conditions for the rapid adaptation of digital technologies due to their dilapidated analog infrastructure, will be particularly affected (Schwab & Ohnesorge, 2019). The *United Nations Conference on Trade and Development* (*UNCTAD*) even expects blockchain technology to make a decisive contribution to the Sustainable Development Goals (SDGs) and to improving the quality of life in developing countries (Freire et al., 2021).

In view of this rapid development in recent years, the question arises as to the concrete potential of this new technology for developing countries and how they can actively benefit from it. Many people in this world still do not have a bank account and thus have hardly any access to financial services. According to the World Bank's latest report from 2017, the number of unbanked adults worldwide is 1.7 billion.

Around 50% of these people live in just seven developing countries (Demirgüç-Kunt et al., 2017). In addition to a lack of financial inclusion, developing countries are also suffering from the consequences of globalization.

By shifting production to developing countries, companies simultaneously externalize costs at the environmental and social level. The *German Federal Ministry for Economic Cooperation and Development* believes that human and environmental rights are still at great risk (BMZ, 2021). In the wake of the COVID-19 pandemic, the situation has deteriorated further, especially for children. Worldwide, more than 150 million children suffer from child labor. In addition, 40 million people are forced to work. Work-related accidents cause around 2.8 million deaths each year. The number of work-related illnesses is 374 million per year (BMAS, 2020).

Many potentials of blockchain technology can be gleaned from the current literature. These are mostly limited to entrepreneurial potential in industrialized countries. Some studies have already identified potential for developing countries. The research is particularly influenced by studies and pilot projects of the United Nations. However, studies in the research field are rarely independent of stakeholders and shareholders in industrialized countries and are aimed at decision-makers in the Western world. Furthermore, in addition to numerous reports on success stories of blockchain implementation in developing countries, there are also some proofs of concepts that highlight the potential of the technology for structurally weak countries. A broad potential analysis of various sectors that examines and highlights concrete opportunities for developing countries does not currently exist. The research question of this study is thus: What are the opportunities for societies in developing countries through blockchain technology? The aim of this paper is to show how developing countries can benefit from blockchain technology.

2 Theoretical Framework

A blockchain is an electronic ledger in which data or events, in a distributed network of computers, are managed independently by the participants (Schlatt et al., 2016). Blockchains are characterized by certain core properties. One characteristic is their decentralization. Centralized systems store data in a central database. In a decentralized system, on the other hand, the data is stored on different, physically separate devices that are connected to each other (Sunyaev, 2020). The aspect of decentralization leads over to the next core attribute of a blockchain, security. Hacking a blockchain can be considered impossible. From a game-theoretical perspective, an attack on a blockchain would be many times more expensive than the profit it would generate (Hosp, 2018b). Blockchain technology is at the same time tamper-proof due to its architecture (BDEW, 2017). The criterion of security is closely linked to the next feature, irreversibility. The data that is stored on the blockchain must be confirmed by the community. Once this process is complete, it is irreversible (Hosp, 2018a). Furthermore, blockchains are notable for their transparency. All transactions can be viewed by the participants of the blockchain at any time. This applies not only to the transactions, but also to the information about who stored the respective data records on the blockchain (Schwarzkopf et al., 2018). Another characteristic of the technology is privacy. Blockchains grant their users pseudonymity. A pseudonym in the form of a public address replaces a user's identity (Kanza & Safra, 2018). Finally, blockchains are based on trust. Participants do not have to trust any central authority. An intermediary that processes the transactions and bears responsibility for their security is obsolete (Bundesnetzagentur, 2019). The system is built on mathematics and cryptography (Hosp, 2018a). In order to transmit information from one party to another, public key cryptography is used in blockchain networks. This works through the interaction of a private key for encrypting a message and a public key for decrypting it (Gayvoronskaya & Meinel, 2020). When sending data, for example transactions, the sender creates a digital signature with his private key specifying the recipient's public key. The information is distributed in the network and stored on the blockchain (Fridgen et al., 2019). In the blockchain network, there are three different roles that participants can take on. In the case of the Bitcoin blockchain, the first group is the users. This group includes all the people who are authorized to make transactions on the network (BDEW, 2017). In addition, there are nodes, units in the network that are connected to other nodes. Their task is to generate transactions in the network. They also check new transactions on the network and forward them to nodes they are connected to. This serves the purpose of spreading the transactions in the network (Zaghloul, Li, Mutka & Ren, 2020). The third group of participants is responsible for building consensus in the network. In blockchain systems, there is no central authority that bears responsibility for the correct execution of transactions. As a result, the decision as to what is correct and what is not lies with the decentralized community. In the case of the Bitcoin blockchain, so-called miners take over this task by checking and verifying transactions (Hosp, 2018b).

More modern blockchains like Ethereum offer the ability to execute smart contracts (Braam et al., 2019). Smart contracts work on the basis of mathematical if-then functions. When a predefined condition is met, the blockchain executes a specific action. This action includes the release of a certain value. A transaction is triggered (Buterin, 2014).

For the use of blockchains in developing countries, the literature places particular focus on supply chains, the public sector, and cryptocurrencies. Due to the increasing interconnectedness of the last decades, supply chains have gained in complexity to a high degree. As complexity and intransparency have increased, so have the risks of global supply chains. Supply chain risks are the product of shock loads and vulnerabilities along the value and supply chain. (Lund et al., 2020). Another problem of non-transparent supply chains is the lack of information about the production conditions. Consequently, it cannot be verified whether the rights of people and nature have been respected (Haupt, Lichter & May, 2021). With the assistance of a blockchain, a good can be traced back to its origin. For this purpose, every participant in a supply chain is connected to the blockchain and receives voting rights. Starting at the lowest level of the value chain, all members enter relevant information on the blockchain in a tamper-proof manner. These are shared with all participants in the supply chain. In order for the blockchain to process relevant data, a connection to the physical world is necessary. With the help of the Internet of Things (IoT), Radio Frequency Identity (RFID) or GPS, the blockchain is connected to the real world. Through smart contracts with predefined conditions, processes can be executed automatically (Krings & Schwab, 2020).

Blockchain technology can be used to optimize and expand the digital infrastructure in the state. Especially in developing countries with efficiency and trust problems, politics and administration could benefit from its use (Freire et al., 2021). One possibility would be to hold elections with the help of a blockchain. Once the vote has been cast, it cannot be manipulated afterwards. Thanks to the transparency of a blockchain, the election results could also be viewed by everyone (Hosp, 2018a). Blockchains can furthermore be used for resource distribution. The demand for resources in developing countries has increased. One use case of blockchain technology in the area of resource distribution is the allocation of aid supplies (Fischer & Bulanda, 2021). The world's largest blockchain-based humanitarian aid project is *Building Blocks* from the *United Nations World Food Programme* (*WFP*). The project is based on the collaboration of different aid organizations, each of which operates a node (vide supra) on the blockchain. Real-time data exchange allows the different entities to collaborate efficiently (WFP, 2022).

In the field of cryptocurrencies, the use of stablecoins has become particularly widespread in developing countries. Stablecoins are characterized by creating a value that is as stable as possible. They are pegged to a specific asset, such as the US dollar or the euro (International Monetary Fund IMF, 2021). The basic idea of blockchain-based cryptocurrency is financial inclusion. No bank account is needed to use cryptocurrencies. Users can make transactions using a smartphone, among other things (Freire et al., 2021). In addition to private use, cryptocurrencies can also be established as legal tender. Central bank digital currencies (CBDCs) are an alternative to the classic monetary system (Bank for International Settlements, 2021). In addition to the introduction of a CBDC, there is the possibility of accepting a cryptocurrency of a public blockchain as an official means of payment. On September 7, 2021, El Salvador became the first country in the world to declare Bitcoin as legal tender (Alvarez et al., 2022).

3 Research Methodology

In carrying out the present investigation, the special method of an integrative review was chosen. Such a review aims to create an overview of the state of knowledge of emerging topics and to subject them to a critical examination. On this basis, preliminary concepts and initial models can ideally be created. The method is also characterized by its creative character in data collection. Thus, the aim is not to collect all published data of an object of investigation and to compare them precisely with each other. Rather, the method aims to show perspectives of different fields and research designs (Snyder, 2019). Therefore, the integrative review is the only approach that allows a combination of data from different empirical and theoretical methods. The approach stands out particularly for its potential to provide information for policy and other practice-related endeavors. Consequently, it contributes to theory building and is directly applicable to policy and practice (Whittemore & Knafl, 2005). Finally, the results are evaluated on the basis of a systematic comparison. The various contents of the sources for the respective use cases are compared with each other and opportunities and risks are highlighted. Similarities and differences between the authors are highlighted.

The analysis of this paper follows the recommendation to structure the results of an integrative review hierarchically according to research design. Evidence from meta-studies has the highest quality level and is therefore evaluated with priority. This is followed by results from individual studies with an experimental design, non-experimental studies, case studies, as well as experience reports and, finally, statements from experts (Stetler et al., 1998).

4 Results

According to a qualitative study by Freire et al. (2021), blockchain is capable of improving supply chain risk management. When complemented with technologies such as the IoT, it can reduce inspection times of containers, among other things. This is made possible by accurately documenting the temperature, movement, and opening of doors of containers. In this way, blockchain can contribute to SDG 1 (No Hunger) and 2 (Health and Well-being). A similar conclusion was reached in a comprehensive case study comparison by Kshetri (2021a). Blockchain technology can increase supply chain transparency by making opaque value chains visible through seamless, real-time recording. On a technical level, this circumstance simultaneously ensures that problems with the documentation of sustainability indicators can be eliminated and that consumers can be provided with a clearer picture of their supply chains. An analysis by Krings and Schwab (2020) supports the findings of the previous sources by demonstrating the potential of blockchains for secure origin verification of goods. This is a necessary condition for the sustainable production of goods and contributes to the twelfth SDG (Sustainable Consumption and Production).

Furthermore, according to Krings and Schwab (2020), blockchain technology can bring cost savings to producers and facilitate access to international trade. The result is economic growth, which in turn promotes the achievement of the eighth SDG (Decent Work and Economic Growth). Moreover, blockchain enables SMEs from developing countries to document production steps in a cost-effective manner. This promotes their integration into global value chains in line with SDG 9 (Industry, Innovation and Infrastructure). The results on cost-effectiveness are supported by Kshetri (2021a). The study identifies opportunities in the cost-benefit trade-off compared to conventional systems. Labels and certain standards require high investments and transaction costs to measure relevant data. A qualitative study by Kapidani, Bauk, and Davidson (2021) further shows that blockchain is capable of connecting the various stakeholders in the maritime industry of emerging and developing countries. Through real-time tracking, shipping companies and ports have the ability to plan ahead for shore operations and reduce their costs through expedited terminal operations. In parallel with improving security and transparency in trade, the technology could reduce the high incidence of staff-related errors. In another study, Kshetri (2021b) highlights the potential of blockchain technology to bypass middlemen through the automation process. The result would be increased income for economic actors such as smallholder farmers who have limited resources.

In addition to the opportunities outlined above, there are also some challenges for developing countries when it comes to blockchain adoption in supply chains. According to an analysis by Schwab and Ohnesorge (2019), a blockchain only guarantees the storage and transparent processing of data. It does not guarantee the correctness of the underlying data, which requires monitoring of the original data. In this context, Kshetri (2021b) refers to the dependence of smart contracts on high-quality data. If the condition is not met, blockchain applications would only bring minor improvements compared to conventional approaches. A qualitative study by Kopyto, Lechler, Heiko, and Hartmann (2020) further presents the limited resources and know-how of companies in the least developed countries as a barrier when viewed in the short term. Freire et al. (2021) highlight the significant financial burden on particularly weak economies.

For the use of blockchains in the public sector, studies show the potential to fight corruption. According to Freire et al. (2021), this would be the result of reduced human interactions and contribute to SDG 16 (peace, justice, and strong institutions). Like Freire et al. (2021), Schwab and Ohnesorge (2019) highlight the area of automated tax and customs clearance in particular. The properties of completeness and verifiability of data make blockchain an obvious solution and can provide regulators with insights into transaction history (Kshetri, 2021a). At the same time, the lack of technical and financial resources of developing countries emerges as a challenge from a research article by Zambrano (2020) and Freire et al. (2021). Furthermore, Zambrano (2020) and Schwab and Ohnesorge (2019) highlight the need for governments to act to reduce regulatory barriers.

According to studies, the resource allocation use case offers particular potential for increasing the efficiency of humanitarian supply chain management (HSCM). According to a quantitative study by Ozdemir et al. (2020), the networking of different stakeholders such as aid organizations or government agencies improves budget planning and solves interorganizational barriers. Case studies of blockchain-based humanitarian supply chains particularly highlight the cost benefits. According to a status report on the *UnBlocked Cash* project by Oxfam (2020), the cost of aid distribution was reduced by 75% and delivery time was reduced by more than 90%. A case study of the *Building Blocks* project from *WFP* by Zambrano et al. (2018) comes to a similar conclusion. According to the WFP (2022) project report, $2.5 million in bank fees have been saved since the project began.

For the use case of crytocurrencies in the private sector, a quantitative study by Mavilia and Pisani (2020) shows potentials for financial inclusion of developing countries. Extensive documentation and long distances to banks are eliminated when opening an account. In parallel, Kapidani, Bauk, and Davidson (2021) illustrate the social dimension of inclusion with the opportunity of cryptocurrencies to create a payment network that is not subject to restrictions and does not exclude anyone. A report by Kremer (2022) illustrates this with the possibility of using cryptocurrencies to promote the independence of women in Afghanistan. In contrast, Mavilia and Pisani (2020), a qualitative study by Holtmeier and Sandner (2019), and Kapidani, Bauk, and Davidson (2021) can be taken as evidence of the need for legal regulation of cryptocurrencies and crypto application companies to prevent criminal practices.

A case study comparison by Soderberg et al (2022), a mixed-methods study by Lopez and Mendoza (2022), and a qualitative study by Chen et al. (2022) suggest the opportunity for developing countries to use CBDCs to promote financial inclusion among their populations. In contrast, a survey by Alvarez et al. (2022) shows that five months after the introduction of Bitcoin as legal tender in El Salvador, just under 60% of the population has downloaded the government-owned *Chivo Wallet*. 20% of users continued to use the app, after receiving the sign-up bonus of $30 in Bitcoin. Soderberg et al. (2022) cite the dilemma of privacy and central banks' insight into transactions as the biggest challenge of CBDCs. This is complicated by the public's distrust of the privacy of a centrally managed digital currency. According to an expert assessment by Snowden (2021), a CBDC would technically empower the state to monitor transactions and influence payment transactions, as the example of China shows.

5 Discussion

All studies equally affirm, regardless of study design, the potential of blockchain technology to increase supply chain transparency. This allows the finding to be given particular weight in terms of answering the research question. With reference to the findings of the theoretical part of this paper, the relevance of the finding can also be rated as high, since according to Lund et al. (2021), supply chain risks increase with increasing complexity and lack of transparency. Furthermore, based on the results, it can be said that blockchain technology offers companies in developing countries the opportunity to reduce their costs. The various sources list different reasons for this. The highest level of empirical evidence can be attributed to the comprehensive case study comparison by Kshetri (2021a). The study reveals the potential of blockchain as a substitute technology for conventional high-cost systems for measuring and evaluating certain parameters. Also worthy of strong empirical weight are the findings of the qualitative study by Kapidani et al. (2021). The authors were able to demonstrate the opportunity to use technology to more closely connect various stakeholders and thereby make logistics processes more efficient. At the same time, blockchain can replace error-prone tasks performed by humans and reduce costs. It must be critically noted here that the study interviewed experts from the countries of Montenegro and South Africa, representative of the developing world as a whole. In addition, the study focuses on the maritime economy. The results are therefore of little or no significance for developing countries without access to the sea and a distinct tourism industry. The results on cost reduction by Krings and Schwab (2020) should be given less weight, as they are based on the analysis of a research institute and are not based on an empirical study. The results indicate the potential to facilitate access to international trade in the course of cost reduction through blockchain. As a direct consequence, the authors predict positive economic growth in developing countries and thus a contribution to the eighth SDG. Of equal weight to Krings and Schwab (2020) is another study by Kshetri (2021b). The analysis is also not based on empirical research, but can be cited due to its expert status and literature-based foundation. Kshetri (2021b) attributes the cost reduction results to downsized supply chains through blockchain process automation. This would lead to the increase of income of small economic actors such as small farmers. The conclusion can only be agreed with to a limited extent. The exclusion of some actors from a supply chain does not guarantee an equal distribution of cost savings across all value creation stages.

At the same time, the finding of cost savings must be contrasted with challenges that put the extent of the potential into perspective. Both Kopyto et al. (2020) and Freire et al. (2021) find that the cost of implementing a blockchain, due to the limited resources of developing countries, leads to a high financial burden. The finding should be weighted heavily due to the qualitative study design with large case selection of both studies.

Similarly, the findings emphasize risks in data maintenance. Schwab and Ohnesorge (2019) Kshetri (2021b) point out the dependency of blockchain on correct data from the outside world, for example via RFID chips or IoT sensors. However, the weight of this finding should not be overstated, as the sources are an analysis by a research institute as well as an expert assessment.

In order for companies in developing countries to benefit from the cost advantages of using a blockchain in supply chains, they should explore the possibilities of meeting the high resource requirements of a blockchain implementation. The results of Chap. 4 show that the limited resources of developing countries make the cost of implementing a blockchain a high financial burden. At the same time, the results reinforce the potential to minimize the ongoing costs of enterprises through blockchains. To meet resource needs, companies could use existing blockchain solutions from companies that provide small businesses with access to blockchain. Furthermore, various NGO projects are available to promote the use of blockchains in supply chains.

With regard to the research question, it can be stated that blockchain technology has the potential to reduce corruption in developing countries. Kshetri (2021a) was able to prove the possibility for the use of Blockchains in the public sector to fight corruption within authorities. The basis for this is provided by the transparent transaction history of blockchains. The specific benefit for public authorities in tax and customs clearance is illustrated by the findings of Freire et al. (2021) and Schwab and Ohnesorge (2019). By connecting authorities, banks, trade actors, and other stakeholders via a blockchain, human tasks that are prone to corruption would be replaced. Due to the study design, the findings of Kshetri (2021a) and Freire et al. (2021) are particularly strong. The anti-corruption finding can be attributed a high relevance due to the corruption problem listed in the literature base of this paper. Looking at the findings of Zambrano (2020) and Freire et al. (2021), the lack of technical and financial resources of developing countries can be identified as the biggest challenge.

To combat the problem of corruption in developing countries, the use of blockchain in politics and administration is beneficial. The results suggest that blockchain technology is resistant to partisan influence and can increase transparency by disclosing all money flows. Responsible officials in politics and administration can actively engage in planning by creating the technical and legal basis for the use of blockchains.

With regard to the question, the most important finding on resource allocation is the increase in efficiency through blockchains. It should be noted that all findings, apart from Ozdemir et al. (2020), relate to two humanitarian projects run by *Oxfam* and the *WFP*. This allows the findings of Ozdemir et al. (2020) to shed light on the general potential of blockchain in humanitarian projects, while the other sources provide more specific findings. Ozdemir et al. (2020) highlight the improved efficiency of donation management through the use of a blockchain. Zambrano et al. (2018) and WFP (2022) and Oxfam (2020) provide another finding on efficiency. While the WFP (2022) and Oxfam (2020) project reports of shorter delivery times and lower costs in HSCM, the Zambrano et al. (2018) case study shows an increase in efficiency in data processing through blockchain. The findings of the three sources in relation to the *Building Blocks* and *UnBlocked Cash* projects, are weighted less heavily than Ozdemir et al. (2020) due to a lack of empirical research.

With reference to the results on the application area of cryptocurrencies, it can be said that both the private use of decentralized cryptocurrencies such as Bitcoin and the introduction of central bank digital currencies can drive financial inclusion in developing countries. Due to the quantitative and qualitative study design, the findings on the use case of cryptocurrencies in the private sector by Mavilia and Pisani (2020) and Kapidani et al. (2021) are to be weighted particularly heavily. The studies show that cryptocurrencies can facilitate access to financial services and not exclude anyone. For the use case of cryptocurrencies as legal tender, the strongest weight should be given to the findings of Soderberg et al. (2022) and Lopez and Mendoza (2022). The study design (case study comparison as well as mixed-method study) and the practical relevance of both studies to ongoing CBDC projects make the significance particularly high.

At the same time, the findings of Mavilia and Pisani (2020), Holtmeier and Sandner (2019), and Kapidani et al. (2021), which list regulation of cryptocurrencies in the private sector as a challenge, carry strong empirical weight due to the quantitative and qualitative research designs. Somewhat weaker weight should be given to the findings on the negative impact of CBDCs on privacy by Soderberg et al. (2022) and Snowden (2021), as Snowden (2021) is only an expert assessment.

To promote the financial inclusion of developing countries through digital currencies as legal tender, users should be granted extensive privacy. The results in Chap. 4 show the public's distrust of centrally managed digital currencies. Governments and central banks can increase the privacy and data protection of digital currencies by having a digital currency managed in a decentralized manner or by accepting an existing decentralized cryptocurrency, such as a stablecoin, as a means of payment.

6 Conclusion

The aim of this work was to demonstrate the potential of blockchain technology for developing countries. The question in this context was: What opportunities arise for societies in developing countries through blockchain technology? The goal was achieved by using an integrative review to examine various areas of application of blockchain for their opportunities and risks for developing countries. The current research pays particular attention to three areas. These include the use in supply chains as well as in the public sector and the use of cryptocurrencies. The results could show that blockchains are able to increase the transparency of supply chains in developing countries. Moreover, blockchain technology can reduce running costs and make logistics processes more efficient. However, this is offset by the dependency on correct data and the high implementation costs, which is why companies should explore financing options such as cooperations with NGOs or existing blockchain solutions for small businesses. For the use of blockchains in the public sector, this study conducted an analysis of policy and administration use cases and resource allocation. Based on the results, it could be shown that Blockchains have the potential to fight corruption in developing countries through their resistance to manipulation and transparency. Technical, financial and legal limitations could be identified as factors critical to success. Policymakers and responsible officials should therefore work on the technical and legal framework. The evaluation of the results on the scope of resource allocation showed that the use of blockchains can increase the efficiency of humanitarian supply chains and reduce costs. This is visible through the shortened delivery times and reduced need for resources and capacity in aid distribution.

In this study, the potential of cryptocurrencies in the private sector and as legal tender was examined. It could be shown that cryptocurrencies in the private sector and in the form of CBDCs have the potential to drive financial inclusion in developing countries. Regulation of decentralized cryptocurrencies and privacy of digital state currencies has emerged as the biggest challenge. Therefore, it is recommended to establish a decentrally managed digital state currency or accept an existing stablecoin.

The work was able to summarize the results of various studies on sub-aspects of the subject under investigation and thus provide an overview of the possibilities of blockchain technology for societies in developing countries. Previous studies have been limited to specific use cases, areas or sectors. The work mainly follows the results of Freire et al. (2021), who have already shown potentials of some application areas. In doing so, the present study was able to produce more precise and differentiated results, diversifying them by including quantitative studies.

For the area of supply chains, the potentials of cost savings through the use of a blockchain were shown. The reasons range from the elimination of cost-intensive reviews of quality standards, to more efficient logistics processes, to downsized supply chains. Confirmation of the findings based on relevant key figures of companies was not possible within the scope of this study. An investigation of the cost-benefit ratio through ex-post analyses of existing projects could empirically strengthen the findings. In addition, a further investigation could address the open question of which specific sustainability indicators could be validly measured with a blockchain in order to gain implications for practice.

References

Alvarez, F. E., Argente, D. & Van Patten, D. (2022). *Are Cryptocurrencies Currencies? Bitcoin as Legal Tender in El Salvador*. https://www.nber.org/system/files/working_papers/w29968/w29968.pdf

Bank for International Settlements (2021). *Annual Economic Report June 2021*. https://www.bis.org/publ/arpdf/ar2021e.pdf

Bundesverband der Energie- und Wasserwirtschaft e. V. BDEW (2017). Blockchain i*n der Energiewirtschaft: Potenziale für Energieversorger*. https://www.bdew.de/media/documents/BDEW_Blockchain_Energiewirtschaft_10_2017.pdf

Behind the Scenes of Central Bank Digital Currency: Emerging Trends, Insights, and *Policy Lessons*. https://www.imf.org/en/Publications/fintech-notes/Issues/2022/02/07/Behind-the-Scenes-of-Central-Bank-Digital-Currency-512174

Bundesministerium für Arbeit und Soziales BMAS. (2020). *Ergebnispapier der Konferenz „Globale Lieferketten – Globale Verantwortung. Menschenrechte und gute Arbeit in globalen Lieferketten. Der europäische Weg nach vorne: Vorschläge für eine neue EU-Agenda zu*

Menschenrechten und guter Arbeit in globalen Lieferketten. https://www.bmas.de/SharedDocs/Downloads/DE/EU-Ratspraesidentschaft/ergebnispapier-konferenz-globale-lieferketten.pdf;jsessionid=DC7CA67D704FFF8E12E9698440B8A5C7.delivery2-replication?__blob=publicationFile&v=1

Bundesministerium für wirtschaftliche Zusammenarbeit und Entwicklung BMZ. (2021). *Eine Welt – unsere Verantwortung - Globalisierung gerecht gestalten: 16. Entwicklungspolitischer Bericht der Bundesregierung.* https://www.bmz.de/resource/blob/96722/e840c8fca72dabdf371a8e9cab809c13/smaterialie575-entwicklungspolitischer-bbericht-data.pdf

Braam, J., Häberer, S., Häberlen, T., Oberweis, R. & Stadler, T. (2019). *Blockchain sicher gestalten: Konzepte, Anforderungen, Bewertungen.* Retrieved from https://www.bsi.bund.de/SharedDocs/Downloads/DE/BSI/Krypto/Blockchain_Analyse.pdf?__blob=publicationFile&v=3

Bundesnetzagentur. (2019). *Die Blockchain-Technologie: Potenziale und Herausforderungen in den Netzsektoren Energie und Telekommunikation.* https://www.bundesnetzagentur.de/SharedDocs/Downloads/DE/Allgemeines/Bundesnetzagentur/Publikationen/Berichte/2019/DiskussionspapierBlockchain.pdf?__blob=publicationFile&v=1

Buterin, V. (2014). Ethereum White Paper: A Next-Generation Smart Contract & Decentralized Application Platform. https://ethereum.org/669c9e2e2027310b6b3cdce6e1c52962/Ethereum_Whitepaper_-_Buterin_2014.pdf

Chen, S., Goel, T., Qiu, H. & Shim, I. (2022). *CBDCs in emerging market economies.* https://www.bis.org/publ/bppdf/bispap123_a_rh.pdf

Demirgüç-Kunt, A., Klapper, L., Singer, D., Ansar, S. & Hess, J. (2017). *The Global Findex Database 2017. Measuring Financial Inclusion and the Fintech Revolution.* https://openknowledge.worldbank.org/handle/10986/29510

Fischer, V., & Bulanda, M. (2021). *Millionen in Micro Payments. Blockmagazin, 2*(2), 102–103.

Freire, C., Solomon, A., Godunova, M., Ye, W. & Shahsavar, R. (2021). *Harnessing blockchain for sustainable development: Prospects and challenges.* https://unctad.org/system/files/official-document/dtlstict2021d3_en.pdf

Fridgen, G., Guggenberger, N., Hoeren, T., Prinz, W., Urbach, N., Baur, J. ... Wederhake, L. (2019). *Chancen und Herausforderungen von DLT (Blockchain) in Mobilität und Logistik.* https://www.fim-rc.de/Paperbibliothek/Veroeffentlicht/1106/wi-1106.pdf

Gayvoronskaya, T., & Meinel, C. (2020). *Blockchain: Hype or Innovation.* Springer Vieweg.

Haupt, S., Lichter, J. & May, F. C. (2021). *Sorgfaltspflichten entlang globaler Lieferketten: Eine ökonomische Analyse.* https://research.handelsblatt.com/assets/uploads/Studie_BMZ_Lieferkettengesetz.pdf

Hosp, J. (2018b). *Kryptowährungen: Bitcoin, Ethereum, Blockchain, ICO's & Co. einfach erklärt.* FBV.

Hosp, J. (2018a). *Blockchain 2.0. Einfach erklärt: Weit mehr als nur Bitcoin.* FBV.

International Monetary Fund IMF. (2021). Global Financial Stability Report. Covid-19, Crypto, and Climate: Navigating Challenging Transitions. https://www.imf.org/en/Publications/GFSR/Issues/2021/10/12/global-financial-stability-report-october-2021

Kanza, Y. & Safra, E. (2018). Cryptotransport: Blockchain-powered ride hailing while preserving privacy, pseudonymity and trust. In Banaei-Kashani, F., Hoel, E., Güting, R. H., Tamassia, R., Xiong, L. (Eds.), *Proceedings of the 26th ACM SIGSPATIAL International* Conference on Advances in Geographic Information Systems (pp. 540–543). Association for Computing Machinery.

Kapidani, N., Bauk, S., & Davidson, I. E. (2021). Developing Countries' Concerns Regarding Blockchain Adoption in Maritime. *Journal of Marine Science and Engineering, 9*(12), 1–11. https://doi.org/10.3390/jmse9121326

Kopyto, M., Lechler, S., Heiko, A., & Hartmann, E. (2020). Potentials of blockchain technology in supply chain management: Long-term judgments of an international expert panel. *Technological Forecasting and Social Change, 53*(161), 1–13. https://doi.org/10.1016/j.techfore.2020.120330

Kremer, M. (2022, January). Hilft Krypto in Afghanistan den Frauen oder den Taliban?. Kryptokompass, 6(1), 22-27.

Krings, K. & Schwab, J. (2020). Blockchain-Technologie in Lieferketten*: Welche Chancen bietet sie für nachhaltige Entwicklung?*. https://www.idos-research.de/uploads/media/AuS_19.2020.pdf

Kshetri, N. (2021). Blockchain and sustainable supply chain management in developing countries. *International Journal of Information Management, 41*(60), 1–13. https://doi.org/10.1016/j.ijinfomgt.2021.102376

Kshetri, N. (2021). The Economics of Blockchain-Based Supply Chain Traceability in Developing Countries. *Computer, 54*(8), 98–103. https://doi.org/10.1109/MC.2021.3082835

Lopez, M. L. & Mendoza, J. P. (2022). E-Peso. Ex-Post Performance Evaluation: Final Report. https://pdf.usaid.gov/pdf_docs/PA00Z9TJ.pdf

Lund, S., Manyika, J., Woetzel, J., Barriball, E., Krishnan, M., Alicke, K.,...Hutzle, K. (2020). Risk, resilience, and rebalancing in global value chains. https://www.mckinsey.com/~/media/McKinsey/Business%20Functions/Operations/Our%20Insights/Risk%20resilience%20and%20rebalancing%20in%20global%20value%20chains/Risk-resilience-and-rebalancing-in-global-value-chains-full-report-vH.pdf

Oxfam (2020). *The UnBlocked Cash Project: Oxfam Pacific scales blockchain solution to revolutionize humanitarian aid*. https://medium.com/@OxfamUBC/unblocked-cash-oxfam-pacific-scales-blockchain-solution-to-revolutionize-humanitarian-aid-4fb7f2a14f6b

Ozdemir, A. I., Erol, I., Ar, I. M., Peker, I., Asgary, A., Medeni, T. D., & Medeni, I. T. (2020). The role of blockchain in reducing the impact of barriers to humanitarian supply chain management. *The International Journal of Logistics Management, 32*(2), 454–478. https://doi.org/10.1108/IJLM-01-2020-0058

Schlatt, V., Schweizer, A., Urbach, N. & Fridgen, G. (2016). Blockchain: Grundlagen, *Anwendungen und Potenziale.* https://www.fit.fraunhofer.de/content/dam/fit/de/documents/Blockchain_WhitePaper_Grundlagen-Anwendungen-Potentiale.pdf

Schwab, J. & Ohnesorge, J. (2019). *Potenziale der Blockchain-Technologie für die Handelsintegration von Entwicklungsländern.* https://www.idos-research.de/uploads/media/AuS__4.2019.pdf

Schwarzkopf, J., Adam, K., & Wittenberg, S. (2018). Vertrauen in nachhaltigkeitsorientierte Audits und in Transparenz von Lieferketten: Schafft die Blockchain-Technologie einen Mehrwert? In A. Khare, D. Kessler, & J. Wirsam (Eds.), *Marktorientiertes Produkt- und Produktionsmanagement in digitalen Umwelten* (pp. 171–180). Springer Gabler.

Snowden, E. (2021, October 9). Your money and your life: Central Banks Digital Currencies will ransom our future, Retrieved October 26, 2022, from https://edwardsnowden.substack.com/p/cbdcs

Snyder, H. (2019). Literature review as a research methodology: An overview and guidelines. *Journal of business research, 46*(104), 333–339. https://doi.org/10.1016/j.jbusres.2019.07.039

Soderberg, G., Bechara, M., Bossu, W., Che, N. X., Kiff, J., Lukonga, I.,…Yoshinaga, A. (2022).

Stetler, C. B., Morsi, D., Rucki, S., Broughton, S., Corrigan, B., & Fitzgerald,…Sheridan, E. A. (1998). Utilization-focused integrative reviews in a nursing service. *Applied Nursing Research, 11*(4), 195–206. https://doi.org/10.1016/s0897-1897(98)80329-7

Sunyaev, A. (2020). *Internet Computing. Principles of Distributed Systems and Emerging Internet-Based Technologies.* Springer Nature Switzerland.

World Food Programme of the United Nations WFP (2022). Blockchain network for humanitarian assistance: Graduated Project. https://innovation.wfp.org/project/building-blocks

Whittemore, R., & Knafl, K. (2005). The integrative review: Updated methodology. *Journal of advanced nursing, 52*(5), 546–553. https://doi.org/10.1111/j.1365-2648.2005.03621.x

Zaghloul, E., Li, T., Mutka, M. W. & Ren, J. (2020). Bitcoin and blockchain. Security and privacy. *IEEE Internet of Things Journal*, 7(10), 10288-10313. doi:https://doi.org/10.1109/JIOT.2020.3004273

Zambrano, R., Young, A., & Verhulst, S. (2018). Case Study. Connecting Refugees to Aid through Blockchain-Enabled ID Management: World Food Programme's Building Blocks. https://blockchan.ge/blockchange-resource-provision.pdf

Zambrano, R. (2020). Taming the Beast: Harnessing Blockchains in Developing Country Governments. *Frontiers in Blockchain, 2*(27), 1–15. https://doi.org/10.3389/fbloc.2019.00027

The Way Smart Cities, Startups and Impact Hubs Contribute to Gender Equality

Antonia F. Terriuolo

Abstract The purpose of this study is to gain insights into how the Sustainable Development Goal (SDG) number 5, addressing Gender Equality, can be connected to the Smart City concept. Recently, Smart Cities have attracted substantial attention and funding, positively impacting the urban economic process. In this regard, the report delves into how Smart Cities can help cities be innovative, safe, and secure to promote gender equality. Furthermore, the objective of this study is to address the Smart City concept as an innovation promoting greater inclusion, safety, resilience, and sustainability so that cities may prosper and provide equal opportunities to all their residents, whilst putting it into the context of the need to address gender equality on a national level. Moreover, the elimination of gender inequality nationally will have a positive impact on a global scale, providing the relevance of this body of work given the scope of globalization. To analyze these conditions, a case study encompassing the startup Safe & The City is used to illustrate the theoretical framework established. Additionally, two interviews with women in the startup and/or Smart City industry were conducted to reach a conclusion in terms of opinions and suggestions for future action. The findings include that networks exist for entrepreneurs and innovators to build and improve their businesses, which is especially of importance for female entrepreneurs. Additionally, initiatives facilitating communities online help to bring marginalized groups together, which may be inevitably important to improve the prerequisites for female founders in the startup industry. This report highlights that the main idea behind Smart Cities, general awareness, and knowledge of SDGs among the public will most likely speed up the process to a more sustainable world. Lastly, issues discovered in this research may be considered in policymaking, showing their relevance for the social, environmental, and economic sphere.

Keywords SDG's · Gender equality · Smart cities · Innovation · Globalization

A. F. Terriuolo (✉)
Dusseldorf, Germany
e-mail: antoniaterriuolo@gmail.com

R. C. Geibel and S. Machavariani (eds.), *Chances and Challenges of Digital Management*, Springer Proceedings in Business and Economics,
https://doi.org/10.1007/978-3-031-45601-5_9

1 Introduction

Living in a globalized world, we try to remain who we are as individuals while forming important networks around the world so as not to fall behind in the whirlwind that is our economic landscape. Increasing innovations and constantly changing technology force individuals, companies, and governments to adapt and implement the changing nature of everyday life into policy, private, as well as working landscapes. In this respect, Smart Cities have attracted substantial attention and funding over the last few years. Based on the literature, it may be concluded that such innovations have a positive impact on the urban economic process. Since the unique context of each city shapes the technological, organizational, and policy aspects of a city, the concept can be considered an innovation in the technological, managerial, as well as organizational fields. This body of work focuses on this innovation contributing to the development of Sustainable Development Goal (SDG) number 5, addressing Gender Equality. Additionally, the paper examines the implications of the different understandings of the Smart City Concept; for cities' abilities to be innovative, safe, and secure to promote gender equality.

The aim of this report is to address the Smart City Concept as an innovation promoting greater inclusion, safety, resilience, and sustainability so that cities may prosper and provide equal opportunities to all their residents while putting it into the context of the need to address gender inequality, nationally, which in turn will have a positive impact on a global scale. Consequently, providing the relevance of the chosen topic given the scope of globalization mentioned before.

2 Smart Cities: An Approach to Better Living

Given the rise of technology and focus on innovation by regional decision-makers, the concept of Smart Cities provides valuable insights into how a regional area can adapt to the demands of the fast-paced world we live in. In 2018, 55% of the world's population lived in urban areas; this is expected to rise to 68% by 2050 (United Nations, 2018). Moreover, the population's growth and the moving from rural to urban areas have increased the need to manage the environmental, social, and economic sustainability of resources (European Commission, n.d. a) giving rise to the concept of Smart Cities, which may be defined as cities where "investments in human and social capital and traditional (transport) and modern (ICT) communication infrastructure fuel sustainable economic growth and a high quality of life, with a wise management of natural resources, through participatory governance" (Caragliu et al., 2009, p. 50). Generally, ICT refers to Information and Communications Technology. Additionally, the main goal of a Smart City is to optimize a city's functions and promote economic growth while simultaneously improving the quality of life for its citizens by using smart technologies and data analysis. Therefore, Smart Cities highlight important aspects of sustainability, such as the need for responsible resource management using digital technologies, citizen engagement, etc. (European Commission, n.d. a). Consequently, adopting a Smart City Strategy would be beneficial for a local urban area, not only from an environmental perspective but also from a social point of view, as it allows the continuation of human life in that area.

The Smart City Model uses performance indicators describing the factors collected from databases derived from freely available public data and concurs in the assessment of a city's performance as a Smart City (Giffinger et al., 2007). The implementation of the Smart City Model is an ongoing process that requires constant revision to be able to make necessary adjustments. Therefore, implementing a Smart City Strategy today will ultimately influence the way a city and its government do things within a local region in the future, making a Smart City an innovation with potential long-term impact.

The Smart City Marketplace aims to bring cities, industries, Small and Medium-Sized Enterprises (SMEs), and many other Smart City actors together to improve citizens' quality of life, increase the competitiveness of European cities and industries as well as reach European energy and climate targets. Additionally, it focuses on different areas of cross-cutting operations; including sustainable urban mobility, sustainable districts, and building environment, integrated infrastructures and processes in energy, information, and communication technologies, and transport, but also dwells on citizen care, policy, and regulation, as well as knowledge sharing. It also assumes the implementation of integrated planning and management, baselines, performance indicators, standards, and metrics, open data governance, business models, procurement, and funding (European Commission, n.d. b).

3 Defining Smart Cities

Generally, "a city can be defined as 'smart' if it adopts an innovative collaborative governance style, to design urban policies aimed at improving citizen's quality of and at promoting environmental, economic and social sustainability" (Nesti, 2019, p. 289). The discourse around Smart Cities incorporates a sustainability topic of high relevance: the Triple Bottom Line, which integrates social, environmental, and economic spheres (Alhaddi, 2015). Therefore, it provides a new framework for companies to conduct their business and consider more than just their traditional bottom line while highlighting issues like Corporate Social Responsibility (CSR), and the general role businesses play in making the world more sustainable. Furthermore, Smart Cities' main components are civic participation and inclusion (Nesti, 2019), stressing its collaborative approach. This is furthered by the growing population size, as well as the increasing complexity of city management that calls for technological solutions for urban spaces and public services, which is where Smart Cities develop. Moreover, the concept of Smart Cities starts at the national sub-level of a specific city, but given its technological and innovative aspects, it can be connected through networks of cities, towards a national, or even global dimension (Dameri, 2013). From these findings a comprehensive definition can be derived leading to the following: "a Smart City is a well defined geographical area, in which high technologies such as ICT, logistic, energy production, and so on, cooperate to create benefits for citizens in terms of well being, inclusion and participation, environmental quality, intelligent development; it is governed by a well defined pool of subjects, able to state the rules and policy for the city government and development" (Dameri, 2013, p. 2549).

4 Gender Equality in Smart Cities

Wanting to improve gender equality, calls for a multi-stakeholder approach, where knowledge of the local space should be used when creating Smart Cities. More specifically, it means to relate to past experiences within a certain urban environment to improve women's experiences in those areas today and in the future. In this regard, literature talks about *gender-balanced urban technologies* ensuring that women play an active role in the establishment of a safe system, rather than being solely at the receiving end of it (Baskaradas & Reilly, 2019). Given the social nature of gender inequality, Smart Cities also incorporate issues of social sciences by dealing with an improvement of life quality while developing public services that are inclusive in nature, consequently, reducing inequality (Sasanapitak & Amornsiriphong, 2020). This is especially relevant in less developed countries, where women systematically are not given the same chances as their male counterparts.

5 Case Study: Smart Cities and Safe & the City Ltd.

Safe & The City is a personal safety navigation app, designed as a map that points out places that might not be safe or have higher crime rates than other areas (Flockett, n.d.). The startup's mobile app provides real-time notifications from official sources and suggests the safest walking and public transit routes based on public ratings (Safe & the City, 2021a). It allows women to notify someone if an unexpected incident occurs and authorities to discover and mitigate risks based on crowdsourced incident reports (StartUs Insights, n.d.). The focus is on public transport and walkways since it is where someone's safety is most at risk and where the least amount of technology for personal protection exists. Therefore, it integrates safety into its navigation system (Montebello, 2020). Launched in 2017 in the United Kingdom, the app uses information from the metropolitan police focusing on areas that have seen a high number of sexual assaults or harassment in the past, to places where several Anti-Social Behavior Order (ASBO) have been assigned (Flockett, n.d.). Its connection to the Smart City Innovation Concept derives from the use of Perceptual Intelligence to improve women's safety in public and digital spaces (StartUs Insights, n.d.), where Perceptual Intelligence refers to "paying attention to people and the surrounding situations in the same way another person would, thus allowing these new devices to learn to adapt their behavior to suit us, rather than adapting to them as we do today" (Pentland, 2000, p. 35).

The company produces risk estimates for public spaces and makes these available to feed directly into other mobile apps and products. Moreover, the machine learning model continuously scans various data sources across different digital channels. It concerns looking out for, for example, public order threats to find out when a serious incident is unfolding, as it did during the 2019 London Bridge terrorist attack, whereby users within a 5 km radius received notification providing official police guidance within ten minutes (Safe & the City, 2021a). Furthermore, the company turns to Twitter to have faster incident discoveries as Twitter's Application Programming Interface (API) allows ingesting a real-time, filtered stream of Tweets using in-built rules and operations. Each new incident detected is flagged to a member of the company to review for accuracy and measured against several metrics for information reliability. Upon acceptance, positive results are forwarded to the users via their registered webhook endpoints; once live, customers can expect to receive notifications in as little as a few minutes (Safe & the City, 2021b). Additionally, the company focuses on the important issue of street and sexual harassment, centering on the fact that millions of these experiences are minimized, not reported, as women are told that it was 'just' a comment, 'just' a joke or that it is all based on the way women dress, contributing to whether they feel safe to walk alone at night (Harris, 2020). Moreover, the direct connection to the Smart City Concept is shown in the publicly available use of data and its participatory nature.

6 Economics of Innovation

Radical or *disruptive innovations* are innovations that have significant impact on a market and on the economic activity of firms in that market. In Schumpeter's view, *radical innovations* create major disruptive changes, whereas *incremental innovations* continuously advance the process of change (Schumpeter, 1934). *Incremental innovations* concern an existing product, service, process, organization, or method where its performance has been significantly upgraded. Thus, Safe & The City is an *incremental innovation*, as it does not create new concepts or products, but focuses on marginal improvements to what already exists. Additionally, Open Innovations concern the paradigm that firms can and should use external ideas as well as internal ideas and paths to market, as the firms look to advance their technology by combining internal and external ideas into their business model (Chesbrough, 2003). Consequently, Safe & The City can be recognized as an Open Innovation because it does not just rely on internal knowledge (e.g., staff or Research & Development) for its innovation, but also gathers information from its users, partners, and authorities. Lastly, *Industry 4.0* represents the fourth revolution of manufacturing, which takes what was started during the third through the adoption of computers and automation and enhances it with smart and autonomous systems fueled by data and machine learning (Marr, 2018). Safe & The City wants to show how people can report and bring about meaningful change in local areas (2020), highlighting their active contribution to the innovation of Smart Cities and why it could be used as an additional resource for cities to integrate into their Smart City Strategy. Moreover, the direct connection to the Smart City Concept is shown in the publicly available use of data.

7 Innovation and SDGs

Given the report developed by Safe & The City in partnership with UN Women in the United Kingdom, it is possible to gather relevant data in terms of the scope of this body of work. The report focuses on sexual harassment, as it is considered the most frequent form of violence that women experience within the EU. Specifically, 64% of women of all ages and 85% of women aged 16–24, in the UK, have experienced sexual harassment in public spaces; while, not less significantly, 38% have experienced a form of verbal harassment between the ages of 14 and 21. These experiences affect choices, and behaviors and, overall, have a huge impact on women's lives. The UN Women's global program "Safe Cities & Safe Public Spaces" aims to highlight relevant aspects of violence against women in the eyes of private and public institutions, to give voice to otherwise unreported incidents, fueling investments and concrete actions to be taken. Unfortunately, the majority of identified incidents are not considered illegal, which is why efficient legislative intervention is needed to prevent violent actions against women. Additionally, UN Women UK implemented its project "Safe Spaces Now" bringing together shareholders from different sectors accelerating the progress toward safety in public spaces in the UK. Moreover, it is built to generate a growing data picture of the reality of women's safety, going over issues in designing adequate solutions through partnerships with public space owners, and finally scaling the process to create lasting and official change processes (UN Women UK, n.d.). Therefore, Safe & The City helps to make traveling within a certain area safer for women as a marginalized group and thus helps move the respective cities towards becoming a Smart City.

Given the scope of the SGDs, the following targets of SDG number 5 are relevant considering Safe & The City: *Target 2*: "end all violence against and exploitation of women and girls […]; [*Target 8*:] promote empowerment of women through technology; [*Target 9*:] adopt and strengthen policies and enforceable legislation for gender equality" (Ritchie, Roser, Mispy & Ortiz-Ospina, 2018, n.p.). Considering the Safe & The City Innovation, the following additional indicators might be relevant: income, sex, age, race, ethnicity, migratory status, disability, method of transportation, and geographic location. Given the fact that Smart Cities encompass the personal sphere of every citizen, the personal characteristics of minority groups should be used as an indicator of the progress of SDG 5 as well. Specifically, "method of transportation", as well as "geographical location" (rural or urban area) should be focused on based on differing traveling needs between women and men, where Safe & The City provides the first initiative in that direction.

8 Impacts on Socio-Economic Factors

Due to globalization, the world's economy has seen specific changes unrelated to the specificity of locality but have different impacts in different areas around the world. In other words, a developed country failing to keep up with the fast-moving technological innovations will fall behind quicker than a developing country, as it has never caught up with the developed world, to begin with. These changes affect how cities organize themselves, thus affecting city government. In this respect, the Smart City Concept can open new areas of opportunity for the development of the city.

Since the wish to become a Smart City is driven by the international competitiveness driving our economy, through the implementation of Smart City Initiatives, local areas provide new space for businesses and clusters to emerge (Bakici, Almirall & Wareham, 2013). Consequently, providing the local economy with areas of increased productivity and new jobs to take and subsequently, creating new/additional competitivity in the market. Therefore, Smart Cities can act as developers of the local economy and local workforce.

However, experience has shown that the Smart City Concept is often too broad, providing a one-size-fits-all solution when, in reality, the specificities of the locality are very important in determining what is needed and possible in terms of the creation of a Smart City. Moreover, since the concept is relatively new; in-depth research and case studies are still missing (Kitchin, 2014), which are needed to provide a more realistic view of the concept. Generally, the impact on socio-economic factors like productivity, competitiveness, and employment could be immense considering the theoretical application of the Smart City Concept. Therefore, constant revision and adaptation of the strategy are needed to overcome the lack of empirical evidence and fill this hole in the literature.

9 Opinion and Suggestion

During the preparation for this research, two interviews were conducted to give further insights into the framework established. The first interview was conducted with Interviewee 1, CEO, and founder of a platform dedicated to female communities. Additionally, the second interview with Interviewee 2 was done with an employee at an Impact Hub in Germany, who is also a facilitator for #Iamremarkable[1] workshops.

Startup Hubs provide networks for (social) entrepreneurs and innovators to build and improve their businesses. Moreover, it provides a space for collaborating, networking, and exchanging information to connect entrepreneurs and innovators with organizations, and different kinds of people that may accelerate the respective business. Moreover, it is a priority when looking at females in the startup industry

[1] A Google Initiative to empower women and, generally, underrepresented groups to celebrate their achievements. This is regarding their private, as well as professional life.

that they are provided with a space where they can meet and develop their businesses in an environment of support and innovation. The venture of Interviewee 1 provides a platform dedicated to women to better manage their professional networks, as well as enhancing the engagement of their respective communities. Where Startup Hubs can act locally, it is indisputable that big corporations, like Google with their #Iamremarkable initiative, have a much faster and more poignant impact on a global scale. Consequently, providing a safe space, not only for women but all marginalized groups to come together and lift each other up rather than tearing each other down, is of great importance when wanting to improve the prerequisites for female founders in the startup industry.

In terms of Smart Cities, the economic and spatial nature is different in every city, therefore, leading to different conceptions of what the Smart City will look like (Anand & Navío-Marco, 2018). Subsequently, leading to the conclusion that there is no one-size-fits-all solution. Even though many cities have put sensors to use when generating large amounts of data, the issue of being able to analyze and process that data remains. Therefore, the literature suggests a bottom-up publish-subscribe data and integration model, and a data representation scheme in the future (Raghavan, Boung Yew, Lee, Tan & Kee, 2019), further highlighting the importance of citizen participation when creating a Smart City, which is supported by the statement of Anand and Navío-Marco (2018): "A city "smartness" is meaningless unless it is rooted on citizens' participation" (p. 797).

Interviewee 1, who works closely with the French government to work, among other things, toward SDG 5, usually encounters people who do not know what SDGs are in general but do not know what SDG 5 entails, specifically. Nonetheless, gender equality is of great importance also in the context of Smart Cities, as women have distinctively different traveling needs to men, centering around issues of access, safety and/or comfort, and ease of travel (Singh, 2020). Regarding the startup scene, partnerships of affiliations with the local government, based on the startup working towards one or multiple SDGs, can be very helpful, because it provides visibility, as well as credibility to those issues. Moreover, given the participatory nature of Smart Cities, general awareness, and knowledge of the SDGs among the general public will most likely speed up the process to a more sustainable world. Again, the awareness about issues of marginalized groups is to be focused on and is supported by initiatives like Safe & The City, shedding light on previously overlooked issues that are of great importance when wanting to create a safe environment/city for every citizen.

10 Policy Suggestions to Increase Diffusion and Positive Effects of Smart Cities in Context of SDG 5

The issue of policy regarding Smart Cities has been a thoroughly investigated topic in literature. Rogers' (1995) Innovation Diffusion Theory (IDF) focuses on the how, why, and rate of innovative ideas and technologies and their spreading within a social system. Moreover, it highlights the importance of reshaping products and behaviors to better fit the needs of the current times. Therefore, the innovations themselves need to be changed to stay relevant. Additionally, diffusion is also considered to be the process of communication of innovation between the different members of the social system (Wani & Ali, 2015). Subsequently, this theory is in line with the previously mentioned point that it is important to increase awareness of certain issues, like gender equality, within the society to generate public participation in terms of innovation, like Smart Cities.

Moreover, within the Western world shared economies have gained increasing importance, especially within the mobility sector. Consequently, this changed how people, and therefore, also women, move. Additionally, research found that women face higher hurdles and have less access to cost-/time-efficient travel. Subsequently, broad access to mobility apps, like Safe & The City should help to improve access to travel for economically vulnerable groups (Singh, 2020), which must be considered when adopting policies for rapid changes in our economy. Since apps like Safe & The City provide a service, the end customer, and their different lifestyle(-needs) must be kept in mind. In this context, access to digital data and use thereof is especially important today for private, as well as public actors. Moreover, policies need to make use of up-to-date and reliable data to provide citizens with the best possible solutions for the given area. Here, policymakers and other public agents may make use of Geo-Science and Geo-Imaging, which use interactive tools and data to add to the smart information design to further improve the urban planning tools of the city. In terms of demographics, knowledge of clusters within the city and their mobility patterns, combined with social information about those demographics may provide additional insight to use in urban management and policymaking by trying to answer questions about how, when, and, where people interact within certain places within the urban area. Moreover, the use of such data will further the progress toward e-governance influencing smart urban policy (Koutit et al., 2016). Furthermore, the changes in governmental functions should be reflected in governmental policies to provide a seamless transition to e-governments in the future. Additionally, since policies should always be adopted with the citizens' best interest in mind, any policy geared towards making an urban area safer should consider, not only women but all its inhabitants and how to best improve their daily lives. In this context, collected data by companies like Safe & The City and Interviewee 1's company may be used by the government to gain access to a broad spectrum of data that can further be used to make specific policy changes and/or adaptions. Moreover, policy agendas allow for an inclusive policy framework since one policy domain shows a direct linkage to another (Clement & Crutzen, 2021). Consequently, the improvement towards a Smart City in one policy area, for example, women's safety, will have a direct impact on other policy areas leading to a domino effect of positive policy implementations toward a Safe and Smart City.

Both interview partners were asked questions related to the underrepresentation of women in the startup industry, and why they believe that women are a marginalized group to this day. Regarding this, the focus was put on education and upbringing, or change thereof, to be the starting point of changing the narrative of women being the victim of a male-dominated society. Additionally, the importance of representation in different areas of our society to provide positive examples was highlighted. In this regard, it was said that the women's quota may put pressure on organizations to give women the seat at the table they deserve. Other issues regarding the underrepresentation of women in the startup industry that were mentioned are the gender pay gap, the gender confidence gap, and the gender funding gap. The latter is considered especially detrimental because there are fewer female investors. Additionally, female founders generally tend to found businesses of a social nature, which are overlooked by investors who want to focus on more profitable ideas. Furthermore, the issue of gender-sensitive language was raised to be able to think and speak of and about women appropriately.

All the aforementioned issues are areas that may be considered in policymaking and have importance and accuracy since they come from people who feel this type of discrimination daily. Furthermore, shedding light on the value that is provided by listening to marginalized groups; be it in private conversations, or public data gathering.

11 Conclusion

Smart Cities highlight important aspects of sustainability. Within the Smart City Development Model data analyses results are communicated to decision-makers who take appropriate actions. Moreover, the importance of protecting women from violence and emphasizing their participation to create economic empowerment is supported by the United Nations by including gender equality in the development of Smart Cities. Considering the main idea behind Smart Cities, general awareness, and knowledge of the SDGs among the public will speed up the process to a more sustainable world. Therefore, this is in line with the point that it is important to increase awareness of certain issues, like gender equality, within our society to generate public participation in the arena of innovation, like Smart Cities. Furthermore, new tools for city management and planning development have become especially important regarding policy strategies. Therefore, issues discovered in this research may be considered in policymaking and have importance and accuracy since they come from people affected by this type of discrimination. Since we are at the beginning of this urban development project, there are still areas that need to be improved upon. Therefore, concrete analyses are required to assess whether the positive outlook can persist. If it does, it will lead to the reduction of inequality and the creation of safe surroundings for all marginalized groups.

References

Alhaddi, H. (2015). Triple bottom line and sustainability: A literature review. *Businessand Management Studies, 1*(2), 6–10. https://doi.org/10.11114/bms.v1i2.752

Anand, P. B., & Navío-Marco, J. (2018). Governance and economics of Smart Cities: Opportunities and challenges. *Telecommunications Policy, 42*(10), 795–799. https://doi.org/10.1016/j.telpol.2018.10.001

Bakici, T., Amlirall, E., & Wareham, J. (2013). A Smart City Initiative: The Case of Barcelona. *Journal of the Knowledge Economy, 4*(2), 135–148. https://doi.org/10.1007/s13132-012-0084-9

Baskaradas, E. & Reilly, P. (2019, April 25). *In search of a Gender-Balanced approach towards Smart Cities 3.0.* Retrieved from https://www.globalpolicyjournal.com/sites/

Caragliu, A., Del Bo, C., & Nijkamp, P. (2009). Smart cities in Europe. *Journal of Urban Technology, 18*(48), 45–59. https://doi.org/10.1080/10630732.2011.601117

Chesbrough, H. W. (2003). The era of open innovation. *MIT Sloan Management Review, 44*(3), 34–42. https://doi.org/10.12691/jfe-2-5-9

Clement, J., & Crutzen, N. (2021). How local policy priorities set the smart city agenda. *Technological Forecasting & Social Change, 171*(1), 120985–120996. https://doi.org/10.1016/j.techfore.2021.120985

Dameri, R. P. (2013). Searching for smart city definition: A comprehensive proposal. *International Journal of Computers & Technology, 11*(5), 2544–2551. https://doi.org/10.24297/ijct.v11i5.1142

European Commission (n.d. a). *Sustainable urban development*. https://ec.europa.eu/regional_policy/policy/themes/urban-development_en

European Commission (n.d. b). *Smart cities: Cities using technological solutions to improve the management and efficiency of the urban environment.* https://ec.europa.eu/info/eu-regional-and-urban-development/topics/cities-and-urban-development/city-initiatives/smart-cities_en

Flockett, A. (n.d.). *Safe And The City*. https://startupsmagazine.co.uk/article-safe-and-city

Giffinger, R. et al. (2007, October). *Smart Cities ranking of European medium-sized cities.* https://www.researchgate.net/publication/261367640_Smart_cities_-_Ranking_of_European_medium-sized_cities

Harris, J. (2020, October 19). *Safe & the City launches global campaign.* https://geovation.uk/safe-the-city-partner-with-un/

Kitchin, R. (2014). Making sense of smart cities: Addressing present shortcomings. *Cambridge Journal of Regions, Economy and Society, 8*(1), 131–136. https://doi.org/10.1093/cjres/rsu027

Koutit, K., Nijkamp, P., & Steenbruggen, J. (2016). The significance of digital data systems for Smart City policy. *Socio-Economic Planning Science, 58*(1), 13–21. https://doi.org/10.1016/j.seps.2016.10.001

Marr, B. (2018). *What is Industry 4.0? Here's A Super Easy Explanation For Anyone.* https://www.forbes.com/consent/?toURL=https://www.forbes.com/sites%20/bernardmarr/2018/09/02/what-is-industry-4-0-heres-a-super-easy-explanation-for-anyone/

Montebello, L. (2020, October 6). *Safe & The City: A Personal Safety Navigation App That Is Transforming The Way We Get Around The City.* https://www.wewhodo.com/the-sustainable-startup-series-spotlight-on-safe-the-city

Nesti, G. (2019). Mainstreaming gender equality in smart cities: Theoretical, methodological and empirical challenges. *Information Polity, 24*(3), 289–304. https://doi.org/10.3233/IP-190134

Pentland, A. (2000). Perceptual user interfaces: Perceptual intelligence. *Communications of the ACM, 43*(3), 35–44. https://doi.org/10.1145/330534.330536

Raghavan, S., Simon, B. Y. L., Lee, Y. L., Tan, W. L. & Kee, K. K. (2019). Data Integration for Smart Cities: Opportunities and Challenges. In R. Alfred, Y. Lim, H. Haviluddin, C. K. On (Eds.) *Computational Science and Technology. Lecture Notes in Electrical Engineering, vol. 603* (pp. 393–403). Springer.

Ritchie, H., Roser, M., Mispy, J., & Ortiz-Ospina, E. (2018). *Measuring progress towards the sustainable development goals.* https://sdg-tracker.org/gender-equality#targets

Rogers, E.M. (1995). *Diffusion of innovations. (4th ed.).* Free Press.
Safe & the City (n.d.). *Personal Safety: Keep Safe On The Go.* https://www.safeandthecity.com/
Safe & the City (2021 b, April 15). *Q1 20201: Consumer Survey Results.* https://www.safeandthecity.com/blog/consumer-survey-results
Safe & the City (2021 a, March 8). *Announcing the i3 Intelligence Platform.* https://www.safeandthecity.com/blog/announcing-the-i3-intelligence-platform
Sasanapitak, A. & Amornsiriphong, S. (2020). *Smart City: The Role To Create Justice And The Promotion Of Gender Equality.* https://www.ic.kku.ac.th/?page_id=11892
Schumpeter, J. A. (1934). *The Theory of Economic Development: An Inqfuiry into Profits, Capital, Credit, Interest, and the Business Cycle.* Transaction Publishers.
Singh, Y. J. (2020). Is smart mobility also gender smart? *Journal of Gender Studies, 29*(7), 832–846. https://doi.org/10.1080/09589236.2019.1650728
StartUs Insights (n.d.). *Discover 5 Top Startups developing Gender Equality Solutions.* https://www.startus-insights.com/innovators-guide/discover-5-top-startups-developing-gender-equality-solutions/
United Nations (2018, May 16). *67% of the world population projected to live in urban areas by 2050, says UN.* https://www.un.org/development/desa/en/news/population/2018-revision-of-world-urbanization-prospects.html
UN Women UK (n.d.). *Safer Spaces For Women And Girls: A pilot demonstrating partnership, technology and data-driven insights into women's lived experiences of violence and harassment public spaces.* https://www.safeandthecity.com/media/cs2ltsmd/saferspacesforwomen_unw_stc.pdf
Wani, T. A., & Ali, S. W. (2015). Innovation diffusion theory: review & scope in the study of adoption of smartphones in India. *Journal of General Management Research, 3*(2), 101–118.

The Importance of Intelligent OCR Software in a Digital Loyalty Program

Florian Studener, Yeelen Knegtering, Christin Barreira, Oliver Reinking, and Richard C. Geibel

Abstract From the first stamp-based loyalty system in the late nineteenth century up to today's digital cards and barcode coupled systems, loyalty programs have come a long way. With the aim to create incentives and to reward recurring customers, digitisation has changed and eased many processes around loyalty programs but its intentions. Nevertheless, digitisation by means of using OCR offers more than an easily created incentive for customers to either increase or repeat their purchases but offer the additional potential for detailed customer insights, personalised promotions, as well as a huge potential for the reduction of manual labour and reduced turnaround times for the verification and clearing processes within such programs. Within this article we will outline the roll-out of an artificial intelligence (AI) based optical character recognition application programming interface (API) used within a localised loyalty campaign for two shopping centres and highlight the core benefits of a fully automated process. Lastly, we will elaborate on the potential usage of such technologies for the generation of broader customer insights analysis.

F. Studener
E-Commerce Institute, Cologne, Germany
e-mail: florian@klipper.com

Y. Knegtering
CEO Klippa, Cologne, Germany

C. Barreira (✉)
Klaas Management, Lingen, Germany
e-mail: c.barreira@klaas-management.de

O. Reinking
Reinking Consulting, Lingen, Germany
e-mail: oliver@codingjungle.de

R. C. Geibel
E-Commerce Institute, Cologne, Germany

East European University, Tbilisi, Georgia

R. C. Geibel
e-mail: geibel@ecommerceinstitut.de

R. C. Geibel and S. Machavariani (eds.), *Chances and Challenges of Digital Management*, Springer Proceedings in Business and Economics,
https://doi.org/10.1007/978-3-031-45601-5_10

Keywords Loyalty · Digital transformation · OCR · AI · Costumer engagement

1 Introduction

With the reopening of businesses after two years of the Covid-19 pandemic and the closure of entire businesses, offices, and schools, the perspective change in regard to digitisation and the usage of digital tools during and after the Covid-19 pandemic has seen a fundamental shift in many regards. From the introduction to virtual classrooms and video conferences to the QR ordering systems and digitally provided health information, digital acceptance leapt forward by an estimate of five years (Baig et al., 2020). Concomitantly, sales organisations have experienced a massive shift towards digital engagement and remote seller interactions (Bages-Amat et al., 2020) and even newer technologies such as AI driven technologies and services are becoming more and more relevant for organisations, especially in the retail market (MIT Technology Review, CIO vision 2025: Bridging the gap between BI and AI, 2022). These observations clearly display a shift in the acceptance of newer digital tools and technologies within business in general and in particular in the retail and loyalty market segment.

For the latter, these technologies have become of particular interest, as the reduction or elimination of manual labour generated by the reviewing and clearing of proof of purchases allow more cost-efficient offerings, higher throughput, and easier scalability towards clearing services. Additionally automated processes do not require any training of personnel and can, most of the time, be integrated into existing websites and mobile applications as well as be coupled to other automations such as point counting and automated analysis.

2 Theory and Methodology

Optical Character Recognition is defined as the process of classifying optical patterns contained in an digital image corresponding to alphanumeric or other characters. Computerised systems capable of transforming text and patterns into machine-readable data have existed since the 1970s, yet their use in commercial settings has significantly increased since the addition of new emerging technological advances such as Natural Language Processing, Artificial Intelligence, and Machine Learning during the last two to three decades (Tkáč and Verner, 2016. Artificial neural networks in business: Two decades of research. Applied Soft Computing, 38, pp.788–804). The addition of the latter technologies allows broader and a more flexible adaptation to various cases and in particular the recognition, interpretation, and characterisation of documents allow otherwise time-consuming analysis and a faster generation of usable and structured data (Baviskar et al., 2021. Efficient automated processing of the unstructured documents using artificial intelligence: A systematic literature review and future directions. IEEE Access, 9, pp.72894–72,936.).

In our case study, we used a system developed by Klippa App B.V that uses classical rule-based algorithms, Artificial Intelligence and Machine Learning algorithms during and after the optical character recognition to process, recognize and characterise receipts from the individual points of sale located at the two geographical different locations. The combination of these different systems allows high recognition of various receipt designs and addition of individual rules and logic, tailored to the specific use case, such as data verification and implementation of lookup tables. The generated output is given as key-value pairs and structured as a JSON file, which is a common output format for application programming interfaces. Advantages for this kind of file structure are the ease of integration to third party applications, platforms, databases, and common understanding within the developer community. The output was subsequently analysed by the evaluation of a combination of multi-variable true–false analytics of the individual data points, to create a combination of fields that allows a unique identification of every participating merchant.

3 Method

We evaluated a dataset of 73 unique receipts split into two datasets that represented the participants of the to be implemented loyalty campaign. In a first initial benchmark, we parsed the data as image files to the API and evaluated the extraction without the addition of any lookup table or relational objects that can be used to compare the extracted results. The fields of interest were: store name, amount, purchase date, and address. Additionally, a system to exclude or hinders the submission of duplicates as well as fraudulent receipts needed to be implemented. A hash building based on the total amount, the merchant's name, and the date, was therefore implemented to avoid the submission of duplicates as these key-value pairs showed the highest recognition rate overall. A look-up table of relational objects which included the known merchant's name, address, telephone number, and VAT number was added, to ensure that in case any combination of values is identified (i.e. name and telephone numbers), the non-recognised fields will be added automatically from the given list. Lastly, we added a VAT recognition, calculation, and comparison as simple means to avoid the submission of fraudulent receipts.

4 Results

Within our initial test of 73 receipts and without any addition of a look up table or string search algorithms, we recognised 98% of the text-based content correctly and parsed 72.5% of the to-be-evaluated key-value pairs correctly. This also concludes that in 28.5% of the cases, the key-value pair has not been correctly identified.

With the addition of relational objects within a lookup table, we could significantly improve the recognition and correct parsing of key-value pairs up to 95,6%. With the combination of two or more of these identifiers (name and telephone number, or name and VAT number), we were able to identify 99% of the receipts unambiguously with regards to the needed values. Table 1 displays the two test and core results of the test runs. The numerical values are displayed in image 1 for the OCR results without the usage of user data and in image 2 for the OCR results with the addition of user data (Fig. 1).

Figure 2 shows an increased recognition of the combination between the merchant's name and the telephone number as well as the merchant's name and the VAT number. Errors that occurred during the processing did not belong to the same receipt and occurred partially due to missing data on the receipt itself (a telephone number or VAT number that was not displayed on the receipt itself). Nevertheless, these results and combination of these data fields demonstrate the usage of

Table 1 Displaying the percentage of identified TRUE values for the data fields of interest dependent on the addition of no user data versus with user data

Added user data	Merchant name [%]	Address [%]	Total amount [%]	Telephone number [%]	Vat number [%]
No	96,34	36,7	100	70,96	77,41
Yes	100	48,38	100	85,42	80,64

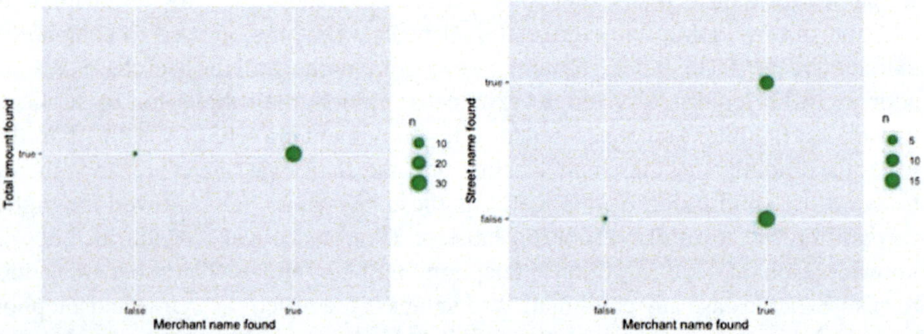

Fig. 1 Multi variable comparison of the OCR -recognition of different data fields without the usage of any user data

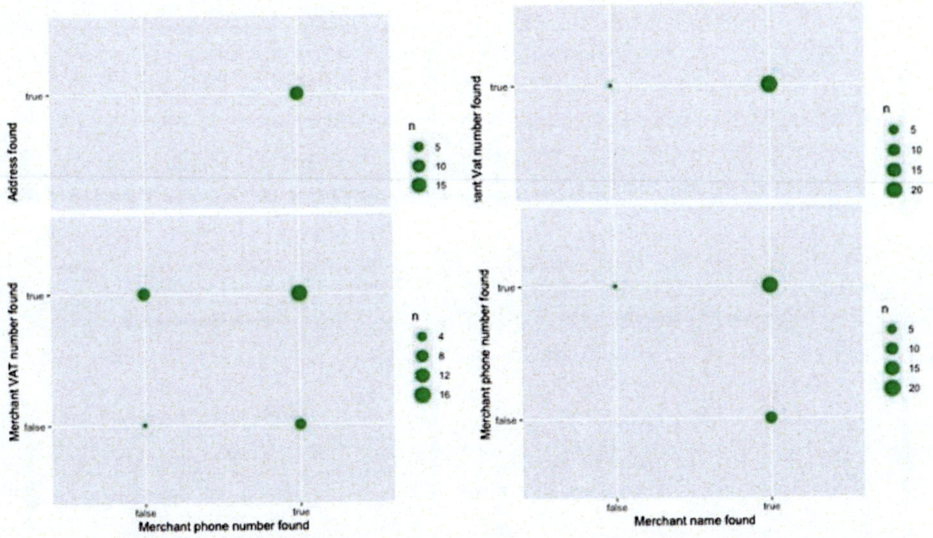

Fig. 1 (continued)

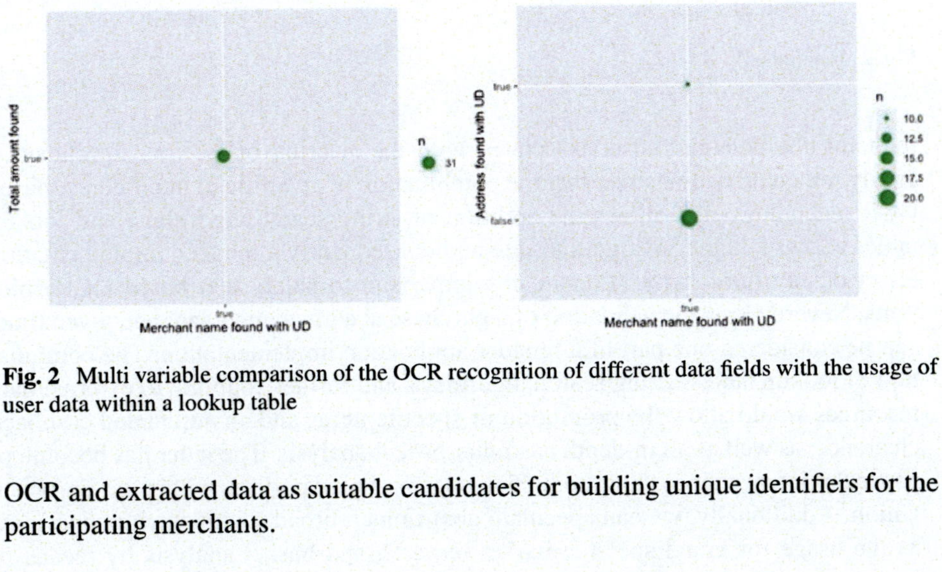

Fig. 2 Multi variable comparison of the OCR recognition of different data fields with the usage of user data within a lookup table

OCR and extracted data as suitable candidates for building unique identifiers for the participating merchants.

5 Conclusion

We have been able to demonstrate the successful implementation and optimisation of artificial intelligence based optical character recognition application program interface within the context and framework of a loyalty campaign for two geographical different shopping malls. Furthermore, the implementation of our solution circumvented the need for any (additional) manual or human labour and therefore have been

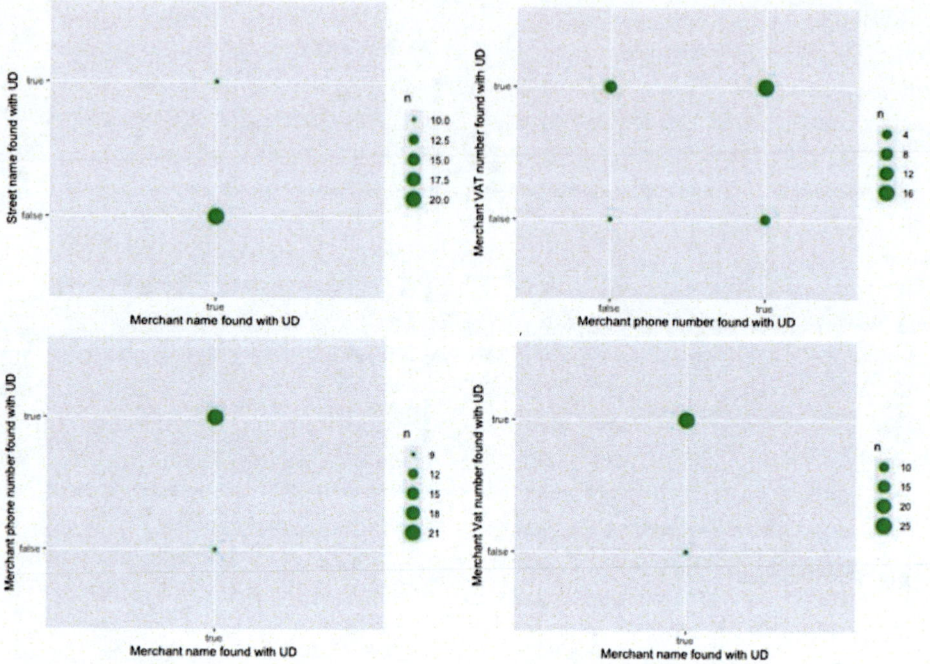

Fig. 2 (continued)

reducing the potential costs associated with the clearing of receipts significantly. Lastly, we could demonstrate that the combination of an artificial intelligence-based OCR technology that allows the addition of string search algorithms and lookup tables allows a higher recognition rate and consequently a reduced implementation effort of any third party IT team in comparison to solely text based OCR solutions. Nevertheless, the validation of a purchase at a given merchant and given time, can be considered one part of a broader application implementation. The combination of lookup tables, string search algorithms and further coupling to external data resources would allow the promotion of specific items and an automated cashback clearance, as well as an in-depth customer basket analysis. The latter has become of particular interest since the introduction of new cookie policies within the European Union. Additionally, we can speculate about much broader implementations, such as the usage for brand specific market research and basket analysis by means of investigating the actual individual purchased items.

References

Bages-Amat, S., & Harrison & Stanley,. (2020). These eight charts show how COVID-19 has changed B2B sales forever. *McKinsey Digital, 14*(10), 2020.

Baig, H., Jenkins, L., & McCarthy,. (2020). The COVID-19 recovery will be digital: A plan for the first 90 days. *McKinsey Digital, 14*(05), 2020.

Baviskar, D., Ahirrao, S., Potdar, V., & Kotecha, K. (2021). Efficient automated processing of the unstructured documents using artificial intelligence: A systematic literature review and future directions. *IEEE Access, 9*, 72894–72936.

MIT Technology Review. (2022). CIO vision 2025: Bridging the gap between BI and AI.

Tkáč, M., & Verner, R. (2016). Artificial neural networks in business: Two decades of research. *Applied Soft Computing, 38*, 788–804.

Blockchain Technology: Its Application in the Financial Sector and Cryptonomics

Thaarun Palaniappan

Abstract Blockchain, the technology behind bitcoin, is revolutionizing various aspects of life, particularly in the finance sector. This study aims to bridge the gap between blockchain and its applications in the financial industry. It explores the concept of Cryptonomics, wherein cryptocurrency miners and users seek to transform the current financial payment structure into digital currency. The study draws information from academic and non-academic sources, utilizing qualitative analysis. Through informative articles, the paper examines the blockchain and cryptocurrency markets, providing readers with up-to-date developments. Numerous ongoing studies and financial use cases demonstrate the numerous advantages of blockchain technology. However, challenges related to security, regulation, and industry application persist alongside its efficiency and self-governance benefits. The paper presents case studies of technology and financial companies utilizing blockchain applications in their business processes and suggests potential future directions for further exploration. Overall, this research sheds light on the transformative potential of blockchain in the financial industry.

Keywords Digitalization · Blockchain · Cryptonomics · Finance industry

1 Introduction

This paper discusses blockchain technology and its impact on the financial sector, including the regulations surrounding cryptocurrency. Blockchain gained popularity in 2017 and continues to grow. Bitcoin and cryptocurrency are widely discussed buzzwords in this field. A blockchain is a secure, distributed ledger that stores transaction information in a peer-to-peer network. Cryptocurrency, a peer-to-peer form of electronic cash, is closely tied to blockchain and remains a contentious topic in finance (Silva & Mira da Silva, 2022).

T. Palaniappan (✉)
Airbus, Hamburg, Germany
e-mail: tharun0704@gmail.com

R. C. Geibel and S. Machavariani (eds.), *Chances and Challenges of Digital Management*, Springer Proceedings in Business and Economics,
https://doi.org/10.1007/978-3-031-45601-5_11

Blockchain technology has its roots in the work of Haber and Stornetta in the early 1990s, leading to the invention of Bitcoin by Nakamoto (2008). Ethereum, developed by Buterin, improved upon the technology with its fast performance and versatile functionality. Smart Contracts, introduced in 2015, revolutionized blockchain applications (Swan, 2015). Today, blockchain has emerged as a transformative technology with diverse applications across industries. It has evolved from securing digital documents to enabling secure transactions, decentralized networks, and automated contract execution (Coingeek, 2021). The journey of blockchain showcases its immense potential and impact on the digital landscape.

To understand the working principle of the blockchain, it is necessary to know some of the fundamental technical concepts that are implicated in blockchain architecture. In blockchain, a peer-to-peer distributed network (P2P) connects nodes, which are computer systems maintained by individuals or organizations (Batra et al., 2019). Transactions form the basic units of the blockchain, containing sender and receiver addresses along with transaction values (Komalavalli et al., 2020, p. 350). Blocks store transaction data and consist of a block header and block body. The block header (Fig. 1) includes important elements such as Hash, Merkel Tree, Timestamp, nBits, Nonce, Parent Block Hash, Block version, and Genesis Block.

A hash is a one-way mathematical function that converts data into a fixed-length output (Drescher, 2017, p. 82). Multiple transaction hash values are grouped into a single *Root Hash* called a *Merkel Tree* (Fig. 2).

nBits validate the block's hash and indicate the difficulty level used in block creation. *The Parent Block Hash* refers to the previous block's header hash and helps maintain the blockchain's integrity. *The Block* version denotes the blockchain version.

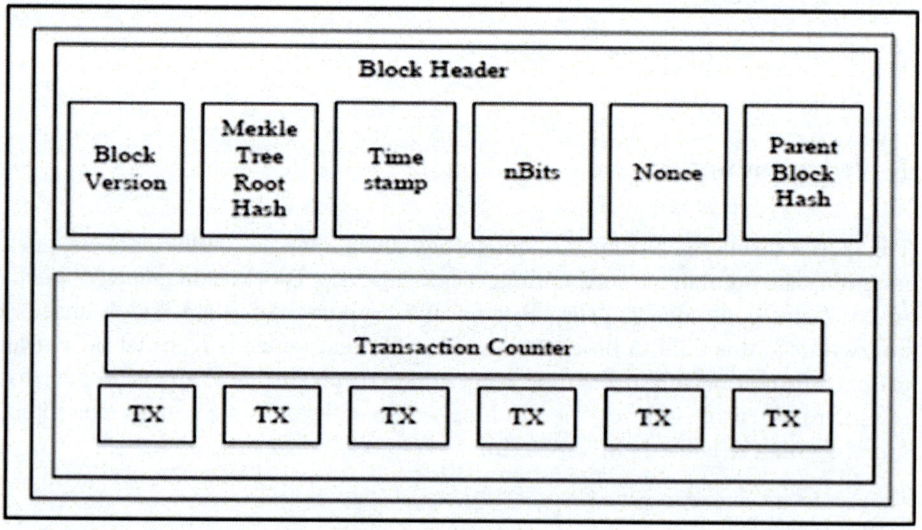

Fig. 1 Blockchain architecture (Zheng et al., 2017, p. 558)

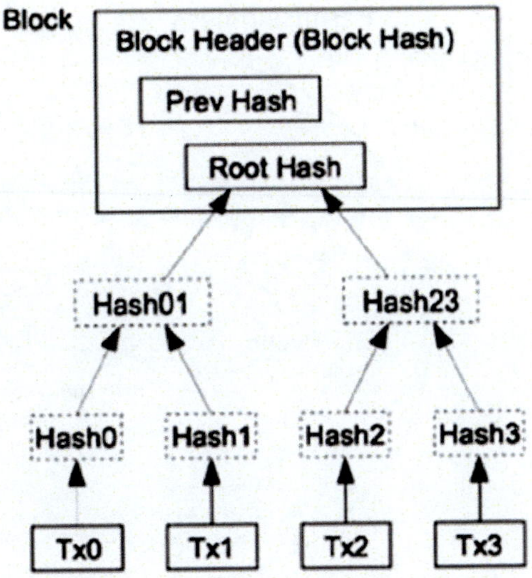

Fig. 2 Transaction hashed in Merkel Tree (Patki & Sople, 2020)

Digital signature technology is used in the distributed network of blockchains to facilitate communication and establish trust between nodes. It primarily uses identity verification, information authenticity, and integrity verification, as well as information non-repudiation.

2 Consensus Algorithm

In centralized networks, transactions are verified by authorized individuals. However, in blockchain's decentralized peer-to-peer network, there is a need for a secure and reliable method to process and verify transactions. To address this, a consensus mechanism was developed. This mechanism allows participants in the network to order and validate transactions they have received. It ensures that a transaction is added to the block only when all participants reach a consensus, confirming its validity and trustworthiness (Wang et al., 2019, p. 22333). This consensus mechanism plays a crucial role in maintaining the security and integrity of blockchain transactions. Proof of Work (PoW) is a mechanism used in the Bitcoin blockchain to secure transactions by solving complex mathematical tasks (Holbrook, 2020b, p. 123). Miners compete to add blocks and earn rewards. Proof of Stake (PoS) is an alternative consensus mechanism where validators are selected based on their ownership of cryptocurrencies or coinage (Sanka et al., 2021, p. 182). Proof of History (PoH) utilizes an internal clock within blocks for automatic timestamping. Ripple Protocol Consensus Algorithm (RPCA) is used in the XRP blockchain for global financial transactions, offering real-time tracking and its own cryptocurrency for asset exchange (Schwartz, Youngs, & Britto, 2018, p. 2). These mechanisms ensure security, efficiency, and functionality in blockchain networks.

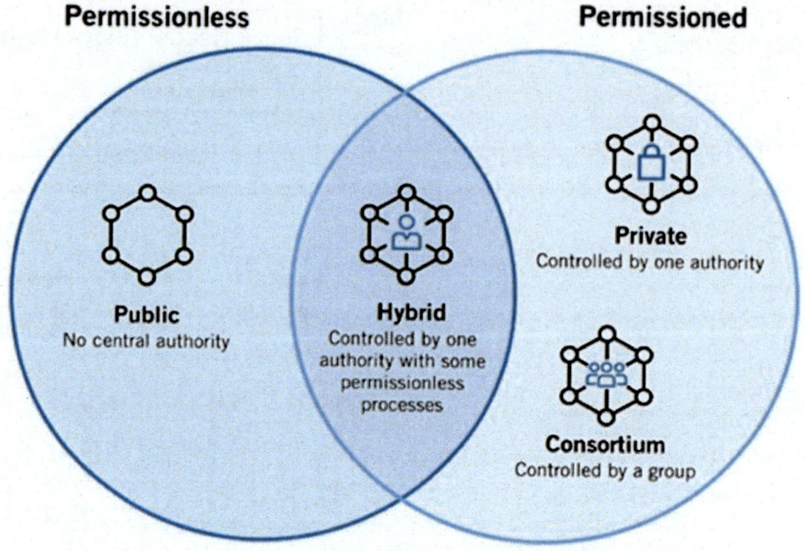

Fig. 3 Blockchain characterization and its types (foley.com, see Wegrzyn & Wang, 2021, n.p)

3 Blockchain Types

Blockchain operates on the principle of providing free access to the network while eliminating intermediaries (European Central Banks 2012, p. 21). However, organizations may want to restrict access to third parties and hackers, making it necessary to differentiate between permissionless and permissioned blockchains (Fig. 3). *Permissionless blockchains* like Bitcoin and Ethereum allow anyone to join and interact with the network, while permissioned blockchains are private and require authorization from a governing group (Gupta, Rakhra, & Singh, 2021, p. 70). Based on these characteristics, blockchain structures can be categorized as private, public, hybrid, or consortium (Fig. 4).

4 Blockchain Layered Infrastructure

The blockchain structure is composed of various complex technologies and components that work together to ensure its smooth functioning. These include mathematical computation, peer-to-peer communication, and consensus algorithms for validation. Unlike centralized systems, blockchain operates without a central authority. Similar to the OSI model used in web protocols like HTTP and FTP, blockchain also follows a layered approach. It consists of five layers, each with specific functions to maintain transparency, efficiency, immutability, and security layers (Cointelegraph, 2021, n.p). Understanding these layers provides a clearer perception of blockchain's workflow.

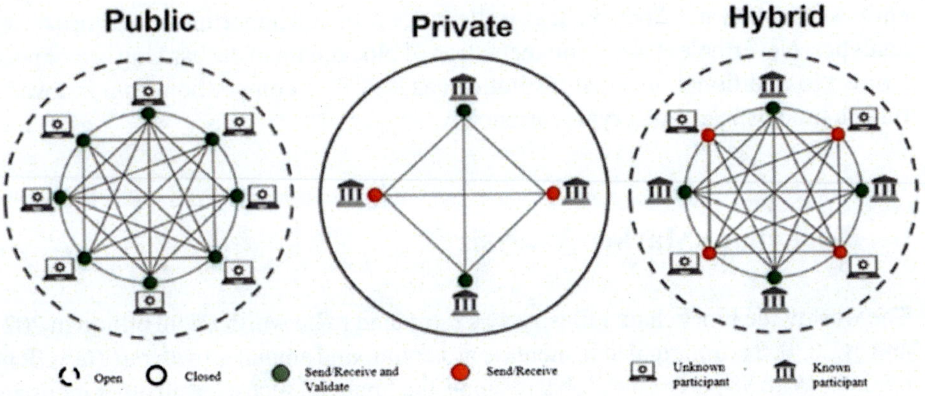

Fig. 4 Public, private and hybrid blockchain (ccecosystems. news, see Plazibat, 2021)

5 Blockchain Application

Blockchain technology serves a similar function to the financial sector, verifying and transferring financial and asset-related information digitally. It offers advantages such as speed, security, transparency, and cost-effectiveness. With the ability to prevent fraud, build trust, and save time and money, blockchain is becoming crucial in the finance industry. Various sectors are actively implementing blockchain applications to leverage these benefits.

Blockchain technology has various applications in the finance sector. It can strengthen cross-border payments by eliminating intermediaries and creating real-time systems like R3's Corda project (Holotiuk et al., 2019, pp. 208–209). Digital asset management benefits from blockchain's ability to record, transfer, and secure assets, with major players like Amazon exploring its potential (Swan, 2015, pp. 75–76). Auditing processes can be automated and enhanced using blockchain, as demonstrated by collaborations between firms like KPMG, IBM, PwC, Deloitte, EY, and Accenture. Crowdfunding platforms can leverage blockchain's security and efficiency, replacing traditional paper documents with a more accessible and secure alternative (Zhu & Zhou 2016, p. 6). Lastly, blockchain implementation in Know Your Customer (KYC) processes streamlines identity verification and facilitates loan approvals, although privacy regulations like GDPR present challenges. Overall, blockchain technology offers transformative solutions across these finance sector domains.

Blockchain technology offers several strengths, including transparency, security, flexibility, independence, automation, and cost-cutting, which enhance the efficiency of financial applications. However, there are weaknesses, such as the inability to easily change codes and encryption, the absence of accountability in data management due to GDPR regulations, and the complexity of understanding blockchain for newcomers (Kapsoulis et al., 2020, p. 3). On the other hand, blockchain presents opportunities for individuals to control their data, reducing reliance on centralized entities like Meta and Amazon. It also allows for research opportunities in big data and analytics. Nevertheless, the implementation of blockchain in the banking sector poses a threat to traditional financial institutions as they face competition from innovative fintech models based on cryptocurrencies.

6 Blockchain Market Analysis

The worldwide blockchain industry was estimated to be worth $5.92 billion in 2021, and by 2030, it is anticipated to increase at a compound annual growth rate (CAGR) of 67.54%. With 38 percent of global revenue, the financial sector led all other industries in dominating the blockchain market. For instance, JPMorgan Chase said that its cryptocurrency, JPM Coin, is being utilized for the first time in a business setting to make payments around the world in October 2020. This technology takes care of some of the applications like cross border transactions, digital identity verification, and credit reporting. For instance, in June 2021, a few banks in India collaborated and established the Indian Banks Blockchain Infrastructure Co. But there is a lack of recruiting skilled people, so the adoption of technology will be delayed and there will be a stagnation in the market for a few years (Grand View Research, 2021, n.p.).

The global cryptocurrency market is expected to grow at a CAGR of 12.9% and reach $46.2 billion by 2032. Major companies in this market include Coinbase, Intel, Nvidia, Ripple, Binance, Coinbase Global Inc., and Bitmain Technologies Ltd. Bitcoin, Ripple, Ethereum, Solana, Cardano, Tether, and U.S. dollar coins are among the leading cryptocurrencies based on market capitalization. The pandemic disrupted the financial system and affected personal income, leading to reduced investment in cryptocurrencies. However, it also increased awareness and understanding of cryptocurrencies among traders. Maintaining legitimacy and the involvement of institutional investors are key challenges in the cryptocurrency market. In 2021, Coinbase reported significant trading volume from institutional clients.

Regulation plays a crucial role in shaping the development of innovations, including the cryptocurrency market. As the crypto market grew, regulators like the SEC became more involved, investigating its increasing funds and market size. The rise of cryptocurrencies garnered public attention, with their total value soaring to $3 trillion and nearly 16,000 cryptocurrencies in circulation. This prompted regulators to implement frameworks to govern the digital market (Hammond & Ehret, 2022, pp. 1–2). However, due to the volatile nature of the market and varying regulations worldwide, staying up-to-date is challenging. Some countries have lifted cryptocurrency bans, while others are in the process of clarifying rules (Fig. 5). Global coordination among policymakers is crucial for establishing a comprehensive regulatory framework.

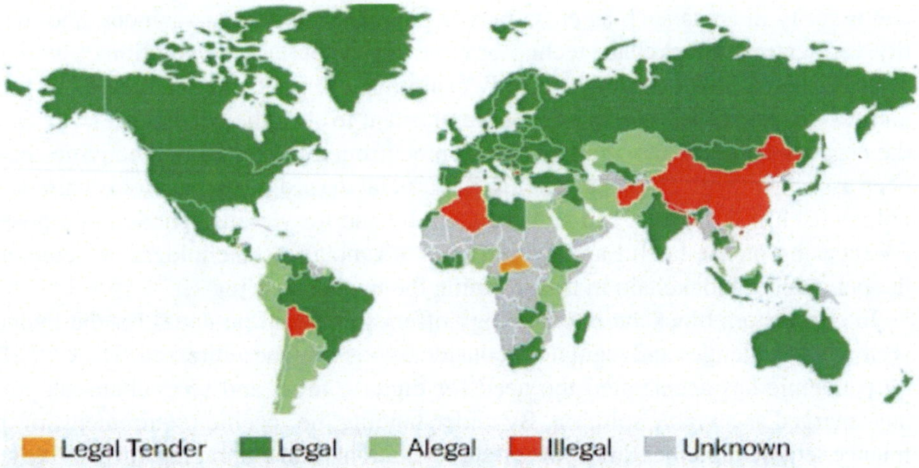

Fig. 5 Cryptocurrency legality map case study. *Source* Bitwar (2022, n.p)

7 Conclusion

The study explores the potential of blockchain technology in the finance sector, recognizing its significant benefits while acknowledging the challenges it faces. The COVID-19 pandemic has highlighted the urgency of digitalization and has prompted the financial industry to consider blockchain adoption as a way forward. The evolution of blockchain technology, including the development of distributed ledger systems, digital signatures, and consensus algorithms, demonstrates its capability to provide secure and decentralized applications.

However, concerns arise when it comes to public blockchains. Security and privacy issues emerge due to the open nature of these networks, raising questions about their suitability for financial applications. Moreover, the energy consumption associated with blockchain, particularly in the case of mining and consensus algorithms, poses environmental challenges that need to be addressed. A SWOT analysis reveals that public blockchains may not be the optimal choice for the finance sector. While they offer transparency and immutability, their limitations in terms of scalability, privacy, and regulatory compliance make them less suitable for financial applications. Therefore, a careful consideration of the specific requirements of the finance sector is necessary when implementing blockchain solutions.

On the regulatory front, there is a global trend towards accepting cryptocurrencies and blockchain technology. Regulators have started recognizing the potential benefits and are implementing regulations to ensure compliance and protect investors. However, there is still skepticism and hesitation in some countries, leading to bans or strict regulations. It is crucial for regulators to understand the technology and its potential impact on the financial system to strike the right balance between innovation and consumer protection. Case studies demonstrate the advantages of blockchain adoption in financial institutions. These include improved efficiency, transparency, and security in areas such as cross-border payments, asset management, and identity verification. Blockchain technology has the potential to revolutionize various sectors beyond finance, such as supply chain management and healthcare. To fully harness the benefits of blockchain, it is important to shift the perception away from the negative associations often tied to cryptocurrencies. While illicit activities have been associated with cryptocurrencies, it is crucial to recognize that blockchain technology itself is a tool that can be used lawfully and for various beneficial purposes. By focusing on the lawful applications and advantages, stakeholders can embrace the potential of blockchain in transforming the financial sector.

In conclusion, blockchain technology offers significant potential for the finance sector, but challenges and regulatory considerations must be addressed. The COVID-19 pandemic has accelerated the need for digitalization, and blockchain adoption has emerged as a viable solution. By understanding the specific requirements of the finance sector, implementing appropriate regulations, and embracing the positive use cases of blockchain technology, the financial industry can unlock the transformative power of blockchain and realize its benefits.

References

Batra, G., Olson, R., Pathak, S., Santhanam, N. & Soundararajan, H., 2019, Blockchain 2.0: What's in Store For The Two Ends—Semiconductors (Suppliers) And Industrials (Consumers)?, viewed 6 July 2022, from https://www.mckinsey.com/industries/advanced-electronics/our-insights/blockchain-2-0-whats-in-store-for-the-two-ends-semiconductors-suppliers-and-industrials-consumers.

Bitwar, 2022, *Bitcoin Legality Map*, viewed 6 July 2022, from https://www.bitrawr.com/terminal/legality-map.

Coingeek, 2021, *Stuart Haber and Scott Stornetta: How Our Timestamping Mechanism was Used in Bitcoin*, viewed 6 July 2022, from https://coingeek.com/stuart-haber-and-scott-stornetta-how-our-timestamping-mechanism-was-used-in-bitcoin-video/.

Cointelegraph, 2021, *A Beginner's Guide To Understanding The Layers Of Blockchain Technology*, viewed 6 July 2022, from https://cointelegraph.com/blockchain-for-beginners/a-beginners-guide-to-understanding-the-layers-of-blockchain-technology.

Drescher, D., 2017, 'Blockchain Basics: A Non-Technical Introduction in 25 Steps', *Apress Berkeley*, 1–255.

European Central Bank, 2012, 'Virtual Currency Schemes', *European Central Bank*, viewed 6 July 2022, from https://www.ecb.europa.eu/pub/pdf/other/virtualcurrencyschemes201210en.pdf.

Gupta, R., Rakhra, A., & Singh, A., 2021, ' Internet of Things Security Using AI And Blockchain', in K. Kant Singh, *Machine Learning Approaches for Convergence of IoT and Blockchain*, pp. 57–91, Wiley.

Grand View Research, 2021, *Blockchain Technology Market Size, Share & Trends Analysis Report by Type (Private Cloud, Public Cloud), By Application (Digital Identity, Payments), By Enterprise Size, By Component, By End Use, And Segment Forecasts, 2022 – 2030*, viewed 6 July 2022, from https://www.grandviewresearch.com/industry-analysis/blockchain-technology-market.

Hammond, S., & Ehret, T, 2022, 'Cryptocurrency Regulations by Country', *Thomson Reuters*, p. 1–37.

Holbrook, J., 2020b, 'Understanding Enterprise Blockchain Consensus', *Architecting Enterprise Blockchain Solutions*, pp. 1–28, Wiley.

Holotiuk, F., Moormann, J., & Pisani, F. (2019). Blockchain in the Payments Industry: Developing a Discussion Agenda Based on Pain Points and Opportunities. In H. Treiblmaier (Ed.), *Business Transformation through Blockchain* (pp. 197–231). Palgrave Macmillan.

Kapsoulis, N., Psychas, A., Palaiokrassas, G., Marinakis, A., Litke, A., & Varvarigou, T. (2020). Know Your Customer (KYC) Implementation with Smart Contracts on A Privacy-Oriented Decentralized Architecture. *MDPI, 12*(2), 1–14.

Komalavalli, C., Saxena, D., & Laroiya, C. (2020). Overview of blockchain technology concepts. In S. Krishnan (Ed.), *Handbook of Research on Blockchain Technology* (pp. 349–371). Elsevier.

Patki, A., & Sople, V. (2020). Indian Banking Sector: Blockchain Implementation, Challenges and Way Forward. *Journal of Banking and Financial Technology, 4*(1), 65–73.

Plazibat, A., 2021, *Blockchain, More Than Just a Hype? – An Introduction To The Blockchain*, viewed 6 July 2022, from https://ccecosystems.news/blockchain-mehr-als-nur-ein-hype-eine-einfuehrung-in-die-blockchain/.

Sanka, A. I., Irfan, M., Huang, I., & Cheung, R. C. C. (2021). A Survey of Breakthrough in Blockchain Technology: Adoptions, Applications, Challenges and Future Research. *Computer Communications, 169*, 179–201.

Satoshi Nakamoto, S., 2008, *Bitcoin: A Peer-to-Peer Electronic Cash System*, viewed 15 July 2022, from https://bitcoin.org/bitcoin.pdf.

Schwartz, D., Youngs, N. & Britto, A., 2018, *The Ripple Protocol Consensus Algorithm*, viewed 6 July 2022, from https://ripple.com/files/ripple_consensus_whitepaper.pdf.

Silva, E. C., & Mira da Silva, M. (2022). Research Contributions and Challenges In DLT-Based Cryptocurrency Regulation: A Systematic Mapping Study. *Journal of Banking and Financial Technology, 6*(1), 63–82.

Swan, M., 2015, *Blockchain : Blueprint for A New Economy*, O'Reilly Media, California.

Wang, W., Hoang, D. T., Hu, P., Xiong, Z., Niyato, D., Wang, P., & Kim, D. I. (2019). A Survey on Consensus Mechanisms and Mining Strategy Management in Blockchain Networks. *IEEE Access: Practical Innovations, Open Solutions, 7*, 22328–22370.

Wegrzyn, K.E., Wang, E., 2021, *Types of Blockchain: Public, Private, or Something in Between*, viewed 6 July 2022, from https://www.foley.com/en/insights/publications/2021/08/types-of-blockchain-public-private-between.

Zheng, Z., Xie, S., Dai, H., Chen, X. & Wang, H., 2017, 'An Overview of Blockchain Technology: Architecture, Consensus, and Future Trends', *IEEE International Congress on Big Data (BigData Congress)*, 557–564.

Zhu, H. & Zhou, Z.Z., 2016, 'Analysis and outlook of applications of blockchain technology to equity crowdfunding in China', *Financial Innovation,* viewed 6 July 2022, from https://doi.org/10.1186/s40854-016-0044-7.

The Impact of Digital Marketing on Consumer Buying Decisions in the Georgian Market

David Sikharulidze and Gvantsa Tsikhiseli

Abstract The main goal of the research is to find out what influence different mechanisms of digital marketing have on the consumer's buying decision. The purpose of the research is to analyze different platforms and find out how they work in the Georgian market. This study investigates digital marketing channels, including, mobile marketing, social media marketing, and email marketing. It examines how various channels affect consumers purchasing decisions in the Georgia market. Questionnaires were compiled based on a simple sampling technique. 200 questionnaires were distributed and 104 completed copies were collected, excluding those that were not filled in completely. The findings of this study showed that digital marketing, including that done through Gmail, social media, and mobile platforms, has a significant influence on consumer purchasing decisions. As the research results showed, In order to maintain their competitiveness in the modern business environment, organizations should develop strategies to use the digital world and technology to influence customer buying decisions.

Keywords Digital marketing · Social Media · Mobile · E-mail Marketing

1 Introduction

E-marketing is a science that has emerged with the development of the internet network. E-marketing solves the tasks that conventional marketing does. The difference is that in the case of e-marketing, the marketer uses the tools and benefits of the Internet.

D. Sikharulidze (✉) · G. Tsikhiseli
East European University, Tbilisi, Georgia
e-mail: d.sikharulidze@eeu.edu.ge

International Black Sea University, Tbilisi, Georgia

G. Tsikhiseli
e-mail: g.tsikhiseli@eeu.edu.ge

R. C. Geibel and S. Machavariani (eds.), *Chances and Challenges of Digital Management*, Springer Proceedings in Business and Economics,
https://doi.org/10.1007/978-3-031-45601-5_12

Marketers have viewed the Internet as a huge laboratory, conducting test after test in an attempt to discover the secret to increasing mining sales and making customers stay loyal. People accepted digital technology because they believed it would make their lives easier, radically transforming the way they make purchase decisions. As a result of digital technology, all of this is changing. people who before believed to word-of-mouth product recommendations of people they trust, now are reading customer reviews, trying to compare products and prices online, and discuss alternatives on social networks. All this not only empowers customers but also allows marketing teams to participate in the conversation that consumers have as they learn about product lines and place orders (Al-azzam & Al-Mizeed, 2021). We use the word "digital marketing" to describe the processes of using digital technology to attract customers and make them stay engaged, analyze their needs, research and raise customer satisfaction levels, and create relevant marketing communications based on that data (Kannan & Hongshuang, 2017).

Digital technologies have had a huge impact on consumers' information gathering, searching, and processing processes, and decision assistance systems can really play a key role in these changing circumstances (Kannan & Hongshuang, 2017).

Murugan believes that consumer behavior will explore the chain of how consumers choose, buy, and use items. The use of digital technology for research has become widespread. Consumers are becoming more selective, and expect the business to make it even more transparent. The reason for this is that the rate of use of technologies as well as the popularization of online channels has greatly increased. In a customer-oriented market environment, consumer purchasing patterns are changing at a faster rate. Consumer behavior varies depending on the product, quality, price, features, status, and age of the customer, among other factors. The changing preferences of the modern consumer, particularly the young, influence shopping patterns because they primarily follow fashion and taste trends. Customers' interactions with brands and requests for services are being greatly influenced by digital innovation. Customers are increasingly communicating through multiple channels, and they expect consistency despite the time, place, or gadget (Murugan, 2021).

Lindh C. believes that users want to get what they want in the simplest way possible, so dealers have to try to make the simplest website to search for the necessary loads. In addition, marketers work on sites that study the frequency of the same product, and the time the product is viewed. Accordingly, the website reads browsing history information, and time and generates similar related products that the consumer was interested in. Websites generate impulse purchases just like the retail stores do, and the impact on the consumer remains the same. Bright flashy advertising, discounts, bonuses, etc. A nice bonus on the first order is a discount on goods and delivery, but you need to collect a certain amount, which drives the buyer into the financial framework (Lindh et al., 2020).

Thus the goal of the research to study the impact of digital marketing tools, on consumer buying decision. This is important since there are very few similar studies about the Georgian market. This study attempts to assess how digital marketing affects consumers' decision-making processes in the Georgian market.

2 Literature Review

The use of electronic technologies in business has the greatest potential but requires proper management. Companies use e-markets to offer their goods or services, marketing research, supplies, etc. at the same time buyers use electronic markets to search for information, choose goods or services, place orders, pay by credit card, or use electronic payment (Liang & Huang, 1998)

Many brands use email marketing as a source of continuous communication with their existing customers. Brands also use email to advertise and attract new customers (Grimes et al., 2007).

The primary function of email as one of the main tools of the internet is of course exchanging information between people for business, personal, etc. in the way of electronic letters. However, at a very fast pace, email acquired a whole new feature and became one of the key ways to advance the brand's marketing (Kimixay et al., 2019). Email is one of the most accessible platforms for real-time communication with customers, product advertising, and building long-term relationships with customers (Pavlov et al., 2008). But it is important to note that marketers must obtain permission from target groups or individuals before sharing product information, rather than send emails anonymously (Kimixay et al., 2019).

Emails that are sent for commercial purposes, but sent without the recipient's permission, fall into the so-called spam (Morimoto & Chang, 2006). SPAM is also characterized as illegal and disrespectful. there is no option to refuse, so governments enacted laws against all this. (Goldman, 2003). Most users are irritated by receiving spam emails. Of course, it makes sense to ask the question—if spam is so annoying to customers, then how does it remain one of the most used and effective sources of marketing communication? PEM is the answer. PEM is mail with commercial content, sent only to those groups and/or individuals who have been permitted to send emails to them (Marinova et al., 2002).

Giving consent to such emails solves several problems at once. For example, the fact that the brand does not bother customers who are not interested, secondly, there does not arise a question of where the company took customers' personal information - in this case, emails. It even protects users from unsolicited emails which is most likely a waste of time for them. With the help of PEM, the user gets the filtered information and thus may save the time he has to spend in search of the product. PEM also allows users to automatically receive notifications about updates made by brands (Merisavo & Raulas, 2004).

Studies have shown that when it comes to email marketing, most people like it when similar emails are informative, voluminous, and also contain various visual or sound effects. Emails like these are less annoying to users because they realize they are getting the information they need. Offering some benefits such as coupons, free shipping offers, or discounts on the first purchase, is an effective way to promote advertiser products (Duffy, 1998).

To understand how effective email marketing is, you must first have well-defined goals and specifically what results in you want to achieve with them. The easiest and most convenient way to find out is through Google Analytics, which can be clicked to find out how many people will move from the link provided in the email to the website, how long the user will stay on the site, specifically which sections they have visited and so on (Hasan et al., 2009).

Mobile applications offer numerous benefits that conventional systems do not like mobile applications that use GPS-generated location services add the feature of identifying the actual location of each user. (Tate et al., 2015).

It's critical to make your website mobile-friendly and optimized for viewing on smaller displays as more people use mobile web browsers on their iPhones, Android phones, and other devices. Many websites still lack a mobile-friendly architecture, causing businesses to miss out on sales from the growing number of individuals who access their websites via mobile devices. Different HTML code sets should be used on your website to recognize the type of device that guests are using and show the page the suitable. It's also essential that mobile content displays quickly because customers are actively using mobile internet, which is expensive. Furthermore, when it comes to mobile applications, we must remember that a smartphone's screen is small, therefore when creating pages for mobile screens, it's critical to reconsider the type of content you're providing. You should show the most valuable information that you believe a mobile device user might want (Scott, 2015).

When creating content for mobile devices, keep in mind that search engines like Google have a special ranking machine for mobiles. As a result, there are tools for search engine optimization techniques aimed at getting your web page ranked highly. Google has a mobile version, that's a unique model from regular Google. It's different in design and markup and provides desired mobile-friendly websites. Set up a map for mobile users, for example, to ensure that Google knows where your mobile is located. This map will be distinct from the usual user's map. You should also utilize geographic descriptors if the site is about a local business. Many customers, for example, simply type 'chocolate' into Mobile Google, and the results frequently include Google Places information. This is because Google has determined that people desire information that is local or near them, or they want a business that serves their specific area (Bhardwaj, 2017).

Today it is clear that social media marketing is more cost effective than traditional marketing channels. Studies showed that social media is one of the most effective marketing tools that is a cheap, fastest, and easy way to share information. For example, Facebook in general, assist the ability attendees to discover local events, stumble upon reviews, and create extra public relationships easily; those elements play a crucial function for organizers and help increase attendance (Kirtiş & Karahan, 2011).

Marketers are taking note of the many different opportunities in social media and are beginning to use new social abilities faster way than ever before. Social media marketing and the mpanies that use it have become more accomplished. One can't afford not to be on social channels when competitors are promoting their products (Neti, 2011).

In some ways social media is quite a difficult thing, it can bring business great success or a failure. Social media users can ask questions, post videos, and pictures, and write down feedback and their opinion, in one word they can become other friends or worst enemies, it depends on their experience of communication with you. Though the main thing is other, the user is no longer in the role of spectator, he has become a direct participant in the process (Aichner et al., 2021).

According to Zenith, the year 2022 will be the year when the ad market on social media will overtake television. The most common way they learn about businesses or goods and services is through social media(Zenitch, 2021).

When it comes to taking their social media expenditures to the next level, there are a couple of things to consider. Consumers are more receptive to commercial offers on platforms like Instagram, but brand discovery marketing makes more sense on content-driven platforms like Reddit and Snapchat. Customers on international vacations are 56 percent more likely to find forums or internet forums, but this may not be the best match for beauty companies, whose customers trust more representation and influencer advice (Dwivedi, et al., 2021).

The following hypotheses were developed and derived from the above literature and theoretical review (see Fig. 1):

H1: Email marketing is positively related to all stages of a purchase decision.

H2: Mobile marketing is positively related to all stages of the buying decision.

H3: Social marketing is positively related to all stages of a buying decision.

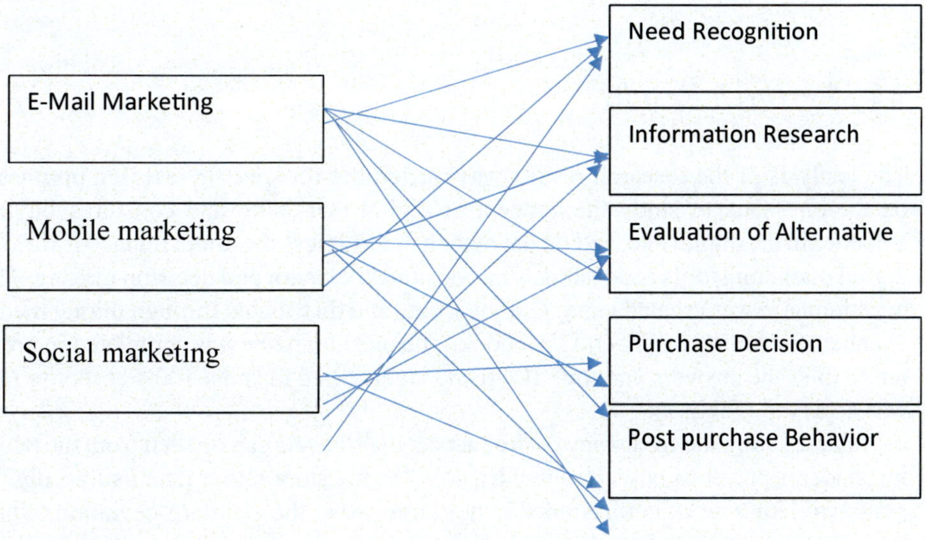

Fig. 1 Research framework

2.1 Research Methodology

A specific quantitative method is chosen in order to choose a workable and comprehensible research approach to achieve the study's main objective. For this study, the questionnaire is the main tool that has been used in this study to understand the impact of digital marketing on consumer buying behavior. The questionnaire began with a cover page and then moved on to closed-ended questions divided into two sections: Sections A and B focus on demographics and social media and the internet.

The association between time spent in the internet and age was discussed in Section A, which was necessary for the participants' gender and age. Section B covered how to interact with customers about a brand by using social media and the internet. The majority of the questions in this section related to consumer purchasing decisions made online. A 5-point Likert scale was used to grade the questions. For our study, we picked an e-mail format that included a link to Google.doc. This way of filling out questionnaires on your own can help you not only contact a huge number of people, but it can also help you use your time more efficiently and effectively (Bryman & Bell, 2011). The population of Georgia is 1,200,000. Accordingly, with a 95% confidence level and a confidence interval of +/- 3, the sampling size will be 383. Data processing will be performed via SPSS software. The main source of data collection is the information obtained from the survey.

2.2 Research Results

The analysis of the research results was carried out for specific research purposes: on the one hand to study the concept of digital marketing and consumer buying behavior in the digital age, and on the other hand to assess the direct impact of various digital marketing tools and channels on consumer behavior and decision making. The questionnaire was created using Google forms and distributed through digital media channels, including Email and Facebook. The questionnaire was completed in order not to miss the answers and thus 104 respondents filled in and a 100% response rate was achieved (Table 1).

Table 2 shows the frequency of product acquisition. As can be seen from the table, respondents prefer to buy a product by going to the store rather than using a digital platform. However, this difference is not large. Also the standard deviation, when you go to the store to buy the product, is lower but even in this case the standard deviation of both variables is not much different from each other.

To test the hypothesis, we used both a simple linear regression equation The dependent variable in the regression equation was the decision-making stages such as the need for information retrieval, evaluation, procurement decision, and post-procurement decision, while the independent variables are: email marketing, mobile marketing, and social media. Table 1 show the regression results that serve to test the hypotheses

Table 1 Demographic profile of respondents

Age	Frequency	Percent	Cumulative Percent
under 19	2	1,9	1,9
20–24	7	6,7	8,7
25–29	27	26	34,6
30–34	33	31,7	66,3
35–39	18	17,3	83,7
40–44	4	3,8	87,5
45 and above	13	12,5	100
Total	104	100	
Gender			
female	80	76,9	76,9
male	24	23,1	100
Total	104	100	

Table 2 Descriptive Statistics of purchase frequency

	N	Mean	Std. Deviation
How often do you buy your product or service online (social media pages, official brand websites, mobile app)?	104	3,20	1,074
How often do you buy a product or service when you visit a store?	104	3,84	1,053

Hypothesis 1: Email marketing is positively related to all stages of a purchase decision.

As can be seen from Table 3, email is positively related to need awareness and this relationship is statistically significant. Email marketing plays an important role in information research. This relationship is also statistically significant. There is also a statistically significant positive relationship between email and product evaluation. Although email marketing has a positive relationship with the buying decision and the post-purchase reaction, however, this relationship is not statistically significant.

Hypothesis 2: Mobile marketing is positively related to all stages of the buying decision.

Table 3 shows the relationship of mobile marketing to all stages of a buying decision. In particular, mobile marketing is positively and statistically significant in terms of need awareness and post-purchase behavior. The impact of mobile marketing on information retrieval, valuation, and sales evaluation is indeed positive but not statistically significant.

Hypothesis 3: Social marketing is positively related to all stages of a buying decision.

Research shows that social marketing has a strong influence on purchasing decisions. In particular, there is a statistically significant positive relationship to social

Table 3 The results of regression model

Hypothesis	Independent variable	Dependent variable	Estimate	Standard error	t-statistic	sig
H 1.1	E-mail	Need Recognition	0,151	0,078	1,941	0,055**
H 1.2	E-mail	Information Research	0,168	0,065	2,588	0,011***
H 1.3	E-mail	Evaluation	0,137	0,066	2,086	0,039***
H 1.4	E-mail	Purchase Decision	0,105	0,076	1,376	0,172
H 1.5	E-mail	Post purchase	0,043	0,069	0,617	0,538
H 2.1	Mobile	Need Recognition	0,184	0,088	2,096	0,039***
H 2.2	Mobile	Information Research	0,078	0,076	1,030	0,306
H 2.3	Mobile	Evaluation	0,088	0,075	0,075	0,249
H 2.4	Mobile	Purchase Decision	0,010	0,088	0,117	0,907
H 2.5	Mobile	Post purchase	0,195	0,076	2,563	0,012***
H 3.1	Social media	Need Recognition	0,473	0,098	4,823	0,000***
H 3.2	Social media	Information Research	0,495	0,078	6,347	0,000***
H 3.3	Social media	Evaluation	0,460	0,080	5,762	0,000***
H 3.4	Social media	Purchase Decision	0,240	0,103	2,333	0,022***
H 3.5	Social media	Post purchase	0,054	0,095	0,574	0,567

marketing in terms of need awareness, information retrieval, evaluation, acquisition decision-making, and post-purchase response.

2.3 Conclusion

This study investigates digital marketing channels for marketers, including retargeting, mobile marketing, and email marketing. It examines how various channels affect how consumers in the Georgian market make purchasing decisions. Through the use of an online questionnaire, the author performed the study. A straightforward sampling technique was used to distribute the questionnaires and collect them from the Georgiaan market. A response rate of 100% was obtained from those who volunteered to participate in the study. The decisions of customers to buy are influenced favorably by three separate factors. Social media is the most significant influence in the customer purchasing choice in the Georgian market among the three digital marketing tools that constitute independent components in this study.

As a result of the study, it was determined that digital marketing channels influence all stages of decision-making. As a result of the research, it is determined that e-mail has a positive and statistically significant impact on decision-making stages such as Need Recognition, Information Research, and Evaluation. As for Purchase Decision and Post purchase, here it has a positive effect, but this effect is not statistically significant and it is not important to take it into account when developing a marketing strategy. As a result of the research, it is also established that Mobile marketing has a positive and statistically significant impact on the stages of decision-making such as Need Recognition and Post purchase. And on such steps as Information Research, Evaluation, and Purchase Decision, it has a positive effect, but this effect is not statistically significant.

And finally, Social media marketing has a positive and statistically significant impact on all stages of decision-making, except for the Post purchase stage, which has a positive impact, but this impact is not statistically significant. Therefore, when developing a marketing strategy, social media is the most powerful tool among the factors influencing the consumer's decision-making process.

References

Aichner, T., Grünfelder, M., Maurer, O., & Jegeni, D. (2021). Twenty-five years of social media: A review of social media applications and definitions from 1994 to 2019. *Cyberpsychology, Behavior, and Social Networking, 24*(4), 215–222.

Al-azzam, A. F., & Al-Mizeed, K. (2021). The effect of digital marketing on purchasing decisions: A case study in Jordan. *The Journal of Asian Finance, Economics and Business, 8*(5), 455–463.

Bhardwaj, D. (2017). The new rules of marketing and PR: How to use social media, online video, mobile applications, blogs, news releases, and viral marketing to reach buyers directly by David Merman Scott. (D. M. Scott:, Hrsg.) Wiley, Hoboken, NJ, 2015,.

Bryman, A., & Bell, E. C. (2011). Business research methods. (3. ed., Hrsg.) NY: Oxford University Press.

Dwivedi, Y. K., Ismagilova, E., Hughes, D. L., Carlson, J., Filieri, R., Jacobson, J., & Wang, Y. (2021). Setting the future of digital and social media marketing research: Perspectives and research propositions. *International Journal of Information Management, 59*, 102168.

Goldman, E. (2003). Where's the Beef-Dissecting SPAM's Purposed Harms. J. Marshal J. Computer & Info. L., L, 22, 13.

Grimes, G. A., Hough, M. G., & Signorella, M. L. (2007). Email end users and spam: Relations of gender and age group to attitudes and actions. *Computers in Human Behavior, 23*(1), 318–332.

Johnson, J. (2022). https://www.statista.com/statistics. https://www.statista.com/: https://www.statista.com/statistics/617136/digital-population-worldwide/

Kannan, P. K., & Hongshuang, L. (2017). Digital marketing: A framework, review and research agenda. *International Journal of Research in Marketing, 34*(1), 22–45.

Kirtiş, A. K., & Karahan, F. (2011). To be or not to be in social media arena as the most cost-efficient marketing strategy after the global recession. *Procedia-Social and Behavioral Sciences, 24*, 260–268.

Liang, T. P., & Huang, J. S. (1998). An empirical study on consumer acceptance of products in electronic markets: A transaction cost model. *Decision Support Systems, 24*(1), 29–43.

Lindh, C., Rovira Nordman, E., Melén Hånell, S., Safari, A., & Hadjikhani, A. (2020). Digitalization and international online sales: Antecedents of purchase intent. Journal of International Consumer Marketing, 32(4), 324-335

Marinova, A., Murphy, J., & Massey, B. L. (2002). Permission e-mail marketing as a means of targeted promotion. *Cornell Hotel and Restaurant Administration Quarterly, 43*(1), 61–69.

Morimoto, M., & Chang, S. (2006). Consumers' attitudes toward unsolicited commercial e-mail and postal direct mail marketing methods: Intrusiveness, perceived loss of control, and irritation. *Journal of Interactive Advertising, 7*(1), 1–11.

Murugan, V. (2021). *Digitalization and Consumers' Behavior Attitudes with Special Reference To Online Purchase in Tiruvarur* (p. 27). Researh Jorney.

Neti, S. (2011). Social media and its role in marketing. *International Journal of Enterprise Computing and Business Systems, 1*(2), 1–15.

Scott, D. M. (2015). The new rules of marketing and PR: How to use social media, online video, mobile applications, blogs, news releases, and viral marketing to reach buyers directly. (7th edition Ausg., Bd. 023). Wiley .

Tate, D. F., Lyons, E. J., & Valle, C. G. (2015). High-tech tools for exercise motivation: use and role of technologies such as the internet, mobile applications, social media, and video games. Diabetes Spectrum, 28(1), 28(1), 45–54.

Zenitch. (2021). Zenitch, (The ROI Agency). Von Global Intelligence: https://www.zenithmedia.com/digital-advertising-to-exceed-60-of-global-adspend-in-2022/#:~:text=Zenith%20expects%20social%20media%20adspend,%25%20and%20television%20at%2021.0%25

The Big Data for Drought Monitoring in Georgia

Marika Tatishvili, Ana Palavandishvili, Mariam Tsitsagi, and Nikoloz Suknidze

Abstract The dangerous hydrometeorological phenomenon—drought is frequent in Georgia. The SPI and SPEI 3, 6 and 12 month drought indices were used to analyze drought frequency and intensity on the territory of Georgia for 1991–2020 year period. The structured data that is the part of big data, of ground hydrometeorological observation network of Georgia have been used to conduct research. The following statistical parameters were calculated: Pearson correlation coefficient (PCC), determination coefficient (R^2), and root mean square error (RMSE) both for the entire period and for months. The correlation coefficient is in a good agreement for all cases, and the absolute deviation shows data scattering, which should be related to the complex relief of Georgia, as well as the heterogeneity of precipitation data distribution. The calculated Standardized Precipitation Index (SPI) for 3 months of Kakheti region was subjected to Machine Learning. A Support Vector Machine (SVM) was selected in the Matlab space—the algorithm for Supervised Machine Learning method. The tenth model showed the best result; using of mentioned model it became possible to determine the drought probability by months at each point. Despite of obtained good parameters, it was necessary to add additional stations, because there was not enough information in the Kakheti region for the correct analysis of Machine Learning avoiding overfitting. The study is important for climate change assessment and hydrometeorological disaster early warning system implementation.

Keywords Big Data · Machine learning · Climate change · Drought indices · Natural hazard

---

M. Tatishvili (✉) · A. Palavandishvili · M. Tsitsagi · N. Suknidze
Institute of Hydrometeorology, Georgian Technical University, Tbilisi, Georgia
e-mail: m.tatishvili@gtu.ge

A. Palavandishvili · M. Tsitsagi · N. Suknidze
Vakhushti Bagrationi Institute of Geography of Tbilisi State University, Tbilisi, Georgia

R. C. Geibel and S. Machavariani (eds.), *Chances and Challenges of Digital Management*, Springer Proceedings in Business and Economics,
https://doi.org/10.1007/978-3-031-45601-5_13

1 Introduction

The hydrometeorological data are collected from a great range of sources and this process increases rapidly with new technologies measuring various environmental data. The first basic environmental data are collected by ground monitoring systems, which consist of vide range of sensor technologies measuring various physical parameters. The weather stations and monitoring systems measure almost all hydrometeorological parameters used in weather prediction and climate change assessment topics. Those include temperature, precipitation, wind velocity and direction, solar radiation, relative humidity and etc.

In Georgia, there exist most of Earths climatic types, from marine wet subtropical climate of west part and steppe continental climate of east part up to eternal snow and glaciers of high mountain zone of Great Caucasus, and also approximately 40% of observed landscapes.

The complexity of the orographic structure of Georgian territory, along with other physical -geographical factors is the cause of wide variety of climates and landscapes. There are almost all types of climates observed on the Globe, from the climate of eternal snows of high mountains and glaciers to steppe continental climate of eastern Georgia and humid climate of the Black Sea coast subtropical zone (Tatishvili et al., 2013).

Such complicated relief has definite influence on air masses motion in atmosphere lower layers. Mainly west and eastern atmospheric processes prevailed over Georgian territory. Thus those climatic zones uphold the formation of different dangerous hydrometeorological phenomena, namely: hailstone, heavy showers, flooding, thunderstorm, draughts, and sea storms. The existing geodynamical and orographic properties of Georgia play major role in the formation of various weather patterns. Such complex relief is one of the main reason of the formation and evolution of various scaled circulation systems and heterogeneous spatial distribution of meteorological elements. This is verified by the fact, that precipitation annual distribution has diverse type, with sharply expressed spatial inhomogeneities (Tatishvili, 2017).

The hydrometeorological ground station observation in Georgia begun on the end of 19-th century gradually increased up to 200 stations at the end of 20-th century. For present there are about 80 ground based automatic weather stations that transmit weather information per 10 min (Fig. 1).

The dangerous phenomenon—drought is a frequent in eastern Georgia. Its frequency in some areas exceeded 40% in the 80-th of the last century by assured estimations. The significant transformation of many types of natural landscapes has been observed resulted from the frequent droughts accompanying the global warming in past decades. The desertification probability of steppe and semi-desert landscape of eastern Georgia by the end of the twentieth century has reached 25–30% (Tatishvili et al., 2021). According to official information, the area of over than 200 000 ha is strongly affected by the intense droughts for present. Property damage caused by drought is also very significant.

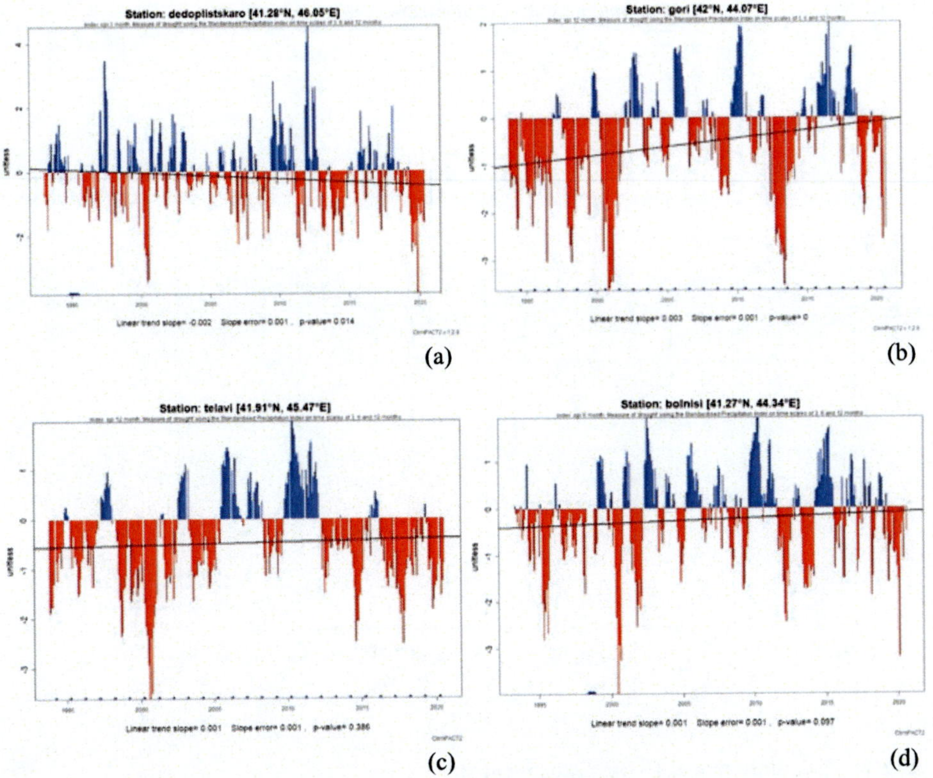

Fig. 1 Drought indices for Dedoplistskaro **a** SPi12, Gori **b** SPI12, Telavi **c** SPI12, Bolnisi **d** SPI6

It is well established, that the main meteorological factors for drought formation are dry weather, high temperature and lack of soil producing moisture. The average time of rainless period with precipitation less than 5 mm most important for agriculture is not more than 10–15 days. Besides, the mean rainfall is not more than 200–300 mm during vegetation period on the lowlands. Nevertheless, producing moisture supply is 50–200 mm per one meter of soil that corresponds to the zone of capillary agro-hydrological humidification and full spring rainfall penetration. At the same time active air temperatures sum exceeds 4000 °C by 10 times and the mean duration of continuous high temperatures more than 30 °C is longer by 4 h.

2 Data and Method

Station data was recovered from the CLIDATA database of the National Environmental Agency (NEA), which has been operating since 2014. Stations were selected based on data continuity and accuracy. After station data validation where data interruption has been detected or measuring sensor transmitted incorrect information

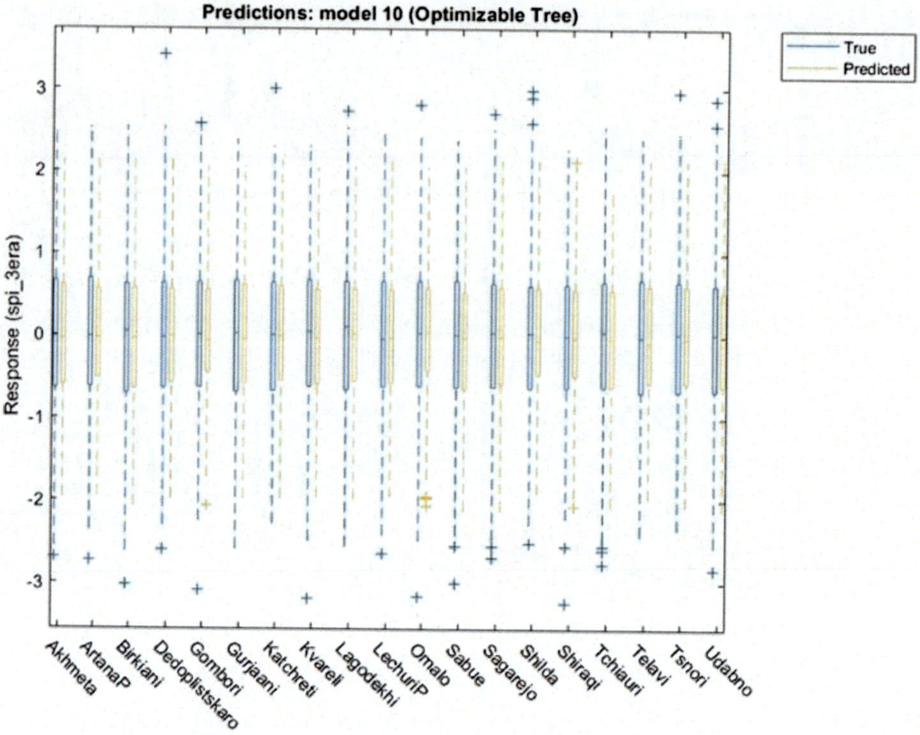

Fig. 2 The trained model 10 for Kakheti region

due to its malfunction they were removed and not analyzed. At the 21 stations the observers monitor data and except human factor the unreliability of the data are minimal, and the rest of them were operated by rain gauge produced by VAISALA (Publish House of Iv. Javakhishvili Tbilisi State University, 2022), which by its design does not measure residual precipitation. The VAISALA weather gauges are the new generation of weighing precipitation gauges. They combine techniques, the latest high-accuracy load cell technology and advanced measurement control algorithms to ensure high performance, both in liquid and solid precipitation used for almost all weather conditions (Publish House of Iv. Javakhishvili Tbilisi State University, 2022).

Drought is one of the most dangerous and widespread natural disasters of all over the globe. Drought in the historical past has become a provocateur for the disappearance of many civilizations (Evans et al., 2018; Kaniewski et al., 2015) and robust migration processes (DeMenocal, 2001). Droughts are characterized by decreased natural water availability in the form of precipitation, river runoff, or groundwater (Babre et al., 2022; Tatishvili et al., 2022a). Difficulties related to the study of droughts are determined by their diverse nature (meteorological, hydrological, ecological, and economic). Accordingly, there are different types of indexes, the complexity of which depends on the availability of the necessary data. The most widely used indices in modern studies are SPI (Standard Precipitation Index) and SPEI (Standard Precipitation Evapotranspiration Index). The SPI calculation uses the

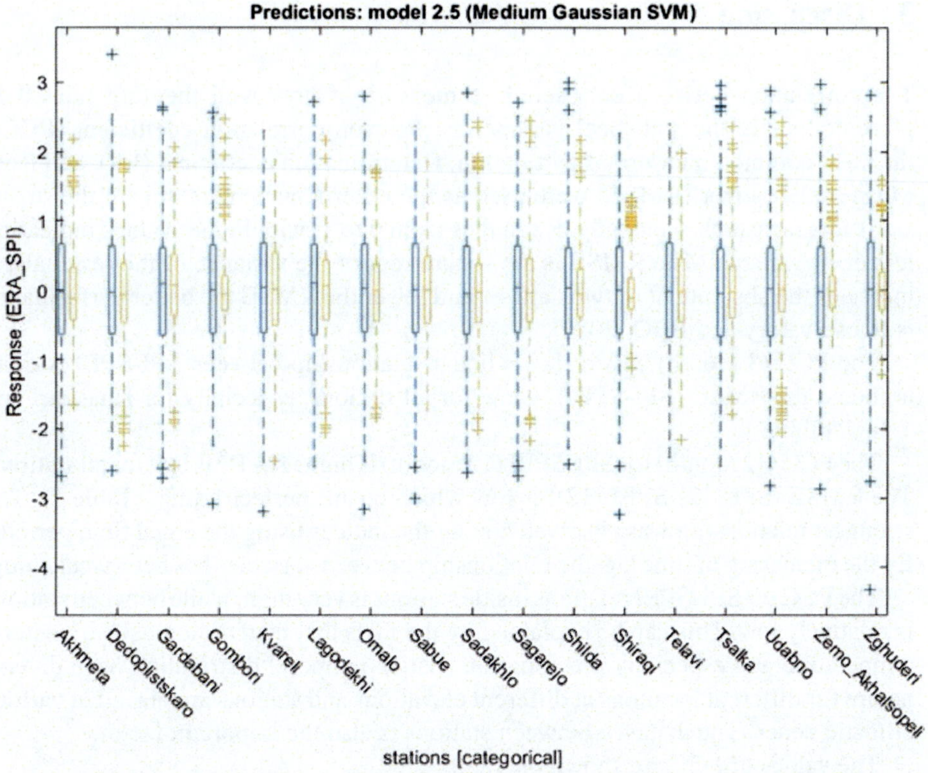

Fig. 3 Advanced SVM prediction Kakheti region model including additional seventeen stations of Kartli region

precipitation data series (McKee et al., 1993), and the SPEI is based on the cumulative water balance instead of precipitation sums (Vicente-Serrano et al., 2010). The SPEI hence represents the standard-normal distributed water balance (Vicente-Serrano et al., 2010), where the temperature is considered along with precipitation (Tatishvili et al., 2022a). To calculate above mentioned indices the ground meteorological station data of Georgian National Environmental Agency was used of 1991–2020 year period. 10 stations have been chosen from data archive that has valid data to calculate indices.

The drought indices are classified according months: 3, 6 and 12. R-stat soft was used for plots. Below are presented several draught SPEI, SPI drought indices plots from selected stations. They represent Kakheti and Kartli regions notable for agriculture: Dedoplistskaro, Gori, Telavi and Bolnisi.

3 Discussion

The correlation between data sets is a measure of how well they are related In presented study the statistical parameters: Pearson correlation coefficient (PCC)-the most common measure of correlation, Determination coefficient (R2), and Root Mean Square Error (RMSE) were used as the criteria, which are among the strong statistical measures. Generally, R2 ranges from 0 to 1, with higher values indicating less error variance. The RMSE is the square root of the variance of the residuals. It indicates the absolute fit of two data set and lower the RMSE the better performance is (Observatory and EDO, 2021).

The PCC (3 month) which shows linear relationship between SPI-SPEI is quite high and the RMSE (SPI-SPEI) is low for all stations, especially for Khashuri and Telavi. (Table 1).

The PCC (12 month) for SPI-SPEI (12 month) is high. The R^2 is low for all stations. The RMSE (SPI (12)-SPEI (12)) is low which means perfect fitting, (Table 2). The strongest relationship was observed among the indices using the equal time periods. By the increasing of time lag, the relationship between variables has been weakening.

The PCC for SPI-SPEI relations inside stations is very high, while between stations is relatively low. This can be explained by the facts that meteorological parameters-temperature and especially precipitation spatial–temporal distribution have diverse nature for different locations at different elevations and stations are placed in various climatic zones. The distance between stations is also the important factor.

The values of PCC are shown on Table 3.

The calculated values of indices give possibility to split negative and positive number or dry and wet day number.It's interesting to count drought and wet day ratio

Table1 Statistical parameters PCC, R2, RMSE for most vulnerable regions according SPI3 and SPEI3

Station/Stat. parameter	Pearson (3)	R^2-SPI	R^2-SPEI	RMSE(SPI-SPE)
Dedoplistskaro	0.94	0.02	0.07	0.01
Gori	0.92	0.01	0.03	0.02
Khashuri	0.91	0.01	0.09	0.01
Telavi	0.96	0.001	0.02	0.01

Table 2 Statistical parameters PCC, R2, RMSE for most vulnerable regions according SPI (12) and SPEI (12)

Station/Stat. parameter	Pearson	R^2-SPI	R^2-SPEI	RMSE(SPI_SPE)
Dedoplistskaro	0.92	0.07	0.22	0.02
Gori	0.84	0.01	0.12	0.01
Khashuri	0.89	0.05	0.28	0.01
Telavi	0.93	0.01	0.04	0.02

Table 3 Pearson correlation of draught indices inside and between stations

Stations	Pearson SPI(3)-SPEI(3)	Pearson SPI(6)-SPEI(6)	Pearson SPI (12)-SPEI(12)
Telavi	0.96	0.94	0.93
Akhaltsikhe	0.93	0.91	0.86
Ambrolauri	0.96	0.96	0.96
Gori	0.92	0.86	0.84
Mta Sabueti	0.98	0.98	0.97
Pasanauri	0.98	0.96	0.94
Poti	0.99	0.98	0.99
Kutaisi	0.98	0.97	0.98
Tbilisi	0.93	0.91	0.88
Telavi-Gori	0.47	0.48	0.54
Axalkhalakhi- Mta Sabueti	0.5	0.50	0.50
Tbilisi -Kutaisi	0.32	0.32	0.45
Tbilisi-Mta Sabueti	0.31	0.31	0.44
Bolnisi-Pasanauri	0.24	0.16	0.26

at each stations. For Akhaltsikhe point wet day number exceeds drought one, severe drought day is approximately 3 and moderate- 50. At Gori station wet day number slightly exceeds drought day number, severe drought day equals 1 and moderate-60. At Telavi point drought day number greatly exceeds wet day number, severe drought day equals 5 and moderate-58. At Tbilisi point drought day number exceeds wet day one, severe drought day is 4 and moderate-62. At Kutaisi station wet day number exceeds drought one, severe drought day is 5 and moderate-55. At Mta-Sabueti both day types are approximately equal, severe drought day is 5 and moderate-54 (Tatishvili et al., 2022b). In Table 4 dry and wet day number for 3 places are presented.

The index values categorize drought intensity in given period. On Tables 5, 6, 7 and 8 SPEI and SPI categories were presented for Telavi, Tbilisi and Gori stations. All SPI, SPEI values are differing from each other and this fact has explanations.

Table 4 Negative and positive day number in Telavi, Tbilisi and Gori for 1991–2020 year period by SPEI3

Telavi	Negat	175	179	178	162	182	190
	Pos	171	164	159	183	160	146
Tbilisi	Negat	177	180	177	166	181	194
	Pos	181	175	172	191	173	153
Gori	Negat	171	171	164	168	170	163
	Pos	175	172	173	176	169	171

Table 5 SPI (3,6,12) and SPEI (3,6,12) categories for Telavi station

Drought indices		SPEI (3)	SPEI (6)	SPEI (12)	SPI (3)	SPI (6)	SPI (12)
Exceptional drought	<-2	5	7	3	15	11	5
Moderate drought	<-1	58	51	53	52	46	58
Exceptional wet	> 2	3	5	2	2	12	9
Moderately wet	> 1	62	58	66	56	49	62

Table 6 SPI (3,6,12) and SPEI (3,6,12) categories for Tbilisi station

Drought indices		SPEI (3)	SPEI (6)	SPEI (12)	SPI (3)	SPI (6)	SPI (12)
Exceptional draught	< -2	4	3	2	10	9	2
Moderate drought	< -1	62	64	62	56	48	44
Exceptional wet	> 2	3	0	2	9	7	14
Moderately wet	> 1	66	68	66	55	62	58

Table 7 SPI3(3,6,12) and SPEI (3,6,12) categories for Gori station

Drought indices		SPEI (3)	SPEI (6)	SPEI (12)	SPI (3)	SPI (6)	SPI (12)
Exceptional draught	< -2	1	3	5	8	7	9
Moderate drought	< -1	63	58	48	54	54	50
Exceptional wet	> 2	4	2	4	5	4	5
Moderately wet	> 1	58	60	55	58	58	51

According to the definition of SPEI the results of surface water deficit may be interpreted as dryness that is the indicator of drought conditions For Telavi that represents dry region irrigation is major concern. The region is significant agriculture producer and intensively uses Alazani river water for irrigation. According SPEI index the region is most subjected to moderate dryness than by SPI.

Tbilisi the capital of Georgia has its own climatic regime known as Tbilisi Cavern (Tsitsagi et al., 2022). It is more subjected to moderate drought conditions.

Gori represents Shida Kartli agricultural regionthat known by its fhruit production. It is undoubtedly under moderate drought conditions.

The obtained results indicate that there is difference between the droughts depicted by the precipitation based SPI and the evaporation influenced SPEI caused by inter annual and seasonal variability of temperature and precipitations trends, land cover, vegetation, irrigation and etc.

Table 8 Statistical parameters of stations/models located on the Kakheti and Kartli regions

Stations	Standard deviation (station/model)	Pearson correlation (station/model)	MAE (station/model)
Shilda	49.53	0.65	59.49
Shiraqi	41.79	0.61	47.16
Surami	35.67	0.53	60.11
Tbilisi	25.257	0.79	13.24
Tchiauri	36.88	0.54	45.30
Telavi	48.51	0.47	64.66
Tetri-tskaro	45.53	0.50	63.08
Tsalka	44.20	0.41	58.92
Tsiteli_Khidi	28.24	0.59	32.20
Tskhinvali	32.622	0.57	54.08
Tskneti	41.40	0.49	48.80
Tsnori	38.92	0.53	49.69
Udabno	31.58	0.543	37.73
Vanati	39.25	0.663	50.25
Vaneli	55.935	0.583	79.235
Zemo Akhalsopeli	41.68	0.693	28.395
Zghuderi	41.698	0.60	39.44

4 Conclusion

The Machine Learning technique is the important module of the growing field of big data science. Through the use of statistical methods, algorithms are trained to make classifications or predictions, and to uncover key insights in data mining projects. These insights subsequently drive decision making within applications and businesses, ideally impacting key growth metrics. As big data continues to expand and grow, the market demand for data scientists will increase. They will be required to help identify the most relevant business questions and the data to answer them (Publish House, 2022).

Overfitting is a concept in data science, which occurs when a statistical model fits exactly against its training data (Publish House, 2022). When this happens, the algorithm unfortunately cannot perform accurately against unseen data, defeating its purpose. Generalization of a model to new data is ultimately what allows us to use machine learning algorithms every day to make predictions and classify data.

The first region that was subjected to ML analysis is Kakheti, which was revealed as the most vulnerable to drough risk. The existed stations data of 1961–1990 year period were subjected to QC on heterogenity and continuality test and only19 stations passed it. Based on these data, the Standardized Precipitation Index (SPI) for 3 months was calculated and then subjected to Machine Learning. In this case, the most optimal result was shown by the “optimized tree”, where the minimum number of leaves is equal to 45, and the training time is 30,296 s, the prediction speed_ ~ 43,000 obs/sec (Publish House, 2022).

The Support Vector Machine (SVM) was selected in the Matlab space, it is the algorithm for Supervised Machine Learning, which allows us to optimize it, for example, we can control the number of divisions in the “machine tree”, which help to achieve the higher accuracy of the model. As it was revealed the tenth model showed the best result, with the using of this model it became possible to determine the drought probability by months at each point. The model was trained based on historical records and for forecasting by moth the new 1990–2020 year period was added.

Despite obtained good parameters, it became needed to add additional stations from adjacent territories, because there was not enough information in the Kakheti region to conduct the correct analysis of Machine Learning. While comparing the model and station data the overfit was detected, this is not valid for the analysis of new data. It became necessary to add the neighbor Kartli region also. In this case it is remarkable that stations that are displayed closely to each other give better results to the model for this two regions. The stations that are far away increase the probability of overfit. Therefore, Machine Learning needs to increase the observation network density- the number of stations, the observation period, as well as the use of satellite data for the region where there is not enough observation is the better choice. Especially for mountainous country where exist places that aren’t suitable to conduct ground observations.

The additional region contains 17 meteorological stations. The SPI (3) drought index uses precipitation data of those stations. The new prediction model has improved parameters: RMSE-0.77, R^2-0.39, MSE-0.58, and MAE-0.60.

The calculated statistical parameters of this two regions stations data and prediction model are enough fitted. Therefore the following is necessary to avoid overfit: increase number of dataset; increase of time study period, more nearest supporting points of observations.

Consequently, to apply the Machine Learning technique it is essential to increase the observation network- the number of stations and also increase the observation period too. As well as use satellite data for the region where there is not enough observation data and station set up is impossible is essential. Such research is conducted firstly for Georgian territory and it’ll be continued using more station data of large period to cover the whole territory. The research results are important for early warning system.

Acknowledgements The authors are grateful to the Georgian National Environment Agency (NEA) for providing the meteorological data.

Funding This work was supported by the Shota Rustaveli National Science Foundation of Georgia (SRNSFG) [FR-21–13962].

References

Tatishvili M., Elizbarashvili E., Meskhia R., Elizbarashvili Sh. Natural Hydrometeorological Disasters, Their Causes and Prevention Measures. The Macrotheme Review. A Multidisciplinary Journal of Global Macro Trends. A Macrotheme Capital Management. LLC Academic Publication, ISSN 1848–4735, v. 2, iss.1, Winter 2013 (January)., France, pp. 148–154.

Tatishvili M. Developing Weather Forecasting System in Georgia. Ecology & Environmental Sciences, 2 (7), 2017, https://doi.org/10.15406/mojes.2017.02.00046.

Tatishvili, M. R., Megrelidze, L. D., & Palavandishvili, A. M. (2021). Study of the Mean and Extreme Values, Intensity and Recurrence Variability of Meteorological Elements Based on the 1956–2015 Observation Data. Journals of Georgian Geophysical Society, 24(2). https://doi.org/10.48614/ggs2420213325

Ana Palavandishvili Evaluation of natural disasters using machine learning and big data for Georgia. International Conference of Young Scientists "Modern Problems of Earth Sciences". Proceedings, ISBN 978–9941–36–044–2, Publish House of Iv. Javakhishvili Tbilisi State University, Tbilisi, November 21–22, 2022, pp. 111–115. http://openlibrary.ge/handle/123456789/10263

Evans, N. P., Bauska, T. K., Gázquez-Sánchez, F., Brenner, M., Curtis, J. H., & Hodell, D. A. (2018). Quantification of drought during the collapse of the classic Maya civilization. Science, 361(6401). https://doi.org/10.1126/science.aas9871

Kaniewski, D., Guiot, J., & Van Campo, E. (2015). Drought and societal collapse 3200years ago in the Eastern Mediterranean: A review. In Wiley Interdisciplinary Reviews: Climate Change (Vol. 6, Issue 4). https://doi.org/10.1002/wcc.345

DeMenocal, P. B. (2001). Cultural responses to climate change during the late holocene. In Science (Vol. 292, Issue 5517). https://doi.org/10.1126/science.1059827

Babre, A., Kalvāns, A., Avotniece, Z., Retiķe, I., Bikše, J., Jemeljanova, K. P. M., Zelenkevičs, A., & Dēliņa, A. (2022). The use of predefined drought indices for the assessment of groundwater drought episodes in the Baltic States over the period 1989–2018. Journal of Hydrology: Regional Studies, 40. https://doi.org/10.1016/j.ejrh.2022.101049

McKee, T. B., Nolan, J., & Kleist, J. (1993). The relationship of drought frequency and duration to time scales. Preprints, Eighth Conf. on Applied Climatology, Amer. Meteor, Soc., January;

Vicente-Serrano, S. M., Beguería, S., & López-Moreno, J. I. (2010). A multiscalar drought index sensitive to global warming: The standardized precipitation evapotranspiration index. Journal of Climate, 23(7). https://doi.org/10.1175/2009JCLI2909.1

Tatishvili M., Palavandishvili A., Tsitsagi M., Gulashvili Z., Suknidze N. Drought Evaluation Based on Spei, Spi Indices for Georgian Territory. International Conference of Young Scientists "Modern Problems of Earth Sciences", Proceedings, ISBN 978–9941–36–044–2, Publish House of Iv. Javakhishvili Tbilisi State University, Tbilisi, November 21–22, 2022a, pp. 119–121.

Copernicus European Drought Observatory (EDO): https://edo.jrc.ec.europa.eu/

Tatishvili, M. R., Palavandishvili, A. M., Tsitsagi, M. B., & Suknidze, N. E. (2022b). The Use of Structured Data for Drought Evaluation in Georgia. Journals of Georgian Geophysical Society, 25(No.1). https://doi.org/10.48614/ggs2520224806

Mariam Tsitsagi, Zaza Gulashvili,Nana Bolashvili, Marika Tatishvili, Nikoloz Suknidze

RELATIONSHIP BETWEEN NORMALISED DIFFERENCE VEGETATION INDEX, PRECIPITATION AND DROUGHT INDICES (CASE OF KAKHETI, GEORGIA) 22nd International Multidisciplinary Scientific GeoConference SGEM 2022 https://doi.org/10.5593/sgem2022/4.1/s19.46

Marika Tatishvili,Zurab Khvedelidze, Inga Samkharadze, Ana Palavandishvili. Atmosphere processes and climate parameters variation in River Mtkvari basin Int. Sc. Conf. "Natural Disasters in Georgia: Monitoring, Prevention, Mitigation". Proc., Tbilisi, 2019, pp. 117–121. http://dspace.gela.org.ge/handle/123456789/8648

References

Comparative Characteristics of Transformation of the Digital Economy in Georgia

Mikheil Tokmazishvili

Abstract The study reviews the dynamics of the digital economy's transformation process in Georgia, as well as its impediments throughout the pandemic and post-pandemic periods. According to a comparative analysis, the digital economy transition in Georgia is characterized by four major components and ten indicators, which include infrastructure building, the creation, usage, and global distribution of technology and digital services, and the growth of human resources and security. It is demonstrated that in contrast to other nations where digital business was founded on the implementation of internal company projects and then spread throughout the world, its emergence in Georgia was founded on the active engagement and intervention of the state. Its growth follows a "from top to bottom" pattern. The introduction of digital technologies in the public service sector has been rapid, especially in the prior pandemic period, which ensured providing of big data operations and large amounts of needed medical information and state services during the pandemic, while funding, lack of staff, outdated technologies, reliance on foreign innovations and digital business model shortages remained major problems for entrepreneurs. These issues have been exacerbated in the post-pandemic period when the lessons learned during the pandemic are being corrected by inertia.

Keywords Digital economy · Entrepreneurship · Sustainable development threats · Risks · Digital management · Governmental regulations

1 Introduction

The digital economy is a new type of economic relations, developing in all sectors of the world market. It has become the leading segment and driving force in the growth of the economy.

M. Tokmazishvili (✉)
Faculty of Engineering and Business, East European University, Tbilisi, Georgia
e-mail: m_tokmazishvili@yahoo.com

R. C. Geibel and S. Machavariani (eds.), *Chances and Challenges of Digital Management*, Springer Proceedings in Business and Economics,
https://doi.org/10.1007/978-3-031-45601-5_14

Digital technologies and business models are evolving in all areas of society's economic life. It influences the formation of a new type of entrepreneurship, changes its structure, strengthens competition, and accelerates all phases of business development, starting from the purchase of raw materials to their final consumption and after-sales service. The digital economy goes beyond purely economic processes. Digitization penetrates social processes. The lives of people are increasingly dependent on it, in addition, there is a large-scale introduction of digital technologies in the activities of government organizations. It is a modern global challenge and requires special attention from the state and businesses to enhance its further development.

Theoretically, the digital economy increases labor productivity, facilitates business-to-business, business-to-consumer, and business-to-government communication, information exchange and delivery, reduces transaction costs, reduces product life cycles, production time, promotes innovation development, product sales growth, product quality growth and other.

According to World Bank data, the digital economy is equivalent to 15.5% of global GDP, growing two and a half times faster than global GDP over the past 15 years (World Bank, 2022). Its 10% increase in developing countries affects on GDP growth of these countries by 2.5 times. In this scenario, a 1% increase in information and communication technology results in a 0.4% increase in GDP (Sawng et al., 2021). This process has accelerated in the post-Covid-19 period, although the barriers that developing countries, including Georgia, have to some extent hinder the transformation process.

Digital transformation is developing unevenly in different fields of business and in enterprises of different sizes. Important factors in this regard are the level of awareness, the pace of economic development, the requirements and features of the industry, etc.

2 The Impact of Digital Technologies on Economy

Digital technologies are consumed by individuals and broad layers of society, as well as by businesses and entrepreneurs, and by the state, although it is not fully and directly reflected in the GDP "because the measure is based on what people pay for goods and services" (Brynjolfsson et al., 2019a).

The initiative for the development and cooperation of the digital economy was defined in 2016 at the G20 meeting (EU + 19 countries), and the digital economy concept was outlined as "a broad range of economic activities that include using digitized information and knowledge as the key factor of production, modern information networks as an important activity space, and the effective use of ICT as an important driver of productivity growth and economic structural optimization" (G20 Digital Economy Development and Cooperation, 2016).

In general, the GDP increases with the development of the digital economy. The latter mainly expresses the final value of the products and not the quality of life. The digital economy improves well-being, and in some cases, this positive role is even negatively reflected in the increase in value. A number of products, the production of which has shifted to the digital economy, relatively reduces their cost. For example, mobile phones and smartphones have "mastered" the function of taking photographs. As a result, the production of cameras decreased, and the distribution of images, if earlier it was carried out in material form, today it has become virtual and is distributed free of charge on the Internet. Accordingly, the scope of use of public goods has also increased. The Internet made information a public benefit, which is not fully reflected in the GDP. In the digital economy, society tries to distribute goods for free. The area of public goods and services has increased.

The digital economy's impact on the economy is multifaceted; yet, the digital economy is seen as the primary driver of economic growth in both developed and developing countries.

In the scientific literature, a new expanded meaning of GDP appeared, GDP-B, which quantifies benefits, rather than costs…. as it captures the benefits associated with new and free goods and thus goes "beyond GDP" (Brynjolfsson et al., 2019b).

The qualitative analysis of the impact of the digital transformation process on GDP dominates the scientific literature, whereas its quantitative measurement is considered relatively empirical due to the scarcity of such indicators.

GDP does not reflect the qualitative indicators of products, however, it is reflected in labor productivity in the form of value-added. It indirectly expresses the benefits that entrepreneurs and society receive from the use of digital technologies.

Demand for goods and services created by digital technologies can be determined by sales of digital technologies (smartphones, mobile phones, computers, etc.) and services (internet, applications, software, etc.). In other cases, the use of digital technology is determined by its consumption and the number of hours a person devotes to, say, digital media.

In Georgia, according to our survey, the use of digital applications among students in the conditions of the coronavirus, as a result of the transition to the distance mode of teaching, was determined to be 7–8 h a day on average. It means not only educational platforms, but also social networks, music, etc.

The extent to which people are able to use digital networks and services determines the effectiveness of the digital economy. These skills are higher in young people than in middle-aged or elderly people. Accordingly, the growth of the economy is determined not only by the cost that we pay for technologists and is directly reflected in the GDP, but also by how much it increases the benefits and the quality of life of the society. The latter is not implied the national accounting system.

The effectiveness of using digital technologies in business is related to the cost–benefit assessment and mainly to the extent to which entrepreneurs understand the usefulness of using digital technologies.

There are other indicators that give an initial idea of the total digitization of the economy. For example, number of computers, number of Internet users, speed, etc.

These estimates are conditional, as they do not cover all the opportunities that the digital economy provides. On the other hand, the evaluations are more subjective, as they do not take into account the peculiarities of individual businesses, their area of activity and the preferences of customers. Some customers want to buy clothes not virtually, with pictures, etc. s., but directly by physical contact, while buying construction materials and household items online is more extensive and appropriate.

There is no doubt that the digital economy helps to boost capital and labor productivity and to manufacture goods and services at cheaper prices. As a result, scientists primarily examine how technological advancements effect economic growth.

While existing literature focuses on the influence of ICT on economic development in terms of the number of Internet users, fixed broadband Internet users, and mobile subscribers, these approaches do not completely reflect the fuller dimensions of the digital economy's functioning.

There is currently a wide market for the use of information technology and services, and it is clear that countries with relatively low levels of productivity can benefit from the spillover effect of ICT to close the gap with developed countries, but the use of big data is not possible without integration and globalization, which takes place in conditions of imbalance between technological centers and peripheries, And so developing countriess need to integrate with them (Ganichev et al., 2021).

3 Approaches to Measurement of Transition to Digital Economy

Studies on the transition to a digital economy are diverse from both a macroeconomic and a microeconomic standpoint. And the range of indications of the digital economy's change at the macroeconomic and microeconomic levels is interpreted in various ways.

All researchers in the modern literature depict the change as a dynamic process, with Corvir-19 playing an accelerating role. As a result, they concentrated on how much the Corvirus-19 accelerated digital transformation (Kim, 2020).

From a geographical standpoint, some research have evaluated the effects of COVID-19 on the digital transformation process in the Belt and Road countries, while others have concentrated on developing an index system from a qualitative standpoint. Depending on the degree of development of the digital economy's infrastructure, a country's openness (which includes indicators of export and import), the innovative environment required for the development of digital technologies (which includes indicators of networks and technology use), and the competitiveness of digital technological innovations (which includes indicators of higher education and research and development) are distinguished from one another for this purpose (Zhang et al., 2022).

There are widespread mutual influence models, where the mutual influence of economic growth, information technology infrastructure and investments are discussed (Pradhan et al., 2018),conditions, processes and effects of digital transformation interdependence are reviewed (Ershova et al., 2018) and etc.

Different mathematical models relating to the development of the ICT (information and communication technologies) economy are being created for this purpose, and the outcomes of their impact vary between nations (Remeikiene et al., 2021, 12).

Focus is placed on the following areas in accordance with the spheres of digital transformation: 1. people, and their educational institutions; 2. technologies, and the extent to which they are used in various fields; 3. the integration of digital technologies into business and IT processes; and 4. the legal and institutional framework (Karimov et al., 2012, 354).

In order to facilitate a comparative study, the global researcher's organization agrees that the approach for mapping the digital economy should be uniform worldwide. International Digital Economy and Society Index (I-DESI), Digital Evolution Index (DEI), World Digital Competitiveness Index (WDCI), Boston Consulting Group Economy Digitalization Index (e-Intensity), and ICT Development Index (IDI) are common international methods for assessing digitalization (Karimov et al., 2012, 351). These indicators integrate all the dimensions that demonstrate the production, development, use, and consumption of digital technology and concentrate on different aspects of each.

The Partnership on Measuring ICT for Development (an international, multistakeholder initiative that was launched in 2004) has created a core list of ICT indicators to assist nations in tracking ICT infrastructure, access, and measurement in homes, businesses, education, and government. More than 60 indications are currently on the list. According to the Core List of ICT Indicators (March 2022 edition), they include the following topics: ICT infrastructure and access, ICT access and use by homes and individuals, ICT access and use by businesses, ICT sector and trade in ICT goods, ICT in education, and ICT in government. The alteration of these parameters occurs along with economic and technical growth (Kuzovkova et al., 2019).

In the European Union, there is a common classifier (DESI—digital economy and social indicators). It is based on three structural levels (and 32 indicators) in four directions: human Capital, connectivity, integration of digital technologies, and digital public services (Digital Economy and Society Index, 2022).

4 Methodology for Selecting Evaluation Indicators and Results

All facets of economic and social life are affected by the shift to a digital economy, which is the adoption of digital technologies to alter services or businesses. This process is dependent on the following factors: (a) the state of the technological infrastructure, including software services and networks; (b) the existence of markets, institutions, and global frameworks that encourage digital consumers and producers; and (c) the availability of qualified human resources.

Our methodology divides the digital economy into four broad areas, and its ten indicators describe how technologies are developed, used, and distributed—and, in particular, how far along the transformation process is (see Table 1).

Table 1 Areas of digital economy

1. Infrastructure and competitiveness	2. Technology and global integration	3. Development of human capital	4. Security
1.1. Network Readiness Index 2021 1.2. The population uses the Internet 1.3. Development of cellular connection	2.1. The share of high technologies in exports 2.2. Information and communication technologies (goods) trade 2.3. Export and import of communication tools	3.1. Use of intellectual property 3.2. Services offered by residents 3.3. Rates of research and development	4. Cyber Security Index

The importance and weight of each indicator is different. Their comparison allows to find out the country's strengths and weaknesses. At the same time, we keep in mind the fact that not all statistical indicators are available in Georgia, as well as in other developing countries. Therefore, the analysis is based only on the comparison of existence common indicators.

In order to evaluate the state of the digital economy in Georgia and identify its problems, weaknesses and strengths, we used the comparative method and compared several countries: 1. As Georgia aspires to become a member of the European Union, we took the average indicators of the European Union. Also the indicators of the world; 2. New candidate countries of the European Union—Ukraine and Moldova, together with which Georgia aspires to join the European Union. 3. The leading country of the European Union—Germany, in order to understand how far Georgia is from the advantage country of European Union. 4. In the post-communist space, the successful Baltic states provide an example of what can be achieved in the short term, with neighboring. Turkey as a major trading partner is considering also. For comparison, we used the indicators compiled by the World Bank (World Bank, 2022; World Development indicators).

5 Infrastructure and Competitiveness

5.1 Network Readiness Index 2021

This indicator demonstrates application and impact of information and communication technology (ICT) in economy. Georgia ranks 68th out of the 130 economies included in the NRI 2021. Its main strength relates to Governance (ranks 65) (Georgia, Network Readiness Index, 2021). The best side of Georgia relate to Regulation, Content and Individuals, among others (Ranks 43). The economy's performances in the Quality of Life (Ranks 83), Economy (ranks 89) and Future Technologies sub-pillars (Ranks 114) shows some weakness. According to The Network Readiness

Index (NRI) report the indicators where Georgia performs particularly well include Internet access in schools, Adult literacy rate, and Population covered by at least a 3G mobile network. By contrast, the economy's weakest indicators include E-commerce legislation, rural gap in use of digital payments, and Gross domestic expenditures in R&D (GERD) financed by business enterprise. The introduction of digital technologies in public service sector has been rapid, especially in the prior pandemic period, which ensured providing of big data operations and large amounts of needed medical information and state services during the pandemic, while funding, lack of staff, outdated technologies, reliance on foreign innovations and digital business model shortages remained major problems for entrepreneurs. Although there are portals of municipalities and state structures in Georgia, there are no sectoral web pages. However, every entrepreneur tries to make his website independently, which is associated with large financial costs. During the survey of small and medium-sized entrepreneurs in Georgia, it was revealed that, first of all, entrepreneurs are "afraid" of prices. A serious problem is the shortage of personnel, as well as companies that will work with small and medium-sized businesses (Tokmazishvili, 2021).

5.2 *The Use of the Internet*

In Georgia, 73% of the population uses the Internet, which is one of the lowest rates compared to the EU and candidate countries, the global rate is even lower (60%), while the EU average is 85%. Nevertheless, the growth rate is the highest (122%), which gives hope that this indicator will improve significantly in the short term (Table 2).

5.3 *Development of Cellular Connection*

In Georgia, the use of mobile phones does not lag behind the indicators of other countries (see Fig. 1), and the annual number of fixed network subscribers is 3 times less than the EU average.

6 Technology and Global Integration

6.1 *The Share of High Technologies in Exports*

The share of high technologies in exports is insignificant and amounts to 2–3%, while in the leading countries, in the European Union, and on average in the world, it is several times higher than the average of Georgians.

Table 2 Internet isage by country

	Individuals using the Internet (% of population)			Industrial design applications, resident, by count		
	2015–2019	2020–2021	Growth (2015–2021, %)	2015–2019*	2020–2021	Growth (2015–2021, %)
Estonia	89	89	100	50.6	40	79.1
Germany	86	90	104	41,245.4	35,764	86.7
Georgia	59	73	122	231.4	145	62.7
Lithuania	77	83	108	137.2	106	77.3
Latvia	82	89	109	139.4	141	101.1
Moldova	72			546.4	272	49.8
Turkey	64	78	121	38,428	42,073	109.5
Euro area	81	85	106			
European Union	79	85	107			
Ukraine	59	75	128	4910.2	3228	65.7
World	47	60	129	1,092,440	1,170,800	107.2

*Industrial design applications are applications to register an industrial design with a national or regional Intellectual Property (IP) offices and designations received by relevant offices through the Hague System

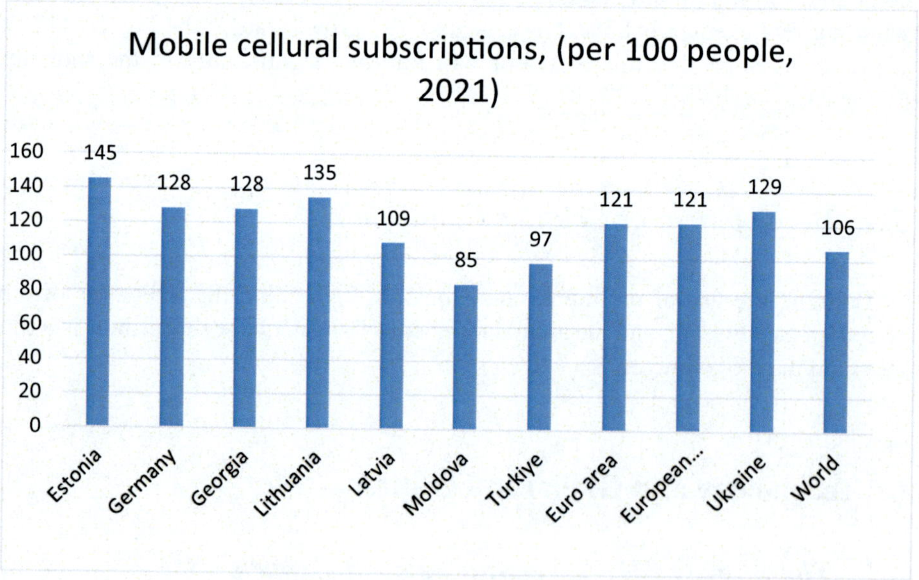

Fig. 1 Mobile cellural subscriptions

Table 3 High-technology exports (% of manufactured exports)

	2015–2019	2020–2021	Growth (2015–2021, %)
Estonia	19.5	20.4	104.5
Germany	16.8	15.5	92.4
Georgia	3.6	2.2	62.9
Lithuania	12.4	12.0	96.6
Latvia	18.3	20.0	109.3
Moldova	3.8	2.2	59.0
Turkey	3.1	3.2	102.3
Euro area	17.0	16.5	97.1
European Union	16.5	16.1	97.6
Ukraine	6.4	5.9	92.1
World	20.6	21.7	105.3

Georgia is an import-dependent country and its exports lag behind almost all comparable countries except Lithuania (see Table 3).

6.2 *Information and Communication Technologies (Goods) Trade*

In information and communication technologies (goods) trade, the share of both imports and exports of Georgia is very low (see Table 4), which indirectly expresses the structure of the economy and the level of digitalization. Before the pandemic, the export-import ratio was relatively higher than during the pandemic.

It should be noted here that despite the low share, the export of services in information technology trade from Georgia is increasing. It is the highest and the growth rate is more than percent, which means that more and more personnel are being trained in the field of information security, who can offer their services to the rest of the world. As a result, in the period of Pandemic export of ICT service exports increased more than in other countries (see Table 5).

According to the data of the National Statistics Service, the export of services in Georgia in 2021 was 61.2% more than in 2020, and imports—25.2% higher than the corresponding indicator of the previous year. In 2021, the positive trade balance is almost 6 times more than the trade balance of 2020. It seems that limitations in doing business that was caused by the coronavirus, enhanced market players to look for services, that can be supplied virtually in distance through digital technologies.

In 2021, telecommunications, computer and information services are in third place (8.5% of the total export of services); The first place in the export of services was taken by travel (48.9%) and the second place is occupied by transport services

Table 4 Information and communication technologies (goods) trade

	ICT goods exports (% of total goods exports)		ICT goods imports (% total goods imports)	
	2015–2019	2020–2021	2015–2019	2020–2021
Estonia	10.0	9.5	9.6	7.6
Germany	4.8	5.1	8.5	8.8
Georgia	0.6	0.4	4.9	4.1
Lithuania	3.8	3.9	5.3	6.2
Latvia	9.7	10.9	9.2	10.8
Moldova	0.3	0.2	3.7	4.7
turkey	1.4	1.0	5.2	4.6
Euro area	4.8	5.1	7.5	8.1
European Union	5.4	5.7	7.9	8.7
Ukraine	0.9	0.7	5.3	6.0
World	12.3	14.3	13.2	15.1

Table 5 Information and communication technologies (goods) service exports (% of service exports, BoP)

	ICT service exports (% of service exports, BoP)		
	2015–2019	2020–2021	Growth (2015–2021, %)
Estonia	10.7	19.1	178.8
Germany	8.9	10.9	121.5
Georgia	2.0	7.2	368.9
Lithuania	5.1	9.2	179.3
Latvia	12.4	19.6	157.9
Moldova	15.4	24.0	156.0
Turkey	2.2	5.2	230.3
Euro area	12.8	18.5	144.5
European Union	12.8	18.1	141.5
Ukraine	20.3	35.7	175.8
World	10.5	15.5	147.2

(32.3%). Besides in 2021 in comparison with 2020 the Costs of using of intellectual property increased more than 5 times, Telecommunication, computer and information services by 86% and other services related to scientific-research and trial-construction activities; consulting services related to management; technical, trade-related and other business services – by 21% (see Table 6).

Table 6 Export of services

Export of services	2020		2021		Change %
	Thous. dollars	% share	Thous. dollars	% share	
Export of services total	1 580,100.8		2 546 837.0	100	61,2
between them					
Costs of using intellectual property	994.7	0,1	6 134.8	0,2	516,7
Telecommunication, computer and information services	113 848.6	7.2	215 876.8	8.5	89.6
Other (services related to scientific-research and trial-construction activities; consulting services related to management; technical, trade-related and other business services;	82 308. 4	5.2	99 746.4	3.9	21.2

6.3 *Export and Import of Communication Tools*

A similar conclusion is made when analyzing the export and import of communication tools. The comparative analysis of the countries shows that during the pandemic in Georgia, the export of computers and other communication media services developed faster than the import (see Fig. 2).

Although every country shows a different trend, in the EU and the world as a whole services exports have been given priority.

If we separate the means of communication for commercial purposes and consider the indicators of export–import of technologies in the balance of commercial services, then it turns out that the export–import of technologies in Georgia grew faster than in other comparable countries (see Table 7). There was a particular increase in the pre-pandemic period, although it was reduced for obvious reasons, but the increase was still impressive.

7 Development of Human Capital

7.1 *Use of Intellectual Property*

Georgia has the lowest share of the current account balance of any other post-communist country. This indirectly means that the use of innovative digital technologies is significantly behind developed countries and the European Union as a whole (see Fig. 3).

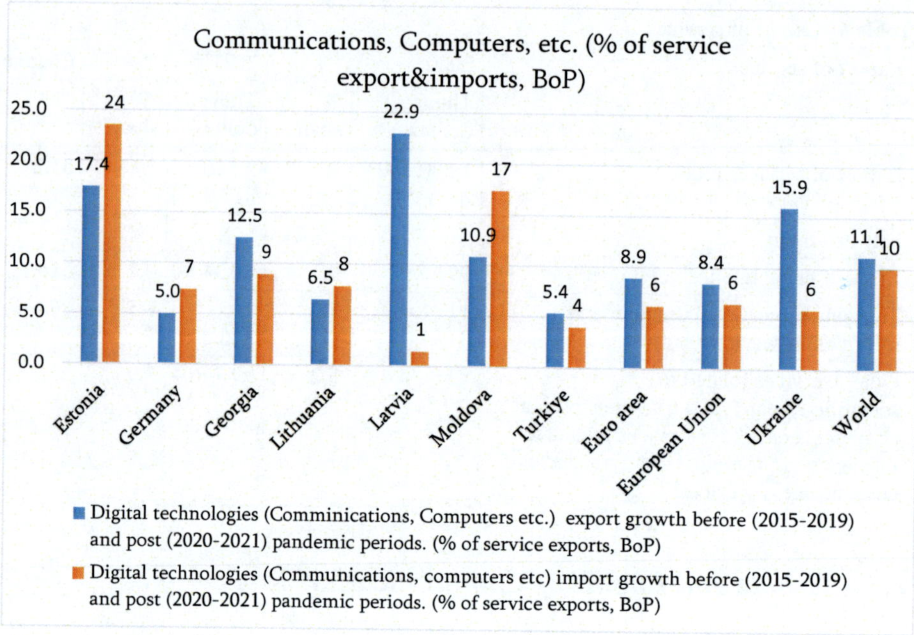

Fig. 2 The export and import of communication tools

Table 7 Growth of export–import of technologies in Georgia

	Digital technologies (Comminications, Computers etc.) export growth (2015–2021,% of commercial service exports)	Digital technologies (Communications, computers etc.) import growth (2015–2021, % of commercial service exports)
Estonia	139	162
Germany	109	115
Georgia	325	182
Lithuania	127	133
Latvia	169	145
Moldova	127	106
Turkey	151	112
Euro area	113	112
European Union	113	112
Ukraine	134	124
World	118	122

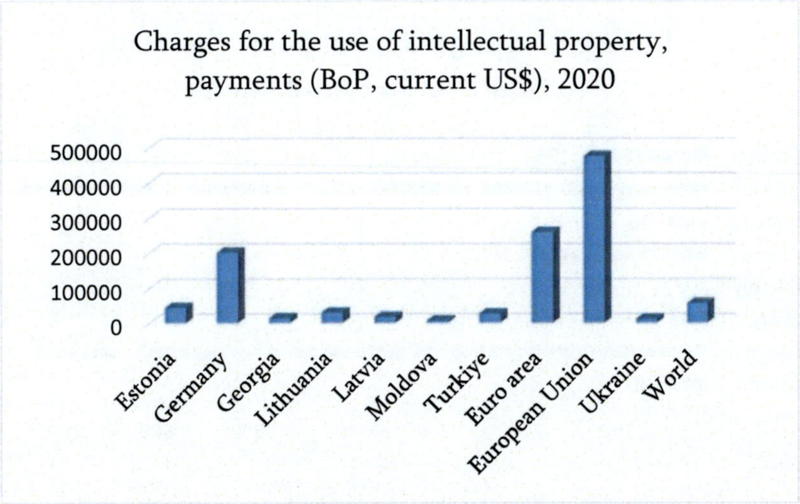

Fig. 3 Charges for the use of intellectual property, payments

However, it should be noted here that the growth of spending on intellectual property in 2015–2021 is much higher compared to all countries except Lithuania (see Table 8). At the same time, expenditure and share of intellectual property in the balance of payments increased especially rapidly in Georgia during the pandemic.

Table 8 Charges for the use of intellectual property, payments (BoP, current US$)

	Growth of Charges for the use of intellectual property, payments (BoP) before (2015–2019) and post (2020–2021) pandemic periods (%)
Estonia	99.1
Germany	117.7
Georgia	126.5
Lithuania	144.4
Latvia	93.7
Moldova	74.2
Turkey	117.2
Euro area	109.0
European Union	109.1
Ukraine	109.7
World	109.6

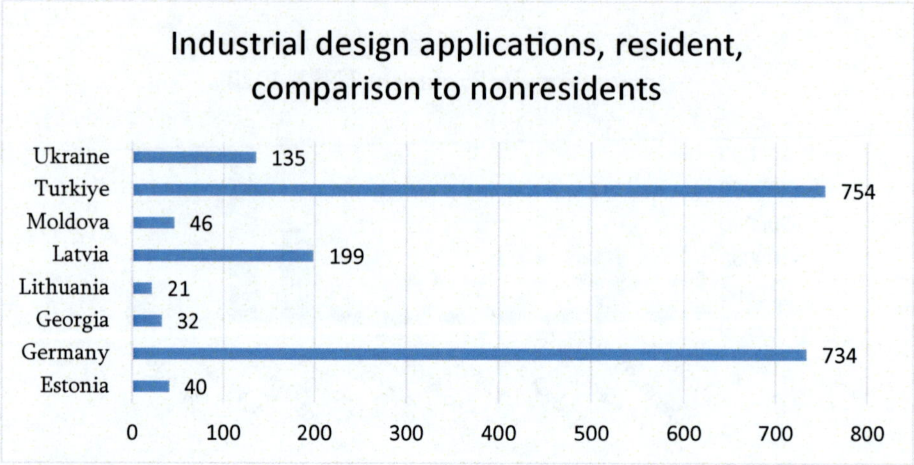

Fig. 4 Industrial design applications, resident, comparison to nonresidents

7.2 *Services Offered by Residents*

It is interesting that the services offered by residents in Georgia make up 32% of non-residents, that is, the country is 3 times more dependent on services provided by non-residents than on local services (Fig. 4)

7.3 *Research and Development*

One of weak side of economy is that Georgia is not distinguished by high rates of research and development. Its share in GDP is only 0.3%, while the EU average is 2.4%, Germany's –3.1% and the Baltic states within 1–2%. This indicator can only be improved in the long term, for which the appropriate political will be needed, which will help Georgia move into the space of advanced technologies (Figs. 5 and 6).

8 Security

Finally, one very important site that assesses positive environment for the development of Digital economy is that according to "The National Cyber Security Index" 2019 by E-governance Academy (eGA) Georgia is ranked 21st position among 130 most advanced and developing economies of the world in terms of national cyber security (Georgia in International Ratings, 2012–2019).

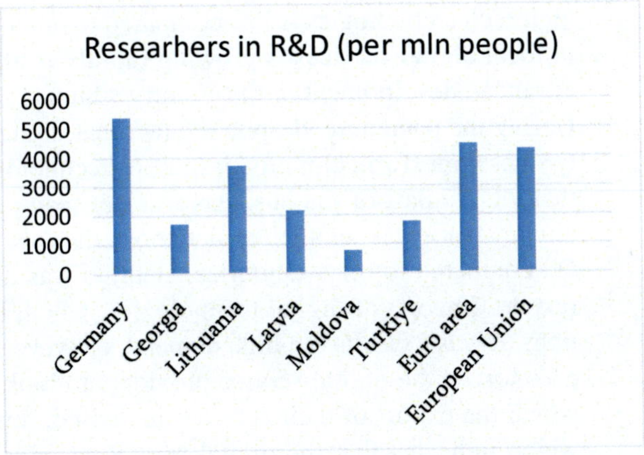

Fig. 5 Research in R&D and R&D expenditure

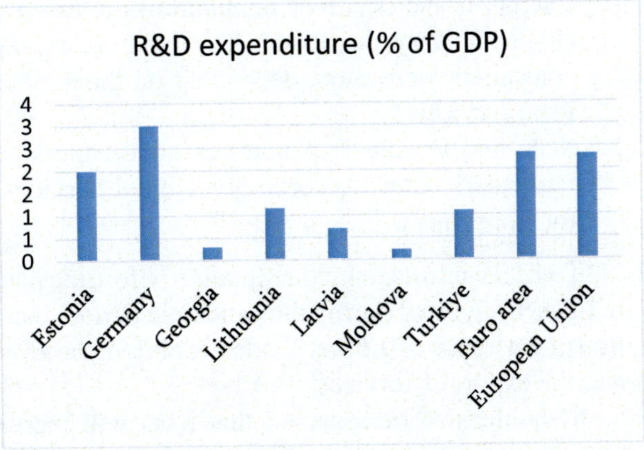

Fig. 6 Research in R&D and R&D expenditure

9 Conclusions

Based on the above data, we can conclude that:

1. In Georgia, the market of digital services in state institutions is relatively developed, although its impact on the quality of life and economy is weak. Coronavirus stimulated Digital services in schools to be well developed. The level of training of young people is high and the country has mobile networks. However, e-law, especially in the commercial field, requires perfection.
2. The use of innovative digital technologies in Georgia lags behind the European Union. However, the expenditure on intellectual property in the tax balance is growing dynamically, the rate of which exceeds the indicators of the European Union and the average world. This positive development is hindered by the fact that in connection with the introduction of technologies in Georgia, there is a great dependence on the foreign market, and the growth rate of the import of

high-tech technologies is low compared to other countries. The fact that the field of local digital services is growing rapidly is also positive, which indicates the advanced development of the country's human resources.

3. During the pandemic, despite the fact that digital technologies were a means of business transformation, the import of technologies decreased, which indicates that a large part of the business was not ready for digital transformation. This circumstance has another explanation: the low activity was due to blockades, but compared to other countries, Georgia was distinguished by a high turnover (export–import) of digital technologies, which indicates that despite of limitations, it was a product in high demand. However, if in other countries the blockades forced the digital service providers to look for new markets, as a result of which the export of their services increased, this was not observed in Georgia, which indicates that the digital service providers in Georgia had difficulty in absorbing foreign markets.
4. Internet usage (share of population) increased during the pandemic, but application delivery decreased. The latter is explained by the fact that Georgian consumers were more dependent on the services of foreign designers than on local services.
5. State and Private Expenditures on Business Research and Development Are Particularly Low. Accordingly, Digital Services Are Still an Expensive Product for Consumers.

If we take into account the situation before the pandemic and the above-mentioned regularities formed during the pandemic period, then we should expect the continuation of the trends of the pre-pandemic period, the growth of the import of technologies and the export of services.

It should also be assumed that risks will increase along with digital transformation, and cybercrimes will increase along with institutional transformation, and fast moral wear of technologies, ecological threats, increase of hazardous waste for the environment, etc. and related regulations, such as the introduction of extended responsibility of the entrepreneur, etc. It will make it more expensive to do business.

In the near term, the Achilles heel of the economy remains the low rates of technology use by small and medium-sized businesses, which may continue in the future if no stimulating measures are implemented. In particular, companies that will serve small and medium-sized businesses can be given tax benefits and exempted from taxes, which will be a great incentive for entrepreneurs to intensify introducing of digital technologies.

References

Ashmarina, S., Mesquita, A., Vochozka, M. (2020). *Digital Transformation of the Economy: Challenges, Trends and New Opportunities.* Berlin: Springer International Publishing. https://doi.org/10.1007/978-3-030-11367-4

Brynjolfsson E.,Avinash Collis A., (2019a), How Should We Measure the Digital Economy? Harvard Business Review, 2019, https://hbr.org/2019/11/how-should-we-measure-the-digital-economy

Brynjolfsson E., Collis A., W. Erwin Diewert, Felix Eggers, Kevin J. Fox (2019b), GDP-B: Accounting for the Value of New and Free Goods in the Digital Economy, *National Bureau of Economic Research, Working Paper 25695.* http://www.nber.org/papers/w25695

Core List of ICT Indicators, March 2022 version, The Partnership on Measuring ICT for Development, https://www.itu.int/en/ITU-D/Statistics/Documents/coreindicators/Core-List-of-Indicators_March2022.pdf

Ershova TV, Hohlov YE, Shaposhnik SB. Methodology for digital economy development assessment as a tool for managing the digital transformation processes. In: *2018 Eleventh International Conference "Management of large-scale system development" (MLSD).* Piscataway: IEEE (2018). pp. 1–3. https://ieeexplore.ieee.org/document/8551846

Ganichev NA, Koshovets OB. (2021), Forcing the digital economy: how will the structure of digital markets change as a result of the COVID-19 pandemic. Studies on Russian Economic Development, Vol., 32, pp. 11–22. https://doi.org/10.1134/S1075700721010056

G20 Digital Economy Development and Cooperation Initiative, (2016), http://www.g20chn.org/English/Documents/Current/201609/P020160908736971932404.pdf

Georgia, Network Readiness Index, 2021, PORTULANS Institute, https://networkreadinessindex.org/country/georgia/

Georgia in International Ratings, 2012–2019, http://www.economy.ge/uploads/publications/economy_774326475d10650591bcb6.91945485.pdf

Digital Economy and Society Index (DESI), 2022, Methodological Note, *European Commission,* https://digital-strategy.ec.europa.eu/en/library/digital-economy-and-society-index-desi-2022

Karimov NG, Khamidova FA, Saydullaev SS, Parpieva RA., (2021), Digital Transformation of the Economy as a New Challenge to Economic Security. In *The 5th International Conference on Future Networks amp Distributed Systems (ICFNDS 2021), December 15–16, 2021, Dubai, United Arab Emirates.* ACM, New York, NY, USA, pp. 348–355, https://doi.org/10.1145/3508072.3508129

Kuzovkova T, Kuzovkov D, Sharavova O., (2019), Transformation of criteria and indicators of digital development of economy and information society. In: *Conference of Open Innovations Association.* Proceeding of the 24th Conference of Fruct Association, pp. 682–687, https://doi.org/10.5555/3338290.3338387

Kim R. Y, (2020), The Impact of COVID-19 on Consumers: Preparing for Digital Sales, IEEE Engineering Management Review, Vol. 48, # 3, pp. 212–218, DOI: https://doi.org/10.1109/EMR.2020.2990115, . https://ieeexplore.ieee.org/document/9076858

Pradhan RP, Arvin MB, Nair M, Bennett SE, Bahmani S. (2019), Short-term and long-term dynamics of venture capital and economic growth in a digital economy: a study of European countries. Technology in Society, Vol. 57, pp. 125–134, https://doi.org/10.1016/j.techsoc.2018.11.002, https://www.sciencedirect.com/science/article/abs/pii/S0160791X18301829

Remeikiene, R., Gaspareniene, L., Fedajev, A., & Vebraite, V. (2021). The role of ICT development in boosting economic growth in transition economies. *Journal of International Studies, 14*(4), 9–22. https://doi.org/10.14254/2071-8330.2022/14-4/1

Tokmazishvili M., (2021), Barriers to Digital Business and Challenges of Social Innovations in Georgia. In the book: Digital Management in Covid-19 Pandemic and Post-Pandemic Times (ed. Geibel RC., Machavariani S.), *Proceedings of the International Scientific-Practical Conference* (ISPC 2021), Springer Proceedings in Business and Economics, pp. 3–13, https://doi.org/10.1007/978-3-031-20148-6.

Sawng Y., Kim P, Park JY, (2021), ICT investment and GDP growth: Causality analysis for the case of Korea, *Telecommunications Policy*, Vol. 45, Issue 7, https://doi.org/10.1016/j.telpol.2021.102157. https://www.sciencedirect.com/science/article/pii/S0308596121000616

Zhang J., Zhao W., Cheng B., Li A., Wang Y., Yang N., and Tian, Y, (2022), The Impact of Digital Economy on the Economic Growth and the Development Strategies in the post-COVID-19 Era: Evidence From Countries Along the "Belt and Road", *Frontiers in Public Health, Health Economics*, Vol, 10, https://doi.org/10.3389/fpubh.2022.856142

World Bank (2022), Digital Development, https://www.worldbank.org/en/topic/digitaldevelopment/overview

World Development indicators, https://databank.worldbank.org/home.aspx

Rethinking the Traditional Statistical Business Process Model in Central Banks in the Light of Modern Digitization: A Case of Georgia

Nana Aslamazishvili

Abstract Many factors, such as, wars, crises or pandemics strongly contribute to modern economic processes to become more and more unpredictable. Nevertheless, statistics remain the science that must study these processes in whatever direction economic events develop. Thus, it is not enough for statistics to simply play the role of an observer of events. It must itself be designed in such a way as to be somewhat ahead of events in order to be able to assess them immediately and supply policy-makers, businesses or academics with necessary information. On the other hand, the production of digital financial system statistics definitely requires the transformation and digitization of the entire statistical business process model. National Bank of Georgia (NBG) applies such a principled approach to the development of statistics under its mandate. In order to realize the mentioned approach, NBG implemented the project SebStat which stands for statistics of NBG. This study shows how the SebStat project solved the above problem by digitizing the statistical business process at the central bank.

Keywords Digitization · SebStat · GSBPM · Banking statistics · SNA

1 Introduction

In today's rapidly evolving informational era digitization of statistical activity is crucial. It "... has two different types of impact on statistics: the first relates to its potential uses for statistical production and the second to the ability of current statistics of keeping track of the digital economy" (De Bonis & Piazza, 2020. p. 29). This study provides Georgian experience in this field over the last decade, from the viewpoint of production of banking statistics.

N. Aslamazishvili (✉)
National Bank of Georgia, Tbilisi, Georgia
e-mail: aslamazishvilinana@gmail.com

R. C. Geibel and S. Machavariani (eds.), *Chances and Challenges of Digital Management*, Springer Proceedings in Business and Economics,
https://doi.org/10.1007/978-3-031-45601-5_15

This paper proposes a novel approach for statistical production in the country's financial system, based on two main pillars: standardization of the Data Structure Definition (DSD) mechanism and optimization of the GSBPM through digitization. Implementation of these two solutions in combination brought successful results to the Georgian banking system's practice and made easier prospects for further statistical innovations from both methodological and practical points of view.

Section 2 of this paper provides literature review and the problem statement is presented. Section 3 describes the proposed methodology. Section 4 presents results while Sect. 5 is dedicated to conclusions.

2 Literature Review

Relatively detailed ways and methods of digitization of statistical business processes in the field of banking statistics are rarely described in relevant publications (Aslamazishvili, 2013; De Bonis & Piazza, 2020). Moreover, getting acquainted with the practices of various countries, it was identified that for the most part, the emphasis is on the automation of individual stages of producing banking statistics, and not on the digitization of the entire statistics business process model. Such a trend is probably related to the fact that statistical business process issues, on the one hand, and digital technologies, on the other, are developing independently of each other.

It is also important to note that recommendations from international organizations regarding digitization are mainly addressed to national statistical offices and less to central banks (PARIS21, 2022). Furthermore, such recommendations still focus on questionnaires rather than more modern methods of data collection (UNCTAD, 2020).

However, before we start thinking about digitization of the statistical business process, it is necessary to define the structure of the information to be collected. In this regard, it is important to note that the most fundamental and accurate recommendations given in the System of National Accounts (SNA). We are talking about a series of important and, in our opinion, fundamental questions, which sound like this: "Who does what, with whom, in exchange for what, by what means, for what purpose, with what changes in stocks?" (EC et al, 2009. p. 16).

It is worth mentioning that this issue remains undeservedly neglected in methodological and practical studies of statistics, except for some of them. Moreover, in the latter it is interpreted somewhat incorrectly. For example, some authors refer to it as a combination of simple links (Hundessa & Alemayehu, 2020. p.63), while the SNA recommends to organize accounting of economic flows and stocks in such a comprehensible way, which "… would provide an enormous amount of information describing the complete network of economic interrelations" (EC et al., 2009. p. 16). Thus, we found this to be a key clue to how to collect the detailed information necessary to get a comprehensive economic picture, which we used as an excellent idea in the process of defining the granular structure of financial data, and standardize set of stages of GSBPM, on the other hand.

Thus, we found that in relation to the issues discussed in this paper, there is a significant gap that does not serve the requirements of the modern statistical business process model and solves the problem only one-sidedly: either only by digitizing individual processes, or by modifying the questionnaires while maintaining outdated collection methods and so on.

3 Proposed Methods and Approaches

The information model that forms the core of SebStat was developed taking into account international statistical standards, guidelines (such as SNA, Monetary and financial statistics manual and compilation guide, GSBPM, etc.) and requirements, Statistical Data and Metadata Exchange (SDMX) concepts, on the one hand, and own developments concerning the principles of statistical production, statistical domains, classifications, IT architecture, and other own approaches and experiences, on the other.

3.1 Data Structure Defining Mechanism

To improve monetary policy analysis based on reliable statistics, NBG decided in 2010 to request the balance sheet data from the individual commercial banks according to the content of the sectoral balance sheet of depository corporations (IMF, 2016. pp. 342–359), i.e. taking into account a balance-sheet-like structure, according to the instrument, the currency of denomination, and the counterpart sector. Moreover, data was requested both in terms of stocks and flows, and were expanded to take into account local characteristics and requirements (see Fig. 1). It can be considered that this is one of the best approaches for the further development of monetary and financial statistics, including compilation of the financial account.[1]

In terms of data structure definition, as we have already mentioned above, developing the right questioning technique is important, as recommended in SNA. After that it is possible to develop the schematic structure of data for any statistical domain.

Ordering of items/digits in the data structure is essential in order to better understand particularly what is requested from the respondents. On the other hand, correct ordering of items helps to trace clearly the logic of requested information. For instance, the schematic structure of the bank balance sheet items is as follows (see Fig. 2):

After describing the structure of the data, it is a particularly responsible task to choose the right classifications for each digit. It is essential that this happens in Phase 2 ("Design") and not in Phase 5 ("Process") as described by the GSBPM (see Fig. 3). Therefore, the digitization task requires some sub-processes of the GSBPM

[1] For details see: https://nbg.gov.ge/en/statistics/interactive.

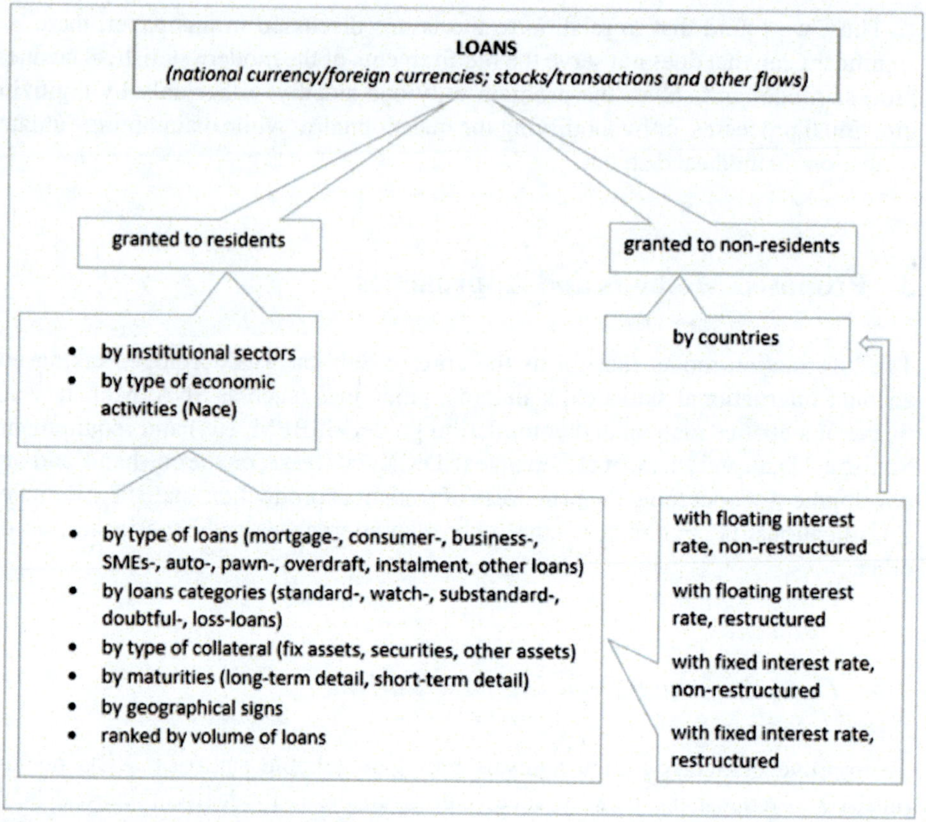

Fig. 1 Data granulation example for loans

to be moved to another place, for example sub-process 5.2 ("classify and code") to be moved under the "Design" phase, as classifications play an important role on the data structure definition stage.

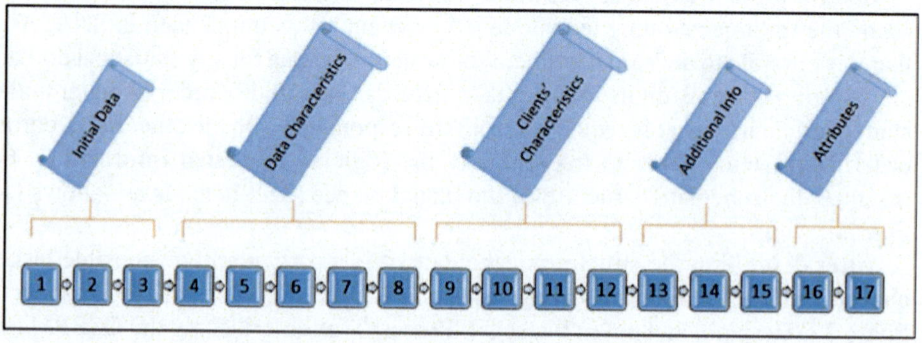

Fig. 2 Schematic structure of balance sheet data within the SebStat

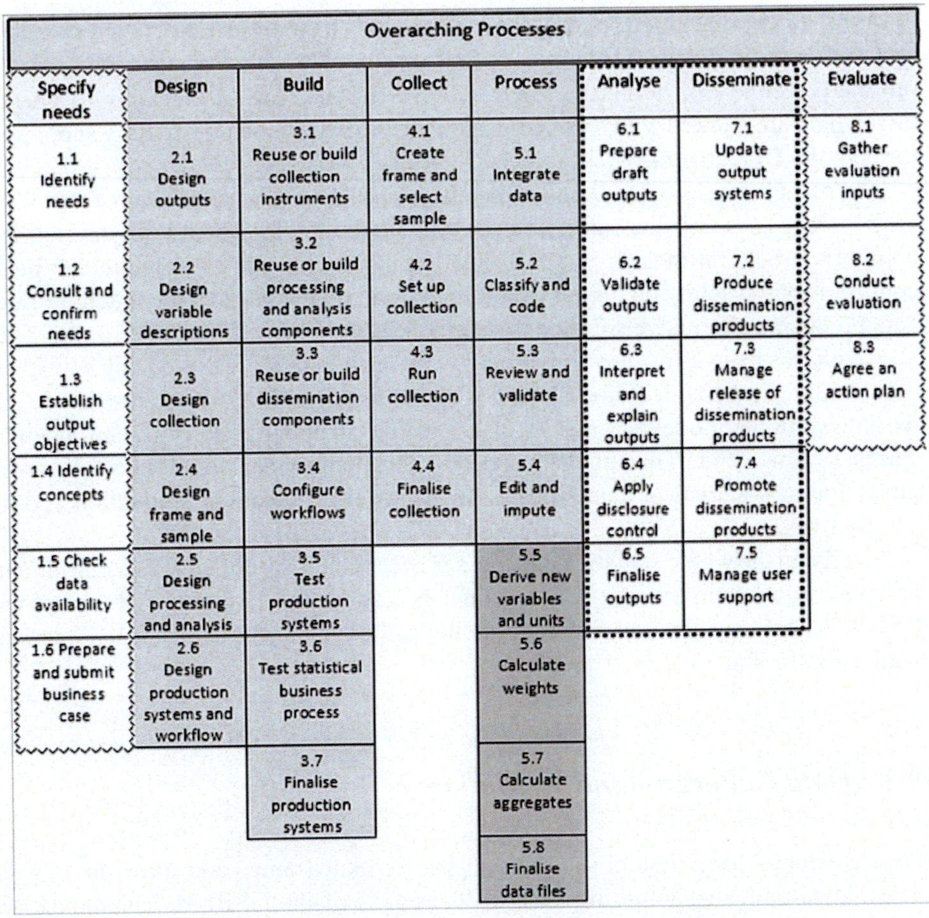

Fig. 3 Scheme of the generic statistical business process model (GSBPM)

3.2 *The GSBPM Modification and Streamlining*

Since our goal was to digitize workflows within a statistical business process framework, we have found that there is no better international standard for this than the GSBPM. Indeed, as is known, the GSBPM is intended to guide the planning of surveys and other statistical operations by systematically considering all processes and the workflow from initial preparatory steps to dissemination, documentation and archiving (UNCTAD, 2020, p. 71). This choice helped us to create a digitized model of the statistical business process for all statistical domains under the NBG's mandate, using IT technology.

In order to follow the GSBPM framework, our IT architecture was constructed in accordance with them. Thus, phases 2–5 ("Design", "Build", "Collect", "Process") of the GSBPM that we have digitized within the framework of SebStat (Fig. 3) have been marked with a light grey.

Another solution was found for phases 6 and 7 ("Analyse" and "Disseminate") and this involves Business Intelligence (BI) support. Nevertheless, this does not rule out the possibility of doing the same within SebStat. Thus, digitization of phases 6–7, which are marked with a dotted line on the GSBPM scheme, are fully supported through the BI platform.

The sub-processes 5.5–5.7 under the phase 5 ("Process") have been marked with a dark grey. These are the sub-processes that can be implemented both through the appropriate SebStat module and BI. This is a good example of how the SebStat's concept is based solely on digital technologies and on the basis of the latter, it offers data producers alternative solutions as well.

All phases from 2 to 7 are predefined by the standardized way and any statistical data family can be added or enhanced without significant effort and resources. All workflows in the model act in accordance with a predetermined consistent manner and there is no need to invent again special concepts, standards and rules for implementation new statistical data families. It makes easy statistical production and its perspectives.

Finally, in the whole statistical business process chain described above, the human being plays a role in the first ("Specify needs") and last ("Evaluate") phases of the GSBMP. These are the phases when intellectual engagement is necessary (marked with a zigzag line).

3.3 *Data Collection and Validation*

Data collection tools, established within the SebStat framework, allow us to predefine data matching logic in phase 2 ("Design") of the GSBPM. The validation process is fully automated and it begins immediately when the respondent starts uploading the file. If the error is found in the file, a special message will appear on the respondent's desktop, announcing that "Check N x is detected in the file". The respondent should follow the given link and find a Check N x scheme in the system, which looks as follows and correct appropriate data is given:

If	Family in (PCS) AND Freq in (MM) AND Bt in (IS, AQ)
Then	Tt not_in (AA,XX,ZZ,Z1, Z2, CA, CL, CP, CO)

In addition, data validation procedures, established within the SebStat, completely exclude item non-response because in case of omissions, the respondent will not be able to upload the requested information.

Data validation procedures also exclude data duplication, which is a very important feature of the SebStat. This exclusion is established in the "Design" phase that changes old statistical data collection practice significantly.

4 Results

Digitization and optimization of statistical business processes significantly changes the culture of statistical production in the central bank. Standardization of statistical business processes simplifies planning and implementation of statistical work and leaves more time for intellectual activities, such as, data analysis, development of innovative solutions, etc.

Introduction of Sebstat fundamentally changed the entire process of production of banking statistics, from the planning of statistical work to the dissemination of data. There is no misinterpretation or non-response with required data. Respondents are provided with the predefined scheme of data structure for reporting. In addition, there is a special module on the data producers' side that monitors the situation immediately if there are any problems while uploading the data by data providers.

The processes and procedures are well documented and posted on the SebStat portal. Thus, it can be used to specify appropriate quality information about banking statistics. On the other hand, it makes all workflows understandable and simplifies transferring of knowledge and experience to others.

Communication with data providers is fully automated. Any feedback from data producers to data providers and vice versa is managed by the system, that saves time and resources significantly.

As it is known, many developing country NSOs still disseminate data only in the form of numerical tables, limiting the comprehension of results to less "statistically literate" audiences (UNCTAD, 2020). However, despite this, NBG also coped with this task thanks to the successful integration of SebStat with BI and practices data dissemination using user-friendly and powerful IT tools for data visualization. This solution certainly provides fast access to data, is evolving and flexible. As for the exchange of information with international organizations, the NBG already cooperates with the IMF in the field of data exchange in the SDMX format. Upon request, similar cooperation is possible with other international organizations as well.

5 Conclusion

Thus, the paper briefly describes the way NBG digitized the statistical business process by successfully combining the main concepts of the SNA and Monetary and Financial Statistics with the GSBPM. NBG's statistical business process model SebStat, which is created as a full-fledged digital workplace, has proven itself especially in the context of Covid-19, when the process of statistical production was not interrupted at all and took place in an absolutely calm and comfortable atmosphere for both data providers and data producers.

To summarize main advantages of our proposed approaches to statistical production briefly, i.e. SebStat features as a whole, they are as follows:

1. The SebStat's concept is based solely on digital technologies and eliminates routine manual intervention in the statistical production, which is a significant achievement in the face of ever-increasing demand for information and insufficient resources;
2. It is designed for the long term perspective, as its conceptual architecture is based on international statistical standards, unified and flexible procedures, digital technologies for data collection, validation, processing and dissemination;
3. It is a user-friendly, flexible and time-saving system for parties involved that creates a brand new and convenient communication environment between data providers and producers;
4. Its methodology, procedures, and workflows are well documented and available on the SebStat portal. The audio/video learning materials regarding SebStat's main principles and implementation features are also posted on this portal, which provides the possibility for continuous training/learning of banking system reporting specialists.
5. The transparency of SebStat as a statistical business process model is directly reflected in the transparency of the published statistical information, which creates the guarantee of the trust of users of NBG statistics.
6. SebStat is flexible for system-to-system communication, which is essential when cooperating with international organizations in the field of information exchange.
7. Easy to share knowledge and experience with colleagues and interested parties regarding digitizing statistical business processes.

Thus, the results of SebStat and the mentioned advantages are a clear confirmation that the digitization of the statistical business process is clearly equivalent to moving the NBG's statistics to a qualitatively new level.

References

Aslamazishvili, N. (2013). Data collecting strategy in the new informational environment. *Conference of European Statisticians.* Geneva: UNECE. Retrieved from https://www.researchgate.net/publication/350213787_DATA_COLLECTION_STRATEGY_IN_THE_NEW_INFORMATIONAL_ENVIRONMENT_Working_paper

Aslamazishvili, N. (2017). *SebStat: System for collection, processing, storage and dissemination of financial and statistical information of the National Bank of Georgia. 2nd edition.* National Bank of Georgia. doi:https://doi.org/10.13140/RG.2.2.28282.16322

De Bonis, R., & Piazza, M. (2020). A silent revolution: How central bank statistics have changed in the last 25 years. Bank of Italy. Retrieved from https://www.bancaditalia.it/pubblicazioni/qef/2020-0579/QEF_579_20.pdf?language_id=1

EC, IMF, OECD, UN & WB. (2009). *System of National Accounts 2008.* European Commission, International Monetary Fund, Organization for Economic Co-operation and Development, United Nations and World Bank.

Hofmann, A. (2018). *Modernized statistical business process models in central banks.* FIS MarketMap FAME Analytic Platform. Retrieved from https://www.slideshare.net/AlexanderHofmann3?utm_campaign=profiletracking&utm_medium=sssite&utm_source=ssslideview

Hundessa, A. Y., & Alemayehu, N. A. (2020). The Current Practices and Gaps in Forest Accounting System of Ethiopia: A Review. *Research Journal of Finance and Accounting, 11*(19).

IMF. (2016). *Monetary and Financial Statistics Manual and Compilation Guide*. International Monetary Fund.

PARIS21. (2022). Digital Transformation of National Statistical Offices. *OECD*. https://doi.org/10.1787/ee4b1b85-en

Solans, D. (2003). *The importance of Eurostat for the monetary policy of the European Central Bank, speech delivered at the academic meeting on the occasion of the 50th anniversary of the Statistical Office of the European Communities, Luxembourg, 16 May 2003*. Retrieved from https://www.ecb.europa.eu/press/key/date/2003/html/sp030516.en.html

UNCTAD. (2019). Digital economy report. Value creation and capture: Implications for developing countries. United Nations Conference on Trade and Development.

UNCTAD. (2020). *Manual for Production of Statistics on the Digital Economy. Revised Edition*. United Nations Conference on Trade and Development.

UNECE. (2013). *Generic Statistical Business Process Model - Version 5.0*. Retrieved from https://statswiki.unece.org/display/GSBPM/GSBPM+v5.0

Digitalization in Education

An Analysis of the Relationship Between Sustainability Focus and Grit in German Entrepreneurs

Antonia F. Terriuolo

Abstract The purpose of this study is to delve into the personalities and the values that make up German entrepreneurs. The rising awareness regarding sustainability issues and the wish to counteract them led to the creation of what is known as sustainable entrepreneurship. This type of entrepreneurship tries to solve current sustainability issues through market innovation. With this said, the objective of this study is to find whether a relationship exists between an entrepreneur's sustainability orientation and the existence of sustainable entrepreneurship. Additionally, it sets out to see how a psychological concept like grit, meaning the Perseverance of Effort and Consistency of Interest over a long period of time, influences the relationship between them. To analyze these relationships, the three topics were viewed through the lens of literature review, especially focusing on the perspective offered through the Triple Bottom Line. Moreover, empirical research was conducted by using a questionnaire that had 29 German respondents, defining themselves as entrepreneurs. The results indicate that sustainability orientation is an antecedent for sustainable entrepreneurship. However, a positive relationship between sustainability orientation and grit could not be detected. Therefore, it was found that grit does not play a mediating role between the independent variable (sustainability orientation) and the dependent variable (sustainable entrepreneurship). Moreover, this study highlights the importance of psychological research into the personality of entrepreneurs to foster entrepreneurial action in the future. The second valuable area being the implementation of sustainable behavior into the economy and personal life, benefitting the individual's state of mind, as well as society.

Keywords Grit · Sustainable entrepreneurship · Sustainability focus

---

A. F. Terriuolo (✉)
Dusseldorf, Germany
e-mail: antoniaterriuolo@gmail.com

R. C. Geibel and S. Machavariani (eds.), *Chances and Challenges of Digital Management*, Springer Proceedings in Business and Economics,
https://doi.org/10.1007/978-3-031-45601-5_16

1 Introduction

How do successful people do it? If the readers of this article are anything like its author, they have asked themselves this very question. What differentiates successful people from unsuccessful ones, and how can one strive to be successful in their own right? This is where the psychological concept of grit creates the basis for understanding the personality of those that have achieved their goals. Contrary to popular belief, it is not talent that drives them, but rather a combination of perseverance and resilience, combined with hope, which defines Angela Duckworth's concept of grit (Duckworth & Quinn, 2009). Generally, character traits found in high achievers are defined by a strong interest in their respective field, the desire to reach a high level of achievement, as well as the preparedness to put significant amounts of effort and time into the journey of reaching one's goal (Duckworth et al., 2007).

Moreover, the changing economic landscape in Germany highlights the role entrepreneurs and their startups have as drivers of economic innovation. This provides the basis for this research to find out what drives entrepreneurs, what their personalities look like, and how their personal interests shape and influence the face of their companies.

No matter how entrepreneurs' competencies are defined in detail, research overwhelmingly agrees that entrepreneurial competencies detrimentally impact the business's future success. However, they are not natural occurrences in an entrepreneur's character, but they rather are acquired and developed through experience and by accessing similar competencies by business partners and others (Busenitz & Barney, 1997; Mitchelmore & Rowley, 2008, 2013; Rasmussen et al., 2011). All these findings bring to light a theoretical connection between entrepreneurs and the concept of grit.

Due to the rise in awareness regarding environmental degradation and the interest in preserving life for future generations, shown in the economic, societal, and environmental areas, a change in the way of thinking in terms of these issues is detected; not only in the minds of consumers but also in those of business actors and policymakers. Therefore, a rise in the want and need of implementing sustainability in an organization has been observable. Moreover, the concept of sustainability incorporates challenging conventional practices and thinking in terms of long-, as well as short-term well-being. Additionally, it incorporates an analysis of the core issues when making decisions, while recognizing the connection and interdependencies within the field. Furthermore, it is defined as an open-ended process, though confined through limitations, but also infinite opportunities for creative innovation. It is found within a context of complexity and unpredictable situations, where safety measures are paramount while recognizing crossovers in means and ends in terms of culture, governance, ecology, society, as well as economy (Elliot, 2013; Scoones, 2007). In terms of *sustainability dimensions*, Seghezzo (2009) builds upon the dimensions of *Economy*, *Environment*, and *Society*, which traditionally are represented within the concept of the *Triple Bottom Line*, which will be viewed as the basis for this research.

Consequently, this research sets out to analyze the relationship between an individual's affinity toward sustainability and the occurrence of sustainable entrepreneurship. It is of interest to find out if grit plays an important role in this relationship, and whether it positively influences sustainable entrepreneurship (SE). This body of work wants to fill the literary gap between sustainability orientation, entrepreneurship, and grit, as well as provide implications for the research on entrepreneurs' personalities. Furthermore, it highlights the importance of the malleable nature of one's personality. Additionally, it emphasizes the importance of combining current topics, like sustainability, with new emerging markets.

2 Literature-Based Hypotheses Development

An entrepreneur's impact on the performance of their organization is widely acknowledged, for instance, by Mitchelmore and Rowley (2008). Therefore, it is crucial to understand their behavior to, in turn, predict the organizational behavior, which incorporates the entrepreneur's values into the company culture. Regarding sustainable development, the implementation of sustainability by a company is believed to lead to long-term success, for example, by Gawel (2012). Her study argues that an entrepreneur's sustainability focus facilitates sustainable organizational behavior. Thus, it is hypothesized that:

H1. There is a positive relationship between sustainability focus and sustainable entrepreneurship.

Grit literature illustrates that being gritty is part of one's personality, ergo influenced by values and norms held by the individual. In this context, the character development model by Sweeney and Fry (2012) illustrates how values and beliefs are internalized to form one's identity. Therefore, the Perseverance of Effort and Consistency of Interest within grit are believed to be higher for areas that incorporate an individual's values and beliefs. This research argues that entrepreneurs need to find their frame of possibilities to use their impact to solve current sustainability issues. This led to the assumption that grit influences the occurrence of sustainable entrepreneurship, stemming from a sustainability orientation since entrepreneurs can realize their personal values and beliefs in their own company. Therefore, this study hypothesizes the following:

H2. The relationship between sustainability focus and sustainable entrepreneurship is mediated by grit.

The research framework has been illustrated in Appendix A.

3 Establishment of Entrepreneurs' Demographic Profile Through Data Collection

The quantitative methodology used primary data, which was collected by using a structured questionnaire, where the target population for the study was German entrepreneurs. The European Startup Monitor analyzes the entrepreneurial landscape in Germany in its 2016 country report (ESM, 2016). These statistics were used as a basis for the questions asked to generate the demographic profile. The sample was chosen with the convenience sampling technique making the result ungeneralizable. However, this technique was believed to be suitable due to the nature and context of the study, meaning SE. Furthermore, due to this research analyzing the status of SE in Germany, this sampling technique was also deemed suitable. Moreover, the respondents were chosen based on having founded a business, which they were still leading. It was not tested whether the respondents are entrepreneurs based on a certain scale, but the study relies on the respondents' self-definition as entrepreneurs. The respondents were selected through personal recommendations, LinkedIn, and a university newsletter in the field of entrepreneurship. The study generated a total of 29 respondents, of which one was deemed invalid regarding the open question "What industry is your company in?" but was retained due to the other answers being satisfactory. In the beginning, Microsoft Excel was used for dataset analysis to evaluate the entrepreneurs' general profiles and the company's profile. Later, the program as well as SPSS was used for hypothesis testing. Regarding the entrepreneurs' profiles, 48.3% were younger than 30 years old, 24.1% were 30–40 years old, and 27.6% were older than 40. Most of the respondents stated to be male (62.1%), 34.5% were female, and 3.4% identified as other. Moreover, more than half (55.2%) attained an Undergraduate or Graduate degree, 34.4% had less than an Undergraduate degree, and 10.3% stated their highest educational achievement to be higher than a Graduate degree. In relation to the company profiles, the given answers on the company's industry were adjusted to portray representative categories. The top represented industry was Retail (24.1%), and the second was identified to be Marketing (20.7%). Moreover, 24.1% of the companies exist for less than two years, 20.7% exist for two to three years, and the majority (55.2%) have been in existence for more than three years. Most of the companies have less than ten employees (62.1%), 27.6% have more than 20, and only 10.3% have ten to 20 employees, including the founders. Regarding the average annual turnover, the majority (48.3%) reported having less than 250,000 EUR, and 27.6% stated to generate more than 1,000,000 EUR, closely followed by companies earning between 250,000 EUR and 1,000,000 EUR (24.1%). Lastly, most respondents (75.9%) stated to have founded less than two companies, 13.8% said to have founded two or three companies, and 10.3% responded to have founded more than three companies in the past (Appendix B).

4 Measurement Through Questionnaire and Higher Order Construct Formation

The questionnaire consists of 30 items measured using a five-point Likert scale, anchored from 1(= strongly disagree) to 5(= strongly agree), except for the grit scale which was anchored from 1(= not at all like me) to 5(= very much like me). Sustainability focus was measured by also adopting the items of Hooi et al. (2016), who named it *sustainability orientation*, where they adopted the six-item scale from Kuckertz and Wagner (2010). The respondents' grit levels were measured by adopting the ten-item scale from Duckworth (2017), where five items measured the Consistency of Interest, and the Perseverance of Effort was measured by the other five items of the scale. Each of the dimensions of SE were measured by items adopted from Hooi et al. (2016). Fifteen items measured SE, constructing the *Triple Bottom Line*, the researchers adopted four items for the economic impact from Ahmad and Seet (2009). Additionally, seven items were taken for measuring society impact. Lastly, four items to measure the environmental impact are all taken from Turker (2009). The variables' internal consistency was deemed to be satisfactory. The Cronbach's alpha was calculated before adjustment and shall be used as a first assessment of the variables' internal consistency. Since the scales concerning SE were adapted from Hooi et al. (2016) without making any changes to them, the following remains to be true: "sustainable entrepreneurship has been modelled to be a higher order formative construct, formed by the three first-order constructs, namely, economic, environment and society" (p. 1625). Regarding the second-order reflective construct grit, it was modeled with two first-order reflective constructs (Consistency of Interest and Perseverance of Effort).

5 How Are Sustainability Focus, Grit, and Sustainable Entrepreneurship Related?—Data Analysis Results

Regarding the assessment of the respondents' grit levels, the method suggested by Duckworth (2017) was used. Hereby, the points given for each question (ranging from 1 to 5) are added together and are subsequently divided by ten. Therefore, a result of 5 would suggest an extremely high level of grit, whereas the lowest possible score of 1 suggests the opposite. Moreover, a score of 4.1 puts the respondent into the 70% percentile, meaning that the individual is grittier than 70% of the adults in the given sample. The results of this survey were compared to a sample of American adults. Within the given sample a large range of grit scores was detected, ranging from 2.9 (18% percentile) to 4.8 (97% percentile). Significantly, a higher frequency of responses was detected regarding the grit scores of 3.2 (4 respondents), 3.5 (6 respondents), and 3.9 (5 respondents). In other words, entrepreneurs are grittier than 26.5% (grit score 3.2), 40% (grit score 3.5), and 60% (grit score 3.9) of American adults, respectively. However, it was found that, on average, German entrepreneurs have an average grit score of 3.6, suggesting that they are, on average, grittier than roughly 44% of American adults (Appendix C). Moreover, it could be assumed that grit levels in older people would be higher compared to those of younger people. However, this could not be seen in the given sample, due to the range of grit scores being 3.2 (lowest) to 4.8 (highest) in the age category "Older than 40" (indicated by the number 3 on the y-axis). Again, the highest possible grit score is 5, and the lowest is 1 (Duckworth, 2017). Therefore, the theory of grit growing with age through life experience, as suggested by Duckworth et al. (2007), was not supported among the surveyed German entrepreneurs (Appendix D).

In terms of the analysis of the measurement model, for this study, the convergent and discriminant validity of the measurement model were tested, where Khan et al. (2016) provide the reasoning for doing so. To adequately assess the convergent validity, the following was pursued. For reflective scale measurement the convergent validity, factor loading, composite reliability (CR), and average variance extracted (AVE) were measured, with reference to Rahman et al. (2015). For this study, the factor loading cut-off value was set at 0.5, as suggested by Hair et al. (2010), which led to the exclusion of nine items: SF 4 and SF 6 (Sustainability focus); CI 2 (Consistency of Interest); PE 1, PE 2, and PE 5 (Perseverance of Effort); EC 4 (Economic); as well as SC 4 and SC 6 (Society). Moreover, the convergent reliability was deemed satisfactory, based on its range between 0.764 and 0.930 being above 0.7, with reference to Hair et al. (2010). The higher-order construct grit, a reflective second-order factor is represented by seven first-order items with reflective scale measurement, whereas the higher-order construct sustainable entrepreneurship is a formative second-order factor, represented by twelve first-order items, also with reflective scale measurement. Regarding the first, the CR was not calculated since it was not needed for the assessment of the discriminant validity later. However, in this context, the CR scores of the first-order constructs Consistency of Interest (CI) and Perseverance of interest (PI) are satisfactory. Generally, Hair et al. (2013) suggest that composite reliability shall be considered instead of Cronbach's Alpha, which is why this study adopted this approach. The latent variables' AVE, where Hair et al. (2010) recommended a level of 0.5, was deemed satisfactory since it ranged from 0.544 to 0.675. Regarding the formative scale measurement, and as suggested by Hair et al. (2011), the p-value and t-value were assessed to show whether the indicators have a significant effect on the latent variable, in this case, sustainable entrepreneurship. To run the analysis, a bootstrapping procedure for multiple regression was used with 2000 resamples, with reference to Yu (2002). For the confidence interval function in SPSS, the Bias Corrected accelerated (BCa) was used as a more accurate approach to estimating the 95% confidence interval level, as suggested by Fox (2008). Additionally, the variance inflation factor (VIF), showing the multicollinearity of the indicators, was examined to assess the convergent validity. Moreover, VIF values should be below 3.33, with reference to Diamantopoulos and Siguaw (2006), which they are. Even though, only the Economic results show a p-value of <0.01, Environment and Social, were retained due to the VIF meeting the requirement, as done by Hooi et al. (2016). Therefore, the convergent validity regarding the formative scale measurement is fulfilled (Appendix E). After analyzing the convergent validity, the discriminant validity regarding the reflective scale measurements was conducted. To confirm the discriminant validity, the Fornell-Larcker Criterion was adopted, regarding which the squared root of each latent variable's AVE is supposed to be higher than the correlations of the other latent constructs with reference to Fornell and Larcker (1981). The results show that the discriminant validity for the three given constructs (sustainability focus, grit, and sustainable entrepreneurship) can be deemed satisfactory. Summarizing these findings, it can be said that both convergent and discriminant validity for this study are adequate (Appendix F). Regarding the structural model, it is analyzed based on the path coefficient and value of R^2 to measure its predictive power, with reference to Rahman et al. (2015). Furthermore, a Sobel test was conducted for testing the mediating relationship in the model, with reference to Sobel (1982).

5.1 Analysis of the Direct Relationship Between Sustainability Focus and Sustainable Entrepreneurship

Sustainability focus was found to be positively correlated with sustainable entrepreneurship with a ß-value of 0.551 ($p < 0.01$), consequently, leading to H1 being supported. This result suggests that an entrepreneur's individual sustainability focus favors undertaking the creation of sustainable entrepreneurship. These findings support remarks made by Haldar (2019), stating that for *ecopreneurship* and sustainable entrepreneurship to occur, sustainability orientation and/or personal motivation are required as internal factors to enable SE. Moreover, the R^2 of sustainable entrepreneurship was 0.303, meaning that 30.3% of the variance can be explained by sustainability focus, more specifically by its Environment, Economic, and Social dimension. Based on guidelines by Cohen (1988) on interpreting the R^2, the value of sustainable entrepreneurship is substantial.

5.2 Analysis of the Mediating Relationship Through Grit

To analyze the mediation relationship within the model, a bivariate regression analysis was conducted between the independent variable sustainability focus and the mediator grit. It was revealed that the direct effect between the two was statistically unsatisfactory, with a significance value of −0.475. For the sake of completeness, the analysis was carried out completely. Consequently, a multiple regression analysis with sustainability focus and grit as predictors and sustainable entrepreneurship as the dependent variable was conducted to estimate the effect between sustainability focus and sustainable entrepreneurship (ß = 0.710, standard error = 0.246), and, additionally between grit and sustainable entrepreneurship (ß = −0.255, standard error = 0.353). To further estimate and test the indirect effect for statistical significance a Sobel test was conducted, as mentioned previously. Unsurprisingly, the ß-value (−0.701) and significance level of 0.257 ($p > 0.01$) were insufficient. Thus, H2 was rejected. These results of the study indicate that grit is not a mediating factor between sustainability focus and sustainable entrepreneurship, and a positive relationship between sustainability focus and grit cannot be identified (Appendix G).

6 Discussion

The goal of this research was to analyze the relationship between sustainability focus and sustainable entrepreneurship, as well as see whether a possible presence of a mediating role of grit between the two could be detected. The findings of the empirical study imply that sustainability focus is an antecedent for sustainable entrepreneurship. Thus, supporting the statement made by Ploum et al. (2018), finding that pro-environmental behavior values are antecedents for being able to identify opportunities for sustainable development. Additionally, what it also suggests is that an entrepreneur's personal values and beliefs influence how they shape their ventures, with reference to Gawel (2012). Consequently, the assumption that an individual that advocates for sustainability in their private life does so as well in their professional life, can be made. Since the mediation analysis was not significant, the empirical study's results do not show that entrepreneurs are generally grittier than American adults. As previously stated, the entrepreneurs in this sample might be, for instance, in the 60% percentile, meaning that they are grittier than 60% of the American adults in the given sample. However, they might also be grittier than just 26.5%, among other scores. These fluctuations may be accountable to grit scores being highly individual, as suggested by Duckworth (2017), meaning that the higher or lower grit level is not attributed to the fact that the respondents are entrepreneurs, but rather to other factors making up their personality in the moment of questioning. Future research should take into consideration a larger sample size to prove or disprove the assumption that entrepreneurs are, on average, grittier than other adults. Furthermore, the results of this research cannot identify a positive relationship between sustainability focus and grit. This is perhaps due to two factors. First, the grit scores among German entrepreneurs are significantly lower than expected, compared to American adults. Based on other publications, for instance by Duckworth et al. (2007), grit correlates with personality traits associated with entrepreneurs, namely conscientiousness. Thus, it was assumed that entrepreneurs generally exhibit higher grit levels than the average adult, but this was not reflected in the sample. Regarding the demographic profile of the sample, an indicator for the lower grit scores is the fact that 75.9% founded fewer than two companies. However, this might also be due to 48.3% of the respondents being less than 30 years old. Nonetheless, the companies owned by the respondents can be considered small, since 48.3% generate less than EUR 250,000 on average, and 62.1% have less than ten employees. In conclusion, a sample of entrepreneurs with higher grit levels and economically more successful companies, i.e., average revenue above EUR 250,00, might lead to the positive relationship between sustainability focus and grit, which should be the focus of future research. The suggestion that this might already be achieved by having a bigger sample size leading to a higher average grit score can be made, based on the variance in grit scores in the smaller sample. Secondly, respondents were chosen based on their self-assessment of being entrepreneurs, which was not measured statistically. Therefore, there might perhaps be a questionable relationship between entrepreneurship and sustainable entrepreneurship because it is not clear if respondents would be classified as entrepreneurs, based on scales adopted, for instance, by Cardon et al. (2012). In other words, if the respondents were not defined as entrepreneurs, based on the literature, this could be the reason for lower grit levels than expected. Additionally, sustainable entrepreneurship could then not occur, since entrepreneurship is considered its antecedent, with reference to Hooi et al. (2016). In the context of the German entrepreneurial landscape, the European Startup Monitor finds that 66.2% of the startup founders advocate for social engagement, and 57.4% of those value economically sustainable development of the business (ESM, 2016). Therefore, a trend towards sustainable entrepreneurship was already detected in 2016 and is assumed to become stronger in the next years. Thus, German entrepreneurs will benefit from developing a sustainability focus to adapt to current market changes. Those market changes are represented in the changing mindset of consumers as well, where, especially in Germany, businesses receive an advantage when positioning themselves as sustainably responsible, with reference to Maignan (2001). Moreover, given the long-term nature of sustainability, it is assumed that it will provide the business with a long-term advantage, since life is sustained for future generations, opening doors to future revenue generation. Grit is developable, with reference to Duckworth (2017), and in the context of this research, the level of displaying Consistency of Interest and Perseverance of Effort cannot be too high. Therefore, entrepreneurs would also benefit from consciously developing their grit level, which is assumed to positively correlate with the success of the venture, with reference to Butz et al. (2018). Since sustainability entrepreneurship focuses on personal skill and initiative, it is clear why it provides the starting point for societal change. In other words, entrepreneurs are needed to develop environmental and/or social innovations to achieve market success, and subsequently, societal change toward a more sustainable future for all.

7 Limitations

There are two major limitations to the current research. Generally, this study relied on a self-report questionnaire, for which the limitations are well known, with reference to, for example, Paulhus (1991). Consequently, the study relied on the respondents' self-assessment of being entrepreneurs and might not theoretically be classified as such. Therefore, the need to restructure the model by changing the variables was identified to correctly assess if respondents can theoretically be categorized as entrepreneurs as well. It is proposed to set the independent variable as entrepreneurship, and consequently, have two dependent variables, namely sustainable entrepreneurship, and grit, with the mediator still being sustainability focus, leading to two new hypotheses with a mediation role of sustainability focus. Lastly, the sample size of 29 may be considered too small, therefore, this research should be redone with a bigger sample size to get a more accurate result. A sample size of 200 is suggested, with reference to Hair et al. (2010) (Appendix H).

8 Conclusion

Entrepreneurs have always been drivers of innovation by providing the market with solutions to existing problems. One of those problems, with increasing importance in recent years, has been the issue of sustainability. Sustainable entrepreneurial action can bridge the wish for economic success and innovative ecological problem-solving. The importance of sustainability, embodied in personal goals and preferences by the entrepreneur, is thus reflected in the venture's goals and objectives. Therefore, the company is influenced by the entrepreneur's personality, which is supported by the empirical research finding, that sustainability orientation acts as an antecedent for sustainable entrepreneurship. Since the entrepreneur's personality (made up of a moral code, values, norms, etc.) detrimentally influences the company they found, it led to the inclusion of the third dimension of grit into this body of work. To answer the question, "How do successful people do it?" posed in the very beginning, it can be said that it comes down to their personality and their willingness and readiness to work on achieving a goal over a long period of time. In other words, they view success as a marathon, not a sprint, and do not give up, even when disappointed. Moreover, generally, a high level of grit has been found to correlate with entrepreneurial behavior, which led to the assumption that a high level of grit would enhance the level of sustainable entrepreneurship, especially in those with a pre-existing sustainability focus. Against the previous assumption, this sample of entrepreneurs was, on average, grittier than just 44% of American adults. Additionally, no positive relationship between sustainability focus and grit could be detected. However, the notion that grit acts as a mediator between the two variables should not be discredited, due to this sample size being too small. Moreover, an adjusted framework could prove that respondents truly are entrepreneurs. Therefore, this study should be redone according to the new framework with a larger sample size to better test the hypotheses. Additionally, another focus of future research could be the lack of previous literature on the question of whether gender generally influences grit levels, which was not part of this research due to the limited space provided. Practically, this research has shown the importance of sustainability and personality research in the entrepreneurial field. Regarding grit and its practical implication, personality is the antecedent for entrepreneurial action. Thus, highlighting the importance of parental figures and educators fostering grit in young people. Moreover, this would benefit the economy in the long term by raising entrepreneurs who will solve future issues through innovative solutions. On another note, sustainability should be supported by a change in environmental policies to provide access to chances for future entrepreneurs. The establishment and changing of existing companies hold a wide range of opportunities for economic pressure on legislation to change regulations and for economic success. But most importantly, pro-environmental behavior leads to personally perceived happiness, with reference to Corral-Verdugo et al. (2011), leading the way to collective happiness for society, while in turn, benefitting our environment for future generations to come.

Appendix A

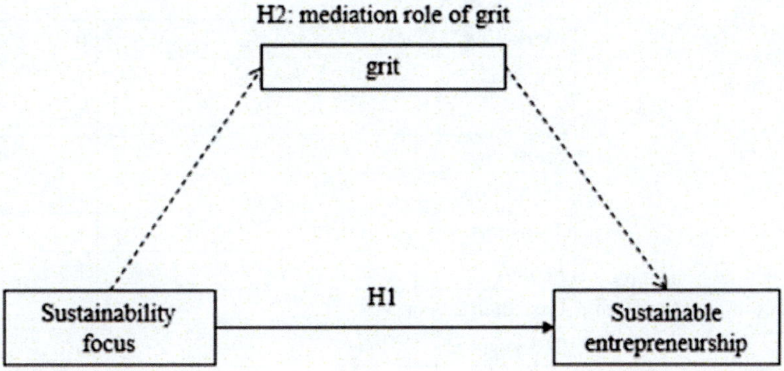

Fig. A.1 Proposed framework

Appendix B

Table B.1 Demographic profile (adapted from Hooi et al., 2016)

Demographic variable	Category	Frequency	(%)
Age	Younger than 30	14	48.3
	30–40 years old	7	24.1
	Older than 40	8	27.6
Gender	Female	10	34.5
	Male	18	62.1
	Other	1	3.4

(continued)

Table B.1 (continued)

Demographic variable	Category	Frequency	(%)
Education	Less than Undergraduate degree (Bachelor)	10	34.5
	Undergraduate degree (Bachelor) or Graduate degree (Master)	16	55.2
	Higher than Graduate degree	3	10.3
Industry (adjusted)	Consulting	2	6.9
	Education	1	3.45
	Engineering	2	6.9
	Event	1	3.45
	Finance	3	10.3
	Food & Beverage	2	6.9
	Marketing	6	20.7
	Pharma	1	3.5
	Retail	7	24.1
	Sport	1	3.45
	Technology	1	3.45
	Transport	1	3.45
	Invalid	1	3.45
Age of company (years of establishment)	Less than 2 years	7	24.1
	2–3 years	6	20.7
	More than 3 years	16	55.2
Number of full-time employees	Less than 10 employees	18	62.1
	10–20 employees	3	10.3
	More than 20 employees	8	27.6
Average annual turnover	Less than 250,000 EUR	14	48.3
	250,000–1,000,000 EUR	7	24.1
	More than 1,000,000 EUR	8	27.6
Number of startups founded	Less than 2 companies	22	75.9
	2 or 3 companies	4	13.8
	More than 3 companies	3	10.3

Appendix C

Table C.1 Summarized grit scores

	Grit score	Percentile (%)	Frequency
Lowest	2.9	18	1
	3.2	26.5	4
	3.5	40	6
	3.9	60	5
Highest	4.8	97	1
Average	3.6	44	

Appendix D

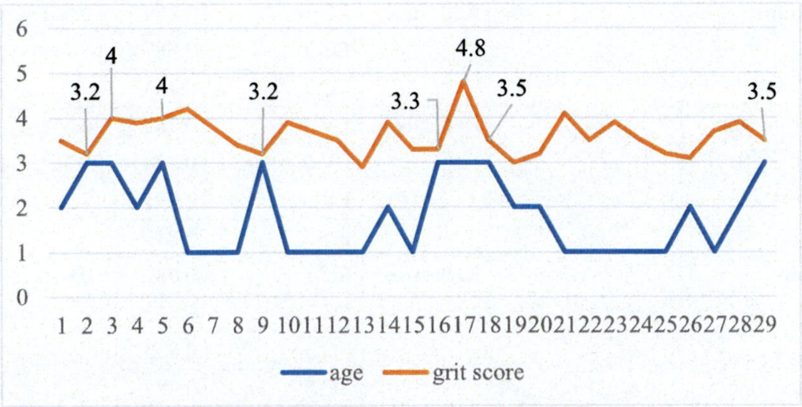

Fig. D.1 Relationship of age and grit scores in German entrepreneurs

Appendix E

Table E.1 Measurement model (adapted from Hooi et al., 2016)

First-order constructs	Second-order constructs	Scale type	Item	Factor loading	AVE	CR
Sustainability focus		Reflective	SF 1	0.840	0.663	0.886
			SF 2	0.728		
			SF 3	0.924		
			SF 5	0.749		
Consistency of interest		Reflective	CI 1	0.860	0.599	0.856
			CI 3	0.702		
			CI 4	0.816		
			CI 5	0.706		
Perseverance of effort		Reflective	PE 3	0.856	0.620	0.764
			PE 4	0.712		
			PE 5	0.538		
	Grit	Reflective			0.544	
Economic		Reflective	EC 1	0.809	0.675	0.861
			EC 2	0.887		
			EC 3	0.764		
Environment		Reflective	EV 1	0.762	0.653	0.930
			EV 2	0.720		
			EV 3	0.891		
			EV 4	0.849		
Society		Reflective	SC 1	0.782	0.616	0.889
			SC 2	0.722		
			SC 3	0.835		
			SC 5	0.787		
			SC 7	0.794		
				p-value	t-value	VIF
	Sustainable entrepreneurship	Formative	Economic	< 0.001	3.550	1.429
			Environment	0.287	1.190	1.038
			Social	0.144	2.361	1.025

Appendix F

Table F.1 Discriminant validity of construct (adapted from Hooi et al., 2016)

Constructs	SF	Grit	SE
Sustainability focus (SF)	*0.814*		
Grit	0.555	*0.738*	
Sustainability Entrepreneurship (SE)	0.638	0.349	*Formative*

Appendix G

Table G.1 Summary of hypotheses testing (adapted from Hooi et al., 2016)

Hypothesis	Relationship	ß	Standard error	t-value	p-value	Decision
H1	SF → SE	0.551	0.448	3.427	0.002	*Supported*
		Sobel Test (z-value)				
H2	SF → grit → SE	– 0.701	0.258	–	0.483	*Not supported*

Appendix H

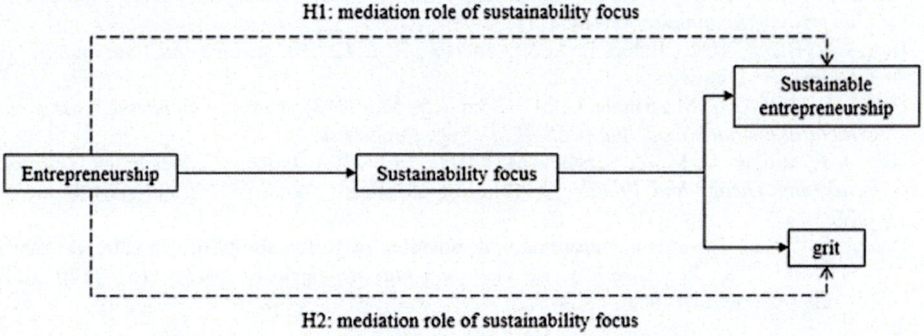

Fig. H.1 Adjusted framework for future research

References

Ahmad, N. H., & Seet, P. S. (2009). Understanding business success through the lens of SME founder-owners in Australia and Malaysia. *International Journal Entrepreneurial Venturing, 1*(1), 72–87. https://doi.org/10.1504/IJEC.2009.023821

Busenitz, L. W., & Barney, J. B. (1997). Differences between entrepreneurs and managers in large-organizations: Biases and heuristics in strategic decision-making. *Journal of Business Venturing, 12*(1), 9–30. https://doi.org/10.1016/S0883-9026(96)00003-1

Butz, N. T., Hanson, S., Schultz, P. L., & Warzynski, M. M. (2018). Beyond the big five: Does grit influence the entrepreneurial intent of university students in the US? *Journal of Global Entrepreneurship Research, 8*(15), 1–16. https://doi.org/10.1186/s40497-018-0100-z

Cardon, M. S., Gregoire, D. A., Stevens, C. E., & Patel, P. C. (2012). Measuring entrepreneurial passion: Conceptual foundations and scale validation. *Journal of Business Venturing, 28*(3), 373–396. https://doi.org/10.1016/j.jbusvent.2012.03.003

Cohen, J. (1988). *Statistical power analysis for the behavioral sciences* (2nd ed.). Lawrence Erlbaum Associates.

Corral-Verdugo, V., Mireles-Acosta, J., Tapia-Fonllem, C., & Fraijo-Sing, B. (2011). Happiness as correlate of sustainable behavior: A study of pro-ecological, frugal equitable and altruistic actions that promote subjective wellbeing. *Research in Human Ecology, 18*(2), 95–104.

Diamantopoulos, A., & Siguaw, J. A. (2006). Formative versus reflective indicators in organizational measure development: A comparison and empirical illustration. *British Journal of Management, 17*(4), 263–282. https://doi.org/10.1111/j.1467-8551.2006.00500.x

Duckworth, A. L., & Quinn, P. D. (2009). Development and validation of the short grit Scale (grit-S). *Journal of Personality Assessment, 91*(2), 166–174. https://doi.org/10.1080/00223890802634290

Duckworth, A. L., Peterson, C., Matthews, M. D., & Kelly, D. R. (2007). Grit: Perseverance and passion for long-term goals. *Journal of Personality and Social Psychology, 92*(6), 1087–1101. https://doi.org/10.1037/0022-3514.92.6.1087

Duckworth, A. L. (2017). *GRIT: Why passion and resilience are the secrets to success* (2nd ed.). Vermilion.

Elliot, J. A. (2013). *An introduction to sustainable development* (4th ed.). Routledge.

ESM (European Startup Monitor). (2016). *European Startup Monitor 2016—Country Report Germany*. https://europeanstartupmonitor.com/esm/country-reports/

Fornell, C., & Larcker, D. F. (1981). Evaluating structural equation models with unobservable variables and measurement error. *Journal of Marketing Research, 18*(1), 39–50. https://doi.org/10.1177/002224378101800104

Fox, J. (2008). *Bootstrapping regression models: Appendix to An R and S-Plus companion to applied regression*. https://socialsciences.mcmaster.ca/jfox/Books/Companion-1E/appendix-bootstrapping.pdf

Gawel, A. (2012). Entrepreneurship and sustainability: Do they have anything in common? *Poznan University of Economics Review, 12*(1), 5–16.

Hair, J. F., Black, W. C., Babin, B. J., & Anderson, R. E. (2010). *Multivariate data analysis* (7th ed.). Pearson Prentice.

Hair, J. F., Hult, G. T. M., Ringle, C. M., & Sarstedt, M. (2013). *A primer on partial least squares structural equation modeling (PLS-SEM)*. Sage Publishers.

Hair, J. F., Ringle, C. M., & Sarstedt, M. (2011). PLS-SEM: Indeed a silver bullet. *Journal of Marketing Theory and Practice, 19*(2), 139–151. https://doi.org/10.2753/MTP1069-6679190202

Haldar, S. (2019). Towards a conceptual understanding of sustainability-driven entrepreneurship. *Corporate Social Responsibility and Environmental Management, 26*(6), 1157–1170. https://doi.org/10.1002/csr.1763

Hooi, H. C., Ahmad, N. H., Amran, A., & Rahman, S. A. (2016). The functional role of entrepreneurial orientation and entrepreneurial bricolage in ensuring sustainable entrepreneurship. *Management Research Review, 39*(12), 1616–1638. https://doi.org/10.1108/MRR-06-2015-0144

Khan, E. A., Dewan, M. N. A., & Chowdhury, M. H. (2016). Reflective or formative measurement model of sustainability factor? A three industry comparison. *Corporate Ownership and Control Journal, 13*(2), 83–92. https://doi.org/10.22495/cocv13i2p9

Kuckertz, A., & Wagner, M. (2010). The influence of sustainability orientation on entrepreneurial intentions – investigating the role of business experience. *Journal of Business Venturing, 25*(5), 524–539. https://doi.org/10.1016/j.jbusvent.2009.09.001

Maignan, I. (2001). Consumers' perceptions of corporate social responsibilities: A cross-cultural comparison. *Journal of Business Ethics, 30*(1), 57–71. https://doi.org/10.1023/A:106433928640

Mitchelmore, S., & Rowley, J. (2013). Entrepreneurial competencies of women entrepreneurs pursuing business growth. *Journal of Small Business and Enterprise Development, 20*(1), 125–142. https://doi.org/10.1108/14626001311298448

Mitchelmore, S., & Rowley, J. (2008). Entrepreneurial competencies: A literature review and development agenda. *International Journal of Entrepreneurial Behaviour and Research, 16*(2), 92–111.

Paulhus, D. L. (1991). Measurement and control of response Bias'. In J. P. Robinson, P. R. Shaver, & L. S. Wrightsman (Eds.), *Measures of personality and social psychological attitudes* (pp. 17–59). Academic Press.

Ploum, L., Blok, V., Lans, T., & Omta, O. (2018). Exploring the relation between individual moral antecedents and entrepreneurial opportunity recognition for sustainable development. *Journal of Cleaner Production, 172*(1), 1582–1591. https://doi.org/10.1016/j.jclepro.2017.10.296

Rasmussen, E., Mosey, S., & Wright, M. (2011). The evolution of entrepreneurial competencies: A longitudinal study of university spin-off venture emergence. *Journal of Management Studies, 48*(6), 1314–1345. https://doi.org/10.1111/j.1467-6486.2010.00995.x

Rahman, S. A., Amran, A., Ahmad, N. H., & Taghizadeh, S. K. (2015). Supporting entrepreneurial business success at the base of pyramid through entrepreneurial competencies. *Management Decision, 53*(6), 1203–1223. https://doi.org/10.1108/MD-08-2014-0531

Scoones, I. (2007). Sustainability. *Development in Practice, 17*(4–5), 589–596. https://doi.org/10.1080/09614520701469609

Seghezzo, L. (2009). The five dimensions of sustainability. *Environmental Politics, 18*(4), 539–556. https://doi.org/10.1080/09644010903063669

Sobel, M. E. (1982). Asymptotic confidence intervals for indirect effects in structural equation models. *Sociological Methodology, 13*(1), 290–312. https://doi.org/10.2307/270723

Sweeney, P. J., & Fry, L. W. (2012). Character development through spiritual leadership. *Consulting Psychology Journal: Practice and Research, 64*(2), 89–107. https://doi.org/10.1037/a0028966

Turker, D. (2009). Measuring corporate social responsibility: A scale development study. *Journal of Business Ethics, 85*(1), 411–427. https://doi.org/10.1007/s10551-008-9780-6

Yu, C. H. (2002). Resampling methods: Concepts, research, and evaluation, *Practical Assessment, Research, and Evaluation, 8*(8), n.p. https://doi.org/10.7275/9cms-my97

Exploring Opportunities for the Enhancement of International Academic Collaboration

Christoph Neu

Abstract This research deals with international academic collaborations in higher education, primarily focusing on the Trans-Atlantic Virtual Exchange and Collaboration (TAVEC) project. The "Corona Virus Disease 2019" (COVID-19) pandemic did not only have an impact on the economy, such as remote working within companies but also on higher education institutions, such as methods to enable distance learning. The educational system had to accomplish a paradigm shift that had an impact on both students and the faculty staff. To conduct an international academic collaboration with another universities, higher education institutions had to decide on a concept for collaborating virtually. Therefore, the international Business school of Hochschule Fresenius (HSF) and the Adelphi University (AU) in New York started a collaboration that consisted out of a virtual collaboration and a mobile component. This concept, which is a fusion of virtual collaboration and a physical meeting between the project partners, is called "Blended Mobility". Still, international academic collaborations, such as TAVEC may face challenges during the process. Aspects such as time difference and cultural backgrounds need to be considered while implementing such an international academic collaboration. The research of this thesis has shown that the mobility component of the TAVEC project did have an impact on the students' learning experiences. In addition to that, the integrated workshops and lectures held by faculty staff from both universities and guest speakers, led to a knowledge increase and exchange, as well for the students and the faculty staff. Further recommendations, can be given, based on a number of surveys, that have been conducted concerning the previous two TAVEC projects (TAVEC I and II). Further recommendations for potential marketing strategies can be given and new marketing tools are being introduced. Furthermore, the potential process of TAVEC III is being explored and suggested.

Keywords Digitalization · International · Project · Education · Collaboration

C. Neu (✉)
E-Commerce Institut, Cologne, Germany
e-mail: christoph.neu93@gmail.com

R. C. Geibel and S. Machavariani (eds.), *Chances and Challenges of Digital Management*, Springer Proceedings in Business and Economics,
https://doi.org/10.1007/978-3-031-45601-5_17

1 Introduction

The following scientific article will examine opportunities for the enhancement of an international academic collaboration. In order to visualize these potential improvements, a case study will be presented within this article.

How can international academic collaborations in higher education be enhanced in general, and how is the virtual collaboration between Hochschule Fresenius (HSF) and Adelphi University (AU) conducted and can be improved in the future? The relevance of international academic collaborations is given due to the increased international focus of higher education institutions and the special challenges caused by the difficult situation regarding the Corona Virus Disease 2019 (COVID-19).

The goal of increasing internationalization is an integral part of many areas of society, particularly for higher education institutions. Germany is among the most popular host countries for internationally mobile students worldwide. In 2018, the number of international students at German universities was 375,000 (Wahlers, 2019, p. 18).

According to a study conducted by the "Deutscher Akademischer Austauschdienst" (DAAD, n.d.), whose results and framework conditions were used to measure internationalization at 20 universities, Germany performed well in terms of its national framework conditions and promoting transnational education. Still the international student mobility in Germany can be improved. Germany could not meet its requirement of 50% of students staying abroad by 2020, achieving only 30% (Forschung & Lehre, 2019).

In that context, this research analyzes a project called TAVEC, a collaboration between the universities HSF (Germany) and AU (USA). This case study will show, how far international academic collaborations have evolved as a virtual collaboration.

2 Higher Education

The term "Higher Education" is described by the Cambridge dictionary as follows: "An education at a college or university where subjects are studied at an advanced level" (Cambridge Dictionary, n.d.a). This overview of the meaning of higher education also differentiates those institutions where a higher education can be achieved. There are multiple ways to earn a higher education degree. Depending on which career a person wants to follow, that person may need a certain kind of higher education (Boughey & Mckenna, 2021, pp. 1–3).

A major driver of the interest in higher education is the evolving globalization (Boughey & Mckenna, 2021, pp. 1–2), which can be defined as an increase of trade across the world, especially made by large companies producing goods around the world (Cambridge Dictionary, n.d.b). Further social components are the reduction of social differences and the better integration of social fringe groups (McDonnell-Naughten & Paunesu, 2022, p. 19).

2.1 The Scope of Higher Education in Germany

Through the growth of the global economy, the demand has risen to learn new skills and expand skillsets, and the demand for new knowledge has grown. Interest in attending universities has increased as governments around the world have wanted to support the notion of being "fueled by knowledge" (Boughey & Mckenna, 2021, p. 3).

Therefore, universities received support from governments, and governments invested in opportunities for higher education. As the number of students and their interests grew, the different study programs increasingly diversified and specified (Boughey & Mckenna, 2021, pp. 3–4). Through increased interest in higher education and the increase of study opportunities, the target group of universities extended, meaning that not only elite students from wealthy families could study, but also students with less financial resources (see Sect. 2.2 for further) (Boughey & Mckenna, 2021, p. 3). Higher education has to exhibit the current status of knowledge development to prepare students for an ever-changing future. For example, the curricula should focus on global knowledge and competencies (Jacobs et al., 2021, p. 353). Furthermore, internationalized curricula should be offered to students to foster internationalized learning experiences that embrace locality and diversity. (Jacobs et al., 2021, p. 354). Currently, many universities have adopted an internationalization strategy, supported also by politics. Internationalization offers advantages within the area of higher education. It can increase research quality and educational purposes, such as teaching and leraning. (Wahlers, 2019, p. 6). A better higher education also has an impact on social components. One aspect is for example the ensurence of job opportunities for young people. Therefore, higher education institutions should draw up a strategy plan on how, one the one hand social needs can be satisfied, and, on the other hand new job offers can be created. As an example, many higher education facilities run research offices and innovation departments within their campuses (McDonnell-Naughten & Paunesu, 2022, pp. 13, 19).

2.2 Challenges and Possibilities of Higher Education

The field of higher education not only offers multiple advantages and further possibilities for the students, but also poses multiple challenges.

At the beginning of the COVID-19 pandemic educational institutions, such as universities and other tertiary education facilities, were affected of closures. The consequences of this pandemic affected 1,6 billion learners across the world in more than 190 countries (United Nations, 2020, p. 2). To adapt to these circumstances and to ensure that the educational learning can be continued, universities had to make use of different electronic learning platforms (Wang & Xu, 2022, pp. 113–114). An eLearning platform uses the technology of the internet to create learning opportunities in a virtual classroom. (Gartner Glossary, n.d.). Thus meetings, courses and graduation ceremonies could be conducted, using a digital platform. These new digital possibilities still provide new challenges. Those challenges can be an unstable internet connection and a lack of digital access devices to participate. Another challenge can be considered in the lacking knowledge of the effective usage of digital learning platforms of both students and the faculty staff (Wang & Xu, 2022, p. 114).

In Germany, study programs in state universities are being funded by the state and the costs for pursuing a higher education can be financed through scholarships or student loans. If an aspiring student does not acquire state funding or gets financial support through family members, they must finance the higher education program alone. Self-funding can be an enabler for visiting a higher education institution, but it can also be a financial challenge since financial resources then need to be paid by the students themselves. Moreover, they must invest time to acquire the financial necessities, so the time they have for study can be reduced, which can negatively affect a student's educational performance (Apolinarski & Gwosc, 2020, pp. 120–123). Although many countries provide stated-funded universities and are led by governments who invest in education, the United States and other countries charge high amounts of money for education (DAAD, 2019, p. 3). One reason for the increase in tuition fees is the decrease in state funding. In that context, scholarships were also reduced. Students were required to pay higher fees, regardless of their socio-economic circumstances (Boughey & McKenna, 2021, p. 5).

Especially the high tuition fees in the U.S. cause many students to take out loans. This leads to a steady rise in graduate student debts. Due to the comparatively low tuition fees in Germany, the interest of U.S. Americans in completing an undergraduate bachelor's degree in Germany, is increasing (DAAD, 2019, p. 7).

In the financial context, higher education provides the opportunity of an increased salary, such as up to 84% higher payment for students with a bachelor's level added to their high school diploma in the US (William Peace University, 2019).

Aside from financial reasons to pursue a higher education, educating oneself can also be a personal goal. In that context, students can broaden their horizon and acquire new problemsolving methods. Therefore, an effect of higher education can be the furthering of research in different fields of science. New technologies can evolve, and progress can be made. The next possibility offered by higher education connects to the internationalization of academic collaborations. Despite the knowledge being transferred through the institution, students who participate in international study programs learn more about cultures and international businesses. The students get to extend their network internationally and obtain degrees (William Peace University, 2019).

3 International Academic Collaboration

In recent years, different universities have integrated international cooperation and collaboration into their mission. This knowledge that can be developed through a collaboration will benefit society (de Wit & Deca, 2015, pp. 3–4).

To start an international collaboration and find a global partner, a few steps must be taken. At the outset, both collaborative institutions should participate in a somewhat low-commitment partnership. It is important to identify success factors and consider problems that could arise. The success depends, in part, on mutual trust in the relationship. Therefore, a baseline of trust must be built first, and collaborative work is a good way to foster the relationship. In parallel, collaborating partners should develop mutual interests. Before considering a formal agreement both institutions should negotiate autonomy, the quality of the collaborative work, and academic freedom. Furthermore, the desired outcome of the project should be clarified. Issues such as resources and financing methods should be negotiated upfront. Moreover, both institutions should discuss their core values and goals. In conclusion, it is highly recommended that both collaborating partners strive for a relationship that includes the values of shared interest, mutual respect, and equality of decision making. Moreover, the whole process should be transparent (Antony & Nicola, 2020, pp. 83–84).

3.1 Virtual Collaborations

In comparison to non-virtual collaborations, virtual collaborations rely on digital platforms. Compared to a face-to-face communication, however (Schieffer, 2016, p. 112).

There are different understandings and definitions of the term "virtual collaboration." Coughlin and Kadjer define it as "A process that uses a variety of methods for professionals to work together, pool resources, communicate and share ideas, fostering opportunities for selfdevelopment" (Coughlin and Kadjer 2009 as cited in Schieffer, 2016, p. 110). A virtual collaboration can be conducted with the use of text-based platforms, virtual institutional platforms, a digital knowledge exchange within a group, and further channels or forums simplified using technical equipment (Schieffer, 2016, pp. 110, 113). The opportunity of virtual collaborations lies in the fact that collaborative group members can work on projects from different locations. This is possible because of the use of social networking applications (e.g., Facebook, Google Doc, Google Hangout, Instagram, WeChat, Word Online 365, and Line Group). These virtual platforms are being used as the basis for virtual collaborations (Vanichvatana, 2020, pp. 387–388).

Expressing and recognizing feelings and emotions can be difficult for collaborators, especially when communicating through a text- based-platform (Garrison et al. 2000 as cited in Schieffer, 2016, p. 112). In sum, because of the absence of visual communication and therefore the greater difficulty of interpreting feelings and emotions, virtual communication can allow mistrust to arise among collaboration partners (Schieffer, 2016, p. 112). A critical factor supporting virtual collaboration through these digital communication tools is trust between collaborators (DeRosa et al. 2004; Jarvenpaa and Leidner 1999; Moore 2006 as cited in Schieffer, 2016, p. 112). A foundation of strong trust among members of the collaboration group simplifies both the communication and the extent of an information exchange (Hu et al. 2011 as cited in Schieffer, 2016, p. 112). The critical ability of the members can also result from a strong foundation of trust (Hu et al. 2011 as cited in Schieffer, 2016, p. 112). This is due to the idea of trust and common purpose, being an attribute for a successful collaboration among professional learning communities (Moore 2006 as cited in Schieffer, 2016, p. 112). Furthermore, trust influences the amount of what a participant shares, and how criticism is being accepted (Schieffer, 2016, p. 112).

3.2 *Critical Success Factors for an International Academic Collaboration*

This section analyzes the key performance indicators (KPI) of successful international collaboration. A KPI is a general indicator of performance, focusing on the important components of output and income. Output results directly from the innovative effort of the organization manager, while outcomes are the consequence of innovation (Janger et al. 2017; Aurora and Kaur 2015 as cited in Sutanto et al., 2021, p. 14). Furthermore, in this context, the KPIs specify support of academic study, research, and society (Secundo et al. 2017 as cited in Sutanto et al., 2021, p. 14). A KPI is an identification number expressing a company's relative success and performance. This indicator is used in management and in controlling the company to measure and rate certain processes (Gabler Wirtschaftslexikon, 2018). These KPIs can define the success of an international collaboration. According to Martin (1981 cited by Coombe, 2016, p. 342) critical success factors can also be seen in barriers of successful collaborations. He mentions cost reductions and the degree of attention, the collaborating partners raise for the relevant objectives (Martin 1981 as cited in Coombe, 2016, p. 342).

There are different possibilities that apply to the measurement of success. One possible way of measuring the competencies of a participant of the collaboration is filling out a questionnaire by which students can rate their competencies prior to and after the collaborative project (Kolm et al., 2022, pp. 184–185).

The further indicators to measure the success of an international collaboration are as follows: the number of joint research papers, written by both partner institutions, and the number of research grants awarded through the added strength of the collaboration (Hamdullahpur, 2020, p. 24).

Another factor in measuring collaboration skills in higher education is the engagement of both collaborating partners in the project process (Xerri et al., 2018, p. 589). Student engagement contains the participation of students in several activities within higher education. Examples are the interchange with academic peers and instructors, the class attendance, and the involvement within extra-curricular projects (Schoffstall et al. 2013 cited by Xerri et al., 2018, p. 590). Further critical dimensions in university collaborations include the size, scope, and nature of the integration, as well as their intensity (Gunn, 2015, p. 13).

The KPI for a university success may include the five-year graduation rate (Badaway et al. 2016; Peter 2014 as cited in Sutanto et al., 2021, p. 14).

To measure the degree of internalization, an indicator could be the extent to which higher education facilities recruit students and academic teaching staff from different countries into their faculty study-program. Recruiting foreign students can be considered difficult for these countries, that do not have a high amount of foreign students yet. Therefore, universities develop solutions of making their study program more attractive for international students. An approach could be the offer of providing courses in the English language. Therefore, all foreign students can participate in the study program, without being forced to speak the language of the country, where the university is located. A further indicator is the amount of short-term exchanges of students in order to benefit from the travel study. The third indicator is the offer of foreign language teaching. In that context, the amount of students that enrolled in a foreign language course can be measured. In addition to that the variety of different languages can be measured as well. The fourth indicator is the international scope of the teaching faculty. Therefore, it must be evaluated where the faculty members come from and from which institution, they received their academic degree (Zajda & Jacob, 2022, pp. 7–8).

3.3 Networking Opportunities Through International Academic Collaborations

Academic collaboration provides the opportunity for students to extend their network to students from another university. According to Agranoff and Mcguire (2014 as cited in Ryu, 2014, p. 633), the term "networking" refers to the individual behavior of participants who want to activate, frame, mobilize, and interact in a network setting among each other. Networking requires more frequent interactions with partner and the way that a networking partner is selected may affect collaborative procedures and the success of the collaboration (Ryu, 2014, p. 633). If students can improve their existing network and extend it, they can raise intercultural awareness and gather new opportunities for innovation and research methods (Lanford, 2020, p. 92).

A further networking opportunity is the co-authoring between researchers who can help each other in publishing a scientific paper (Al-Youbi & Zahed, 2020, p. 5). The idea of a coauthorship collaboration is that the partners, who are collaborating, can distribute their financial expenses and resources. In addition to that, they can combine each other's knowledge. In that context, they can share their skills and develop new approaches to solve research problems. Moreover, transnational, or global problems can be considered (Khor & Yu, 2016, p. 1096).

4 TAVEC Project

The TAVEC was founded as an academic collaboration between the HSF in Cologne and AU in New York.

To enable an academic collaboration, the HSF decided to use the technology and opportunities of social media to connect students from the HSF and AU (TAVEC website, n.d.).

The TAVEC project offers a shared collaborative platform on which both students from HSF and AU work together on a joint project to approach a common goal (Hochschule Fresenius, 2021). The process of this project enables students from both countries not only to train their soft skills and broaden their horizons (DAAD, 2020, p. 2) in terms of cultural learnings, but also to compare work ethics and the working culture of the US and Germany. An example for a project submission in the Business ethics Master course, is a project which followed the objective of analyzing the company Amazon, regarding their ethical handling with warehouse employees. Therefore, cultural perceptions from German and US students were compared (TAVEC website, n.d.).

As an opportunity enabled by the COVID-19 pandemic, the project is being processed fully digitally using various online channels (e.g., Zoom/Microsoft Office, and WhatsApp) (DAAD, 2020, p. 2; Hochschule Fresenius, 2021).

The TAVEC project features an aspect of blended mobility, meaning that among the different project groups, both the students of HSF and the students of AU have had the chance to visit their counterparts in their home countries (TAVEC website, n.d.). The term "Blended Mobility" refers to the possibility to combine the faces of mobility learning in a different country with learning activities. Those activities are conducted among students with an approximately same age. The learning process is connected to virtual learning and therefore a mixture of online and offline learning. The online activities of the project can be conducted either before-, or after the physical mobility activity (School Education Gateway, 2020). Those activities can be projects that are being conducted between institutions in different countries. The concept of blended mobility has been enabled through a digital transformation and requires a decent amount of planning (School Education Gateway, 2020). A blended mobility project is therefore a virtual collaboration with an added mobility component (DAAD, n.d.b). A blended mobility project can be assessed on the following criteria: the teamwork, peer-to-peer assessment, the individual contribution in the process, the documentation, the report, and the interim and final presentation will be graded (Blended Mobility, 2017).

5 Outlook and Conclusion

The higher education in Germany and in the U.S. are different in some aspects. A major difference is that in the U.S. the degree is connected to high financial expenses, since students in the US must pay high student fees in contrast to German students on higher education state institutions, where they have to pay semester fees but are not charged for student's fees. This financial barrier can be overcome by offering scholarships or parental support.

Furthermore, higher education has the goal of a knowledge increase and exchange. Further opportunities, offered with the pursuit of a higher education, include the internationalization that universities are experiencing as a response to factors such as globalization. The research has shown that students can acquire international skills in an educational and cultural context. International academic collaborations provide opportunities for students to broaden their knowledge by collaborating with students from different countries. Both participating institutions need to communicate their objectives and work on a concept for the project implementation.

In that context, challenges can arise during an international collaboration. Depending on the countries, factors such as time zones must be considered. Especially in a virtual collaboration the digital infrastructure is an important requirement. Much organizational talent is required to organize and process such a collaboration.

These collaborations can also extend the network of students and faculty through co-authorship.

There are many forms of academic international collaborations, a higher education institution can offer. The focus lies on virtual collaborations and the concept of blended mobility. Certain opportunities can be taken to enhance those collaborations, based on the critical success factors of international collaboration and evaluation of methods such as surveys. Especially the meaning of the type of virtual collaborations changed in the times of COVID-19. Through technical devices, such as zoom, google docs or further different text-based or conference platforms, the everyday work could be continued. At first these digital platforms give higher education institutions the possibilities of joined collaborations and therefore increase their degree of internationalization. The use of digital communication platforms allows students from geographical distances- even transatlantic- to work together on a common project. For a virtual project, the access to Wi-Fi and power outlets are necessary and can give students the opportunity for a consistent location for learning and group meetings.

Regarding the internal requirements for the participation in virtual collaboration, students should provide communicational and self-organizational skills. They should also respect the opinions of others and develop trust-based relationships. Trust is especially important when the participants only or partly use text-based communication tools, which make the understanding of feelings and emotions difficult.

To sum up the opportunities to provide virtual collaboration, students and faculty staff profit from a knowledge-sharing and extension. Furthermore, they allow students and faculty members to work from different locations, meaning the project work is not bound to a geographical location. The increased usage of digital communication platforms established a basis for future virtual collaborations and concepts of blended mobility. The aspect of blended mobility has proven motivating for students and is praised by them and by the faculty of HSF and AU. It compromises an opportunity to support the fusion of virtual- and in-person collaboration. In a globalized world, connecting cultures and educational backgrounds can enable innovation and research. Therefore, it is important to further improve international academic collaborations with the use of digitalization as an enabler. Making use of digital virtual platforms tackle challenges such as the regulations through the COVID-19 pandemic, using it as an opportunity to generate new insights and enables international collaborations. Therefore, a recommendation for future projects is to enhance the implementation of many digital platforms and encourage further international academic collaborations.

References

Antony, J. S., & Nicola, T. (2020). The tricky terrain of global university partnerships. In A. Al-Youbi, A. H. M. Zahed, & W. G. Tierney (Eds.), *Successful global collaborations in higher education institutions* (pp. 7586). Springer.

Apolinarski, B., & Gwosc, C. (2020). Studienfinanzierung und studienbegleitende Erwerbstätigkeit als Determinanten des studentischen Workloads: Negative Effekte der Selbstfinanzierung? In D. Großmann, C. Engel, J. Justermann, & T. Wolbring (Hrsg,), *Studentischer Workload-Definition, Messung und Einflüsse* (pp. 119–143). Springer.

Blended Mobility. (2017). *What you need to know about blended mobility.* Retrieved July 7, 2022, from https://blendedmobility.com/en/about

Boughey, C., & McKenna, S. (2021). *Understanding higher educationalternative perspectives.* African Minds.

Bundesministerium für Bildung und Forschung. (2022). *Studium.* Retrieved July 2, 2022, from https://www.bmbf.de/bmbf/de/bildung/VIIambrid/VIIambrid_node.html

Cambridge Dictionary. (n.d.a). *Higher education.* Retrieved July 7, 2022, from https://dictionary.cambridge.org/de/worterbuch/englisch/higher-education

Cambridge Dictionary. (n.d.b). *Globalization.* Retrieved October 20, 2022, from https://dictionary.cambridge.org/de/worterbuch/englisch/globalization

Coombe, L. (2016). Models of interuniversity collaboration in higher education—How do their features act as barriers and enablers to sustainability? *Tertiary Education and Manangement, 21*(4), 328–348.

de Wit, H., & Deca, L. (2015). Internationalization of higher education, challenges and opportunities for the next decade. In A. Curaj, L. Deca, & R. Pricopie (Eds.), *European higher education-challenges for a new decade* (pp. 3–11). Springer.

Deutscher Akademischer Austauschdienst. (2019). *Kurze Einführung in das Hochschulsystem und die DAAD-Aktivitäten.* Retrieved July 4, 2022, from https://www2.daad.de/medien/der-daad/analysenstudien/laendersachstand/usa_daad_sachstand.pdf

Deutscher Akademsicher Austauschdienst. (2020). *DAAD SachberichtZwischennachweis 2020* (pp. 1–8).

Deutscher Akademischer Austauschdienst. (n.d.). *International Virtual Academic Collaboration (IVAC).* Retrieved October 15, 2022, from https://www.daad.de/de/infos-services-fuer-hochschulen/weiterfuehrendeinfos-zu-daad-foerderprogrammen/ivac/

Forschung & Lehre. (2019). *Deutsche Hochschulen besonders international ausgerichtet*. Retrieved October 14, 2022, from https://www.forschung-undlehre.de/politik/deutsche-hochschulen-besonders-internationalausgerichtet-2317

Gabler Wirtschaftslexikon. (2018). *Key performance indicator*. Retrieved July 7, 2022, from https://wirtschaftslexikon.gabler.de/definition/keyperformance-indicator-kpi-52670

Gartner Glossary. *E-Learning*. Retrieved October 10, 2022, from https://www.gartner.com/en/information-technology/glossary/e-learning

Gunn, A. (2015). The European universities initiative: A study of alliance formation in higher education. In A. Curaj, L. Deca, & R. Pricopie (Eds.), *European higher education-challenges for a new decade* (pp. 1330). Springer.

Hamdullahpur, F. (2020). Global citizens for the twenty-first century: The role of international partnerships in university education. In A. Al-Youbi, A. H. M. Zahed, & W. G. Tierney (Eds.), *Successful global collaborations in higher education institutions* (pp. 23–30). Springer.

Hochschule Fresenius. (2021). *Trans-Atlantic Virtual Exchange and Collaboration (TAVEC)*, Online Symposium International Reaching TU Braunschweig.

Jacobs, L., Wimpenny, K., Mitchell, L., Hagenmeier, C., Beelen, J., Hodges, M., et al. (2021). Adapting a capacity-development-in-higher- education project: Doing, being and becoming virtual collaboration. *Perspectives in Education, 39*(1), 353–371.

Khor, K. A., & Yu, L. G. (2016). Influence of international co-authorship on the research citation impact of young universities. *Scientometrics, 107*(3), 1095–1110.

Kolm, A., de Nooijer, J., Vanherle, K., Werkman, A., Wewerka-Kreimel, D., Rachman-Elbaum, S., et al. (2022). International online collaboration competencies in higher education students: A systematic review. *Journal of Studies in International Education, 26*(2), 183–201.

Lanford, M. (2020). Long-term sustainability in global higher education partnerships. In A. Al-Youbi, A. H. M. Zahed, & W. G Tierney (Eds.), *Successful global collaborations in higher education institutions* (pp. 8793). Springer.

McDonnell-Naughten, M., Paunesu, C. (2022). Facets of social innovation in higher education. In C. Paunescu, K-L. Lepik, N. Spencer (Eds.), *Social innovation in higher education-landscape, practises and opportunities* (pp. 9–35). Springer.

Ryu, S. (2014). Networking partner selection and its impact on the perceived success of collaboration. *Public Performance and Management Review, 37*(4), 632–657.

Schieffer, L. (2016). The benefits and barriers of virtual collaboration among online adjuncts. *Journal of Instructional Research, 5*, 109–125.

School Education Gateway. (2020). *Blended Mobility: die Neugestaltung unserer europäischen Zusammenarbeit*. Retrieved October 20, 2022, from https://www.schooleducationgateway.eu/de/pub/latest/news/blendedmobility-europe.htm

Sutanto, S., Christy, A. Y., & Sandi, D. K. (2021). Creative university: A definition and activities management based on the completion of key performance indicator (KPI). *Journal of Technology Management and Innovation, 16*(3), 13–20.

TAVEC website. (n.d.). *TAVEC-Trans-Atlantic Virtual Exchange and Collaboration*. Retrieved October 01, from https://www.tavec-project.com

United Nations. (2020). *Policy Brief: Education during COVID-19 and beyond*. Retrieved July 12, 2022, from https://unsdg.un.org/sites/default/files/202008/sg_policy_brief_covid-19_and_education_august_2020.pdf

Vanichvatana, S. (2020). How social network applications enhancing team project collaborations at home. *Cypriot Journal of Educational Sciences, 15*(2), 386–398.

Wahlers, M. (2019). *Die Internationalisierung der deutschen HochschulenAktuelle Entwicklungen und Trends*. Retrieved October 20, 2022, from https://www2.daad.de/medien/3daadhochschulpolitik_2019_internationalisierung_der_hochschulen_m.wahlers_pp-folien.pdf

Wang, X., & Xu, S. (2022). Global higher education technology trends and opportunities in a post-COVID-19 Context. In J. Zajda, W. J. Jacob (Eds.), *Discourses of globalisation and higher education reformsemerging paradigms-globalisation, comparative education and policy research*, 27 (pp. 113–126). Springer.

William Peace University. (2019). *12 reasons why higher education is important*. Retrieved October 20, 2022, from https://www.peace.edu/news/why-ishigher-education-important/

Xerri, M. J., Radford, K., & Shacklock, K. (2018). Student engagement in academic activities: A social support perspective. *Higher Education,* 75, 589605.

Zajda, J., & Jacob, W. J. (2022). Discourses of globalisation and higher education reforms: Emerging paradims. In J. Zajda, & W. J. Jacob (Eds.), *Discourses of globalisation and higher education reforms-emerging paradigms—Globalisation,comperative education and policy research,* 27 (pp. 1–17). Springer.

E-commerce in COVID-19, Analysis of Legislative Gap in Georgia

Ana Medzmariashvili

Abstract COVID-19 is considered to be one of the biggest crises in modern history and has become the main challenge for businesses. Due to the pandemic, digital transformations accelerated significantly. Commercial activities and social interactions were also shifted to digital space. Despite the contact restrictions, most companies survived their businesses by actively using digital technologies as an alternative channel to interact with their consumers. Moreover, some research presented that consumers indicated a preference for online retailing over physical shopping in the post-COVID-19 future. Of course, this fact will bring to the fore the significance of e-commerce in trade even once the pandemic is over. This paper assesses the impact of COVID-19 on e-commerce businesses across developed or developing countries and analyses the gaps in Georgian legislation to meet the expectations of the digitalization process in light of relevant EU legal acts. Although by Association Agreement Member states of the European Union and Georgia agree that electronic commerce increases trade opportunities in many sectors and Georgia undertakes to introduce new regulations in e-commerce, the initiated draft law of Georgia on "electronic commerce" has not been adopted yet. Furthermore, this paper reviews the effectiveness of the Georgian regulatory framework on electronic contracts and electronic signatures, since they are the main legal mechanisms to regulate e-commerce dealings, identifies ongoing Georgian legislative problems in this field, and indicates more national commitment toward e-commerce reforms to satisfy the fast-growing demands in digital space.

Keywords COVID-19 · E-commerce · Electronic contract · Electronic signature

A. Medzmariashvili (✉)
Faculty of Law and Social Sciences, East European University, Tbilisi, Georgia
e-mail: ana.medzmariashvili@eeu.edu.ge

R. C. Geibel and S. Machavariani (eds.), *Chances and Challenges of Digital Management*, Springer Proceedings in Business and Economics,
https://doi.org/10.1007/978-3-031-45601-5_18

1 Introduction

The implementation and advancement of digital technologies have made an immense impact on the global economy. It created a large range of possibilities, especially, it made communication accessible throughout the world and simplified the way of interaction with different nations.

Some companies and entrepreneurs benefited from that opportunity and launched to interrelate with their customers distantly, by disclosing some details of their products, getting orders, and delivering goods or services to them.[1] This appealing way of doing business pushed companies to shift their activities to the digital marketplace or combine it with the traditional mode of profitable work.

In 1996, UNCITRAL adopted a model law on Electronic Commerce, to simplify the business conducted online by guaranteeing national countries with "a set of internationally acceptable rules aimed at removing legal obstacles and increasing legal predictability for electronic commerce."[2] This event was followed by the adoption of the European Directive 2000/31/EC (the E-Commerce Directive). The main purpose of the document was to make 'online' and 'offline' agreements legally equal.[3]

Some researchers divided the evolution of e-commerce into several stages including, companies' first steps to use the powerful functions of the Internet to spread information on their products and services, respectively, the second phase - receiving orders and giving instructions about the products and services to the consumers and thirdly, handing over the purchased products and services to the consumers by using information technology.[4]

There are various definitions of e-commerce, by WTO Electronic commerce is interpreted as "the production, distribution, marketing, sale or delivery of goods and services by electronic means."[5] In a broader sense, e-commerce is defined as "the sale or purchase of goods or services, conducted over computer networks by methods specifically designed to receive or place of orders. The goods or services are ordered by those methods, but the payment and the ultimate delivery of the goods or services do not have to be conducted online. An e-commerce transaction can be between enterprises, households, individuals, governments, and other public or private organisations."[6]

Commercial operations on websites are categorized as 'active,' 'passive,' or 'interactive.' An "active" website allows a consumer to finish a transaction by going through several stages or pages on that website, such as www.amazon.com. A "pas-

---

[1] E-Commerce: A Short History Follow-up on Possible Trends (2017).

[2] UNCITRAL Model Law on Electronic Commerce with Guide to Enactment 1996 with additional article 5 bis as adopted in 1998.

[3] DIRECTIVE 2000/31/EC OF THE EUROPEAN PARLIAMENT AND OF THE COUNCIL of 8 June 2000 on certain legal aspects of information society services, in particular electronic commerce, in the Internal Market (Directive on electronic commerce).

[4] E-Commerce: A Short History Follow-up on Possible Trends (2017).

[5] WTO Work Programme on Electronic Commerce (1998).

[6] OECD Guide to Measuring the Information Society (2011).

sive" website, on the other hand, serves as nothing more than an information source for potential customers. "Interactive" websites are those that give a combination of information and communication with prospective customers, such as information request options or, as is often supplied, sign-up facilities to gather feedback on products, services, or special offers via e-mail.[7]

The main types of E-commerce transactions are:

- **B2B or BTB (Business to Business)**—transactions through the internet between two or more business partners, such transactions frequently are based on internet systems, which implies business partners take action by using the Internet usernames and passwords for their websites.[8]
- **B2C or BTC (Business to Consumer)/C2B (Consumer to Business)**—transaction is made between the company and consumer, company sells the product to the consumer directly, the best example of B2C type transaction is "Amazon";
- **C2C (Consumer to Consumer)**—a transaction between consumers, e.g. Ebay.com provides a framework where consumers can trade different goods and services with each other;
- **B2G (Business to Government)/G2B (Government to Business)**—Business-to-government e-commerce is broadly described as transactions between businesses and the government. It relates to the use of the Internet for government-related purposes such as public procurement, licensing procedures and other administrative tasks. This type of e-commerce has two characteristics: firstly, the public sector maintains a leading role in developing e-commerce and secondly, it is thought that the public sector is the most in need of improving the efficiency of its procurement system.[9]
- **G2C (Government to Consumer)/C2G (Consumer to Government)**—Transactions between government and consumers;
- **G2G (Government to Government)**—Transactions between government unities.[10]

2 Expansion of E-commerce in the COVID-19 Pandemic

The COVID-19 pandemic period is supposed to be one of the biggest crises in modern history that forced states to take a severe course of action to prevent the spread of the virus and the collapse of the entire medical system. Among a range of harsh restrictions, the lockdown was the strictest one imposed by the governments that significantly declined the operation of almost all sectors in the world. On the other hand, COVID-19 has had a huge impulse on social and behavioral change, since, in that difficult time, digital technologies appeared as an alternative way of

7 Gillies (2008), p. 28.

8 Tofan and Bostan (2022), p. 2.

9 Gupta (2014), p. 4.

10 Gabisonia (2022), p. 222.

communication for socially distant people. Businesses, educational institutions and even public entities moved their services to digital space. This process remarkably improved the difficulties caused by the pandemic.

Although in recent years, E-commerce transactions have gained a sizeable share of overall retail sales, COVID-19 has exponentially accelerated its expansion all over the world, as it kept the economy running during a pandemic. Moreover, such a cost-saving way of shopping turned out to be appealing to some consumers. Many online e-commerce companies also have "benefited" from the pandemic, according to WTO, the US-based e-commerce Company—Amazon gained revenues of US$ 75 billion in the first three months of the year since the start of COVID-19. Alibaba, a Chinese e-commerce platform announced its sales grew by 22% in the first three months of 2020. In addition, MercadoLibre, an e-commerce Company in Latin America acquired a 70.5% year-over-year increase in net revenue in the first quarter of 2020.[11]

In Brazil, approximately 54% of online consumers had purchased food or food-related products online in 2020, a significant increase from only 22% in 2018. Moreover, McKinsey's global consumer survey monitoring the use of digital and low-touch activities during the pandemic indicates that new users accounted for more than half of the growth in online grocery purchasing. In response to COVID-19, 21% of adults in the United States report ordering groceries online or via an application from a local retailer.[12]

Governments have applied a wide range of measures for supporting businesses to adopt digital technologies, good example is the distance business program in Hong Kong and China that funded enterprises to implement IT solutions to advance online business.[13] Furthermore, the Chinese government encouraged digital payments to avoid the spread of COVID-19 and distributed vouchers through WeChat Pay to push immediate spending.[14]

In terms of Georgia, research showed that the COVID-19 outbreak has also increased Georgia's e-commerce market, the lockdowns prompted businesses in Georgia to broaden their online product offerings. Following GALT&TAGGART the local e-commerce market reached GEL 137.9 million in 2020, up to 3.2 times year over year and it would grow to 1.1 billion by 2020–2025. Electronics and household equipment were the most popular categories of Georgia's E-commerce market since companies in this sector began investing in digital platforms before COVID-19 and faced the pandemic more prepared than any other industries.[15]

Studies revealed, that local online retailers' poor customer experience is also a concern—most online sellers lack fundamental elements for comfortable shopping (such as price lists, product availability and regional coverage). Consequently, Georgian citizens spend 3.3 times more on international online stores than on

---

[11] World Trade Report (2020), p. 39.

[12] OECD (2020), pp. 5–6.

[13] World Trade Report (2020), p. 39.

[14] Ib. p. 39.

[15] GALT&TAGGART Research (2021) p. 3.

domestic stores. Improving the whole shopping experience is critical for attracting and retaining customers, and requires significant financial and human resources.[16]

3 E-commerce in Light of the Association Agreement Between Georgia and the European Union

Georgia also undertook the obligation to enact the laws on electronic commerce within the framework of the Association Agreement. The Association Agreement between Georgia and the European Union and the European Atomic Energy Community and their member states was signed on June 27, 2014, the Parliament of Georgia ratified it on July 18, 2014, and the agreement fully entered into force on July 1, 2016.[17]

According to Chap. 6 of the document, (Establishment, trade in services and electronic commerce), the Parties, reaffirming their respective commitments under the WTO Agreement hereby lay down the necessary arrangements for the progressive reciprocal liberalisation of establishment and trade in services and cooperation on electronic commerce.[18]

Part 6 of the Association Agreement covers the issues of E-commerce in detail, Article 127 stipulates that:

1. The Parties, recognising that electronic commerce increases trade opportunities in many sectors, agree to promote the development of electronic commerce between them, in particular by cooperating on the issues raised by electronic commerce under the provisions of this Chapter.
2. The Parties agree that the development of electronic commerce must be compatible with the international standards of data protection to ensure the confidence of users of electronic commerce.
3. The Parties agree that electronic transmissions shall be considered as the provision of services, within the meaning of Sect. 3 (Cross-border supply of services) of this Chapter, which cannot be subject to customs duties.[19]

Notwithstanding above mentioned, the association agreement obligates the parties to maintain a dialogue on regulatory matters raised by electronic commerce, which address the following issues:

- "the recognition of certificates of electronic signatures issued to the public and the facilitation of cross-border certification services;
- the liability of intermediary service providers with respect to the transmission, or storage of information;

---

16 Ib. p. 3.

17 Association Agreement between the European Union and the European Atomic Energy Community and their Member States, of the one part, and Georgia, of the other part (2014).

18 Ib. Chap. 6.

19 Ib. Article 127.

- the treatment of unsolicited electronic commercial communications;
- the protection of consumers in the ambit of electronic commerce, and
- any other issue relevant for the development of electronic commerce.

Such cooperation can take the form of exchange of information on the Parties' respective legislation on those issues as well as on the implementation of such legislation."[20]

To simplify the process of the Association Agreement's implementation, Georgia and European Union prepared Association Agenda 2014–2016 and set a list of priorities in the document, including the establishment of electronic commerce compatible with the clauses envisaged by the Association Agreement. It's precisely indicated in the document, that the parties shall ensure appropriate training and administrative capacity for the approximation of legislation, including the English translation, technical assistance and permanent exchange of information to accomplish the abovementioned purpose.[21]

According to the National Action Plan 2016 for the implementation of the association agenda between Georgia and the European Union, the Ministry of Economy and sustainable development of Georgia had to prepare the draft law of Georgia on Electronic Commerce to approximate it to the EU standards. Based on thorough research and analysis of the EU Directive (2000/31/EC) and with the huge support of the USAID (G4G) project Ministry of Economy and sustainable development of Georgia developed the draft law of Georgia on "On Electronic Commerce".[22] Despite the progressive steps made by Georgia, the adoption of legal regulation in electronic commerce has still remained the main challenge for the country.

The same issue, to make the Georgian e-commerce legal system interoperable with the provisions of the Association Agreement was reflected in the Association Agenda 2017–2020 again.[23] Respectively, Each National Action Plan from 2017–2020 and Implementation of the National Action Plan Annual report from 2017–2020 envisage that the draft law of Georgia "On Electronic Commerce" has been adopted and is ready to be registered to the Parliament of Georgia for adoption. Although six years have passed since the signing of the Association Agreement, Georgia still prolongs the procedure to adopt the new law on Electronic Commerce, whereas, COVID-19 was the apparent example, which showed the unequivocal necessity of having e-commerce regulatory norms in the country.

---

[20] Ib. Article 128.

[21] Association Agenda between the European Union and Georgia (2014–2016).

[22] 2016 National Action Plan Implementation Report. p. 248.

[23] Association Agenda between the European Union and Georgia (2017–2020).

4 Regulatory Norms of Electronic Contract in Georgian Legislation

E-commerce involves numerous transactions. It is critical to examine the issue of preserving their form.[24]

Two essential documents enable the conclusion of electronic contracts in e-commerce and ensure equal treatment to paper-based and electronic contracts. On the one hand, the non-discrimination principle of UNCITRAL model law on electronic commerce provides that the validity of an electronic contract would not be disregarded because its form and functional equivalence principle guarantees the equality of electronic communications to paper-based ones.[25] On the other hand, three fundamental presumptions form the foundation of the e-commerce Directive's understanding of contracts. First, it is assumed that online and offline contracts are functionally identical. For instance, the sale of a book at an online store is to the sale of a book offline in a bookstore. Second, it is believed that the context for online transactions and the context for offline transactions are not substantially different. Finally, following the concept of normative equivalence, the laws that apply to offline transactions should likewise apply to online dealings.[26]

Georgian legislation doesn't classify electronic contracts into a separate category. Currently, there is no unified legal definition of "electronic contracts". However, the term "Electronic" relates to devices that operate on electronic principles or "travel in the form of electrical impulses".[27] Regarding the validity of electronic contracts, under the civil code of Georgia, a contract is considered to be in force if the parties agree on all of its essential terms in the form provided for such agreement.[28] If a specific form for the validity of a contract has been established by law, or if the parties have ascertained such a form for the contract, the contract shall enter into force only if it complies with the requirements of the form.[29] In other cases, the principle of freedom of contract applies, within its framework the parties have the right, to enter into such uncharacteristic and diverse agreements that are not expressly provided for by legislation.[30]

Following the approaches in classical contract law, the offer and acceptance sequence has a central role in contract formation, even though some researchers

---

24 Zambakhidze (2005), p. 114.

25 Gregory (2003), pp. 313–43.

26 Roger Brownsword. The E-Commerce Directive, Consumer Transactions, and the Digital Single Market—Questions of Regulatory Fitness, Regulatory Disconnection And Rule Redirection, pp. 168–169.

27 Mik, Eliza (2011), 324–347.

28 საქართველოს სამოქალაქო კოდექსი, მუხლი 327, ნაწილი I. https://matsne.gov.ge/en/document/view/31702?publication=125.

29 საქართველოს სამოქალაქო კოდექსი, მუხლი 328, ნაწილი I. https://matsne.gov.ge/en/document/view/31702?publication=125.

30 Commentaries on the Civil Code of Georgia, Book III, the general part of the law of obligations (2019), p. 2.

intend that "contract is not coextensive with bargain and that even in a bargain context contractual liability can attach without an offer and acceptance sequence".[31] In Georgian law, a proposal to conclude a contract is supposed to be an offer and a person making such proposal is an offeror, respectively, the consent to accept this offer and enter into the contract is acceptance and the person expressing consent is an acceptor.[32]

A telegraph notice, telecopy, or letter exchange shall also suffice to ensure compliance with the written form of the contract.[33] However, a telegraph notice and a telecopy shall not be sent by only one party. If the party receives a telegraph, or fax and agrees with the requested form, he shall burden himself with sending the reply by providing appropriate details, in other words, the party shall send a response document to the counterparty in the same way e.g. by telegraph notice or fax.[34] Based on the above discussion, a contract concluded electronically, fully satisfies the requirements of a simple written transaction.[35] Still, the legislative rule shall strengthen the functional-equivalent approach envisaged by the UNCITRAL model law on electronic commerce by making the national law clear and regulating the legal relations arising from the formation of electronic contracts in detail.

5 The Legal Recognition of Electronic Signatures in Georgia

The primary concern in the electronic contract formation process is the signature on the document. Since the paperless nature of an electronic contract, a digital signature shall ensure that contracting parties have entered into a binding transaction and protect the authenticity, integrity and privacy of online agreements.[36]

It is worth remarking on the widely accepted method of "technology-neutrality" of electronic signatures, namely, UNCITRAL Model Law on Electronic Signatures embodies the fundamental principle that "no method of the electronic signature should be discriminated against, that is, that all technologies would be given the same opportunity to satisfy the requirements of article 6. As a result, there should be no disparity of treatment between electronically signed messages and paper documents bearing handwritten signatures or between various types of electronically signed messages, provided that they meet the basic requirements set forth in article

[31] Eisenberg (2008), p. 417.

[32] სამოქალაქო კოდექსის კომენტარი, წიგნი მესამე, ვალდებულებითი სამართლის ზოგადი ნაწილი, თბილისი, 2019. გვ.108

[33] საქართველოს სამოქალაქო კოდექსი, მუხლი 328, ნაწილი II https://matsne.gov.ge/en/document/view/31702?publication=125.

[34] სამოქალაქო კოდექსის კომენტარი, წიგნი მესამე, ვალდებულებითი სამართლის ზოგადი ნაწილი, თბილისი, 2019. გვ.107.

[35] სამოქალაქო კოდექსის კომენტარი, წიგნი მესამე, ვალდებულებითი სამართლის ზოგადი ნაწილი, თბილისი, 2019. გვ.106–107.

[36] https://cyber.harvard.edu/olds/ecommerce/transactionstext.html.

6, paragraph 1, of the Model Law or any other requirement set forth in applicable law."[37]

Georgian law on "Electronic Documents and Electronic Trust Services", which was enacted in 2017 and replaced the pre-existing law on "electronic signature and electronic document " defines an electronic document, the different types of electronic signatures and the ways of using them. The main aim to adopt the mentioned law was to harmonise the existing Georgian legal framework with European Union legislation.[38] New law interpreted electronic and material documents separately in the following way: "electronic document - a set of textual, audible, visual or audio-visual information and/or data stored in an electronic form" and respectively, "tangible document - a set of information and/or data on paper or in any other tangible form."[39] The major novation of the law is that it defines various types of electronic signature and electronic seal, namely, the advanced electronic signature is exclusively linked to the signatory and can be used to identify the signatory and a qualified electronic signature is created by using an electronic signature creation device, on the basis of a certificate for qualified electronic signature.[40] As for the advanced electronic seal it is exclusively linked to the creator of a seal and can be used to identify the creator of a seal and qualified electronic seal is created by using an electronic seal creation device, on the basis of a certificate for a qualified electronic seal.

Among the above means of signatures, the digital signature remains the most reliable means of electronic substitute for the manual signature, which satisfies the legal requirement of electronic contract authenticity and integrity. A digital signature is an electronic alternative to a manual signature that performs the same functions and more. It is an identifier generated by a computer rather than a pen. A digital signature is a series of bits generated by passing an electronic communication through a one-way hash function and then encrypting the resulting message digest with the sender's private key.[41]

A digital signature "is linked to the data in such a way, that if the data is changed, the signature is invalidated."[42]

However, in comparison to a digital signature, an electronic signature is less regulated and its standard of use depends on the parties' agreement in each individual case, and contracting parties have to rely on each other's assurance that the signature is in fact reliable.[43]

---

37 UNCITRAL Model Law on Electronic Signatures with Guide to Enactment (2002).

38 Gabisonia (2022), p. 312.

39 საქართველოს კანონი „ელექტრონული დოკუმენტისა და ელექტრონული სანდო მომსახურების შესახებ". https://matsne.gov.ge/document/view/3654557?publication=1.

40 Ib. Art.2.

41 Smedinghoff (1998), 16/NO. 2, p. 7.

42 Smedinghoff and Hill Bro (1999), p. 739. https://repository.law.uic.edu/cgi/viewcontent.cgi?article=1260&context=jitpl.

43 Zambakhidze (2005), p. 127.

6 Conclusion

Governments all over the world have decided to encourage the development of e-commerce as it's supposed to be a positive alternative way of carrying out business activities. Accordingly, legislative measures must follow the expansion process of e-commerce, to ensure retailers streamline their operations in a legally safe environment. Moreover, the COVID-19 pandemic has apparently demonstrated the unequivocal need for the country to have a sound e-commerce regulatory system. First imminent step, Georgia shall take is to adopt the law on e-commerce, since the revision of draft law has been in progress for a long period of time. Furthermore, during pandemic, consumers had to make deals online without proper legally protective norms. Secondly, the legal issues related to the electronic contract must be regulated in detail, since there is only a general indication to various means that suffice the electronic form of contract. Thirdly, although Georgia made a huge progressive step by adopting a new law on "electronic documents and electronic trust services", digital signature still remains the alternative safest way for manual signature. Based on the technology-neutrality principle, all means of signatures should satisfy the developed countries' requirement to be used and recognized broadly in practice not only domestically, but also on an international level and finally, there is a strong need to strengthen digital infrastructure, boost the use of internet services and develop the logistical environment for the expansion of e-commerce in Georgia.

References

Association Agreement between the European Union and the European Atomic Energy Community and their Member States, of the one part, and Georgia, of the other part (2014). https://eur-lex.europa.eu/legal-content/en/TXT/PDF/?uri=CELEX:22014A0830(02)

Association Agenda between the European Union and Georgia (2014–2016). https://www.agenda.ge/files/files/000/eu-georgiaassociationagendaeng.pdf

Association Agenda between the European Union and Georgia (2017–2020). https://www.eeas.europa.eu/sites/default/files/annex_ii_-_eugeorgia_association_agenda_text.pdf

Commentaries on the Civil Code of Georgia, Book III, the general part of the law of obligations (2019). ISBN 978-9941-8-1812-7. http://lawlibrary.info/ge/books/giz2019-ge-civil_code_comm_III_book.pdf

E-Commerce: A Short History Follow-up on Possible Trends. (2017). *International Journal of Business Administration, 8*(7). https://www.sciedu.ca/journal/index.php/ijba/article/view/12573/7748

Eisenberg, M. A. (2008). Foundational principles of contract law, the Oxford Commentaries on American Law, Oxford University Press.

Gabisonia, Z. (2022). Internet Law and Artificial Intelligence, publishing house "World of Lawyers".

GALT&TAGGART Research. (2021). https://api.galtandtaggart.com/sites/default/files/2021-07/report/e-commerce-in-georgia_july-2021_eng.pdf

Gillies, L. E. (2008). Electronic commerce and international private law, A study of electronic consumer contracts.

Gregory, J. D. (2003). The proposed UNCITRAL convention on electronic contracts. *The Business Lawyer, 59*(1). JSTOR. Retrieved October 31, 2022, from http://www.jstor.org/stable/40688198

Gupta, A. (2014). E-commerce: role of e-commerce in today's business (p. 4). https://www.ijccr.com/January2014/10.pdf

https://cyber.harvard.edu/olds/ecommerce/transactionstext.html

Mik, E. (2011). The unimportance of being "Electronic" or popular misconceptions about "Internet Contracting". *International Journal of Law and Information Technology, 19*(4).

OECD Guide to Measuring the Information Society. (2011). https://read.oecd-ilibrary.org/science-and-technology/oecd-guide-to-measuring-the-information-society2011_9789264113541-en#page1

OECD. (2020). E-commerce in the times of COVID-19. https://read.oecd-ilibrary.org/view/?ref=137_137212-t0fjgnerdb&title=E-commerce-in-the-time-of-COVID-19

Smedinghoff, T. J. (1998). Electronic contracts and digital signatures. *Journal of Equipment Lease Financing*. Fall. https://www.store.leasefoundation.org/cvweb/Portals/ELFALEASE/Documents/Products/JELFFall98-1.pdf

Smedinghoff, T. J., & Hill Bro, R. (1999). Moving with change: Electronic signature legislation as a vehicle for advancing e-commerce, 17 J. Marshall J. Computer & Info. L. 723. https://repository.law.uic.edu/cgi/viewcontent.cgi?article=1260&context=jitpl

The civil code of Georgia, Pub. L. No. 786 (1997). https://matsne.gov.ge/en/document/view/31702?publication=125

Tofan, M., & Bostan, I. (2022). Some implications of the development of e-commerce on EU tax regulations. file:///C:/Users/user/Downloads/laws-11-00013%20(1).pdf

UNCITRAL Model Law on Electronic Signatures with Guide to Enactment. (2002). United Nations, New York.

World Trade Report. (2020). Government policies to promote innovation in the digital age. https://www.wto.org/english/res_e/booksp_e/wtr20_e/wtr20-0_e.pdf

WTO Work Programme on Electronic Commerce, WT/ L/274, 30/09/1998. https://docs.wto.org/dol2fe/Pages/SS/directdoc.aspx?filename=q:/WT/L/274.pdf&Open=True

Zambakhidze, T. (2005). Fundamentals of legal regulation of electronic commerce (problems and perspective). Review of Georgian Law 8/2005-1/2.

Creative Solutions in a Saturated Market. How Individual Players Develop Successful Digital Solutions in the Textile and Apparel Industry

Hendrik Müller

Abstract The global textile industry is part of a complex market that plays an important role in the global economy: in the European Union alone the manufacturing industry, employs 1.7 million people and generates a turnover of EUR 166 billion. On the other hand, it is a highly saturated industry on a global scale, as there is an abundance of suppliers in the production process that has led to a constant demand of cheap products and a growing number of shops that sell their products online on the other hand. Due to ever decreasing prices, continuous product innovations are necessary to attract customers. In the light of the fast fashion excesses and their problems ranging from poor quality, defective recycling to human rights problems, customers in recent years are also continuously demanding better quality and sustainable production processes. In the following paper I aim to demonstrate how an individual local player from Germany with stores in Düsseldorf and Essen, can be successful in the fashion market online and in-store with the help of digital solutions alone and attracts customers with a range of special products and a highly individual marketing strategy.

Keywords Textile industry · Digital solutions · Market success · Individual players

1 Introduction

The global textile and apparel industry is part of a complex market that plays an important role in the global economy: in the European Union alone, the manufacturing industry employs 1.7 million people and generates a turnover of 166 billion Euro (European Commission, 2022, October 25). The textile industry can be segmented by application type, i.e., clothing application, industrial/technical application, and

H. Müller (✉)
University of Applied Sciences Fresenius, Idstein, Germany
e-mail: hendrik.mueller@hs-fresenius.de

R. C. Geibel and S. Machavariani (eds.), *Chances and Challenges of Digital Management*, Springer Proceedings in Business and Economics,
https://doi.org/10.1007/978-3-031-45601-5_19

household application, by material (cotton, silk, synthetics, and wool), by process (woven and non-woven) or by geography.

On the other hand, the textile and apparel industry is undoubtedly a highly saturated industry on a global scale, as there is an abundance of suppliers in the production process that has led to a constant demand of cheap products and a growing number of shops that sell their products in retail stores and more and more online. Due to ever decreasing prices, continuous product innovations are necessary to attract remaining and new customers. In the light of the fast fashion excesses and their known problems ranging from poor quality, defective recycling to human rights problems, customers in recent years are also continuously demanding on the one hand, better quality products and the implementation of sustainable production processes on the other.

With the caesura of the Corona pandemic, the textile and apparel industry had to find quick answers to shop closures and national or regional lockdowns. Certainly, the digitization of the whole industry has increased rapidly. As McKinsey has stated in 2022 in their report on the future of the industry: "Online business models were a standout success story of the pandemic. We expect that companies will continue to invest in digital innovation and experiment with fresh approaches to creativity and commerce in 2022" (McKinsey, 2022, 11).

In the following paper I want to demonstrate how an individual local player from Germany, based at Hünxe in North-Rhine Westphalia, has developed a successful business model in the apparel market with a range of special products and a highly individual marketing strategy that offers sales stationary and with the help of digital solutions aiming at a core group of loyal customers.

2 Theory

Before the Covid-19 pandemic, the fashion industry global revenue was estimated between \$1.7 trillion and \$2.5 trillion, according to two different research reports by Euromonitor and McKinsey. While Euromonitor reports that the global apparel and footwear market size shrunk in 2020 by −18.1% (to \$1.45 trillion), while McKinsey states that the fashion and apparel industry suffered a 20% decline in revenues for the 2019–2020 fiscal year (Euromonitor, 2021, March 26; McKinsey, 2022).

The same reports predict nearly 10% of absolute growth in retail e-commerce sales in the period between 2020 and 2025. This is based on he fact that in 2020, 16% of all consumer goods were bought online, more than double that in 2015 (Euromonitor, 2021, March 26). This predicted growth of e-commerce activities will have an everlasting effect on offline sale channels and due to changing consumer preferences, a considerable portion can permanently migrate in the coming years (Deloitte, 2019). By 2030, online purchases of clothing in several large consumer markets (China, US, India, Brazil) could increase to reach 50–70% of the total sales.

For single clothing brands within the industry, digitization not only extends the possible sales channels, but may also help reducing cost structures through data-driven stock management, at the same time enabling new sales fulfilment options based on omnichannel solutions (Gonzalo et al., 2020). Deloitte (2019) also predicts the rise of alternative e-commerce models by 2030 which include such options as re-commerce or rentals which could gain a share of up to 30% by the end of this decade. But the impact of digitalization is not restricted to sales options and customer-oriented services only as Rudrajeet and Jayarthne (2022) have demonstrated convincingly and also affects other steps like the design and sampling development, sourcing, or manufacturing. Also, the stronger adoption of circular economy principles to make the whole industry more sustainable is certainly promoted by digitalization in like manner (ibid.).

The textile and apparel retail trade in Germany recently employed about 340,000 people, the majority of whom are women. The national industry consists mainly of smaller and medium-sized enterprises (SME), including a large number of family businesses, with a total of about 135,000 employees (BMWK, 2022, October 23). The specialized clothing trade as a form of distribution now accounts for only about 40% of total sales, with mail order accounting for an increasingly large share in recent years. The market share of department stores in the retail trade as a whole in Germany, on the other hand, has also fallen significantly in recent years. Yet this development is far from being recent, as already between 1960 and 1998 the share of the total consumption expenditure on textile products of West German private households had fallen from 11.6% to 5.6%. So already in the 1990ies the textile market was clearly considered as saturated (Dömer, 2002, 20). Even more reasons for individual retailers to stand out from the competition with distinctive concepts.

As early as 2001 Lee and Kim have identified three basic conceptual categories concerning the scope of digitization, i.e., the categories of 'technological environment', 'information environment' and 'business environment' (Lee & Kim, 2001, 124/129) and define digitization as the "foundation for better productivity and management efficiency by improving operational conditions and management of material quantity and resources in the industry (Ibid. 129–30). Whereas individual players cannot influence the technological nor the business environment, they are certainly responsible for the third aspect of information and can thereby influence the success of their operations according to their adaptation to digital processes.

This is also true for ongoing innovations like the rapid developments of artificial intelligence within the fashion industry, also on an industrial level (Pereira et al., 2022). On the other hand, it is a fact that smaller and medium sized companies certainly are at a disadvantage compared to larger companies, which can more easily hire specialists in the required fields. Therefore, individual success of SME is even more based on innovative processes, either in the field of production, sales or marketing. As Oliver Behr (2018, 6) has pointed out, "the future of intelligent clothing is not just about combining fashion and technological capabilities, like measuring a person's biometrics and behavior or displaying the product's environmental impact. Rather, it is about combining respective capabilities in a meaningful way to create something valuable for the customer in a holistic way." The development of smart solutions on the product side and within the production and distribution processes will be a decisive step to a company's success.

3 Research Method

This paper is based on the one hand on the analysis of several websites of individual players in the textile market with the result of singling out a Germany based company "Uli Schott. The unknown brand" (ulischott.de) whose owner was interviewed on his individual business approach. The answers to the interview questions were analysed and compared on a qualitative basis in order to come to conclusions and arrive at reliable results, how this individual strategy can lead to market success.

4 Case Study

"Uli Schott The unknown brand": Asked what makes Ulrich Schott's business approach special, he answered that the core idea is to make luxury affordable. He continues, "We take high-quality outer fabrics, high-quality ingredients and have them processed by high-quality manufacturers. In this way, we ensure the highest quality, and the customer gets the most." As the clothes are almost exclusively made in Western Europe and meet the standards of actual demands fairness and sustainability can be guaranteed—"This business idea fits the times very well ". Additionally, as no other wholesaler is needed between the brand and the production, an "excellent price performance, which even someone outside the business understands immediately" can be reached. And this is possible without elaborate marketing campaigns, as the brand relies on word-of-mouth recommendations (i.e. "the unknown brand").

The company has 15 employees in total, of which three workfull-time, four part-time and eight employees are "mini-jobbers". Also, family members are involved directly in the operations: apart from the company owner, his wife does the book-keeping and outlet sales and his son and the daughter are also involved in the business. The company operates two branches, an additional outlet store and online sales via its website. The core processes are also channeled either by Ulrich Schott himself, who accounts for the purchasing and product development and operates the marketing activities together with his son. The distribution goes through sales only: "We don't sell to anyone in retail. This gives us price sovereignty and no surprises as to what the competitor is coming up with."

In terms of digitization, Uli Schott uses Google Ads and Affiliate, which works relatively well according to the owner. Asked about his prognosis about the future development of the industry, he thinks that of the big players, one or two will eventually not survive and others will become even bigger as a result, especially those with a distribution of their own. With expensive marketing activities, brands with cheap products of the fast fashion industry will continue to find their customers, but: "Unknown brands like mine may find friends for life".

Where specialist shops will have increasing problems, Ulrich Schott is convinced that second-hand shopping will become more atttactive and also artificial intelligence will become more important, especially when applied to individual garments.

Asked about the importance of online business via social media or platforms, the assessment of Ulrich Schott is as follows: "Online business within retail is incredibly strong and multichannel offers give the customer immense opportunities to get information online in advance and see the whole collection so that no price surprises can occur. On platforms though, "people search for well-known brands or look for reduced articles."

5 Results and Discussion

The answers to our survey prove that individual solutions can be a key to success within the textile and apparel industry when innovative digital solutions are combined with a cleverly organized supply chain that works without further wholesalers and allows sales that only take place in own shops both stationary and online. Marketing unquestionable plays a major role in the whole process, but in our case it is the alleged renunciation of any marketing activities ("the unknown brand") that arouses curiosity.

6 Conclusion, Limitations, and Further Research

In conclusion, it becomes apparent that success in the fashion industry is not a question of the size of a business. Although the market is saturated in the sense that there are some "big names" which will remain their stronghold in luxury fashion and on the other hand, well-known companies in the fast fashion industry that will stay with their discount prices, there is still enough room for individual players who can secure their piece of the cake. The prerequisite of their success is an innovative approach to production, sales, and especially marketing. In all these areas, digitization offers plentiful of solutions as our case study has shown.

The prospect of this paper is relatively limited at this stage, as only one company could be examined more closely. Further research should therefore focus, also on an international level, on other successful business solutions that may also prove that within the fashion industry, trends and developments are as changeable as fashion itself.

References

Behr, O. (2018). Fashion 4.0—Digital innovation in the fashion industry. *Journal of Technology and Innovation Management*, *2*(1), 1–9.

BMWK. (2022, October 23). Textil- und Bekleidungsindustrie. https://www.bmwk.de/Redaktion/DE/Artikel/Branchenfokus/Industrie/branchenfokus-textil.html

Deloitte. (2019). *Global Fashion & Luxury Private Equity and Investors Survey 2019*. Global Report, Mailand.

Dömer, M. (2002). Ressourcenbasierte Erschließung neuer Märkte: Dargestellt am Beispiel der Textilindustrie, Schriften zu Marketing und Management, No. 43, Berlin: Peter Lang International Academic Publishers. https://doi.org/10.3726/b13638

Euromonitor. (2021, March 26). Five themes for the progression of fashion in 2021 and beyond. https://www.euromonitor.com/article/five-themes-for-the-progression-of-fashion-in2021-and-beyond

European Commission. (2022, October 25). Textiles and clothing industries. https://single-market-economy.ec.europa.eu/sectors/fashion/textiles-and-clothing-industries_en

Gonzalo, A., Harreis, H., Sanchez Altable, C., & Villepelet, C. (2020, May 6). Fashion's digital transformation: Now or never. https://www.mckinsey.com/industries/retail/ourinsights/fashions-digital-transformation-now-or-never

McKinsey& Co. (2022). The State of Fashion 2022, New York City.

Lee, M.-R., & Kim, M.-S. (2001). A study on the digitalization of the fashion industry. *IJCC*, *4*(2), 124–137, 48

Pereira, F., Carvalho, V., Vasconcelos, R., & Soares, F. (2022). A review in the use of artificial intelligence in textile industry. In J. Machado, F. Soares, J. Trojanowska, & S. Yildirim (Eds.), *Innovations in mechatronics engineering. ICIENG 2021*. Lecture Notes in Mechanical Engineering. Springer, Cham. https://doi.org/10.1007/978-3-030-79168-1_34

Rudrajeet, P., & Jayarthne, A. (2022). Digitalisation in the textile and clothing industry. In B. L. MacCarthy & D. Ivanov (Eds.), *The digital supply chain* (pp. 255–271). Elsevier.

Digital Transformation of Organizational Culture of Higher Educational Institutions and Types of Organizational Culture that Academicians and Administrative Personnel Perceive at Their Institutions (Case of Georgia)

Tatia Gherkenashvili

Abstract This study aims revealing culture types that the academicians as well as administrative personnel of Georgian private and public higher educational institutions (HEIs) perceive at their organizations on the basis of the four types of cultures (Clan, Adhocracy, Hierarchy, and Market) given in the Competing Values Framework-CVF by Kim Cameron and Robert Quinn and to identify current problems, barriers, features, trends, and directions of digital transformation of organizational culture of HEIs. The study encompasses totally185 academicians of different faculties and positions (Professor, Associate Professor, Assistant Professor, Assistant) and administrative personnel (from Rectors to technical staff) as participants. The data was obtained through the Quantitative research, mainly—Self-Assessment Questionnaire of organizational culture. Data results was calculated in the Ms. Excel file based on the calculation method. According to the findings obtained by research, dominant type of organizational culture in Georgian Private HEIs is **Market culture** and as for public universities' preferable culture is **Adhocracy culture**.

Keywords Digital transformation · Organizational culture · Competing Values Framework (CVF) · Digital transformation · HEIs

T. Gherkenashvili (✉)
Department of Scientific Research and Development, East European University, Tbilisi, Georgia
e-mail: t.gherkenashvili@eeu.edu.ge

R. C. Geibel and S. Machavariani (eds.), *Chances and Challenges of Digital Management*, Springer Proceedings in Business and Economics,
https://doi.org/10.1007/978-3-031-45601-5_20

1 Introduction

1.1 Organization and Culture

Organization serves as a structure encompassing people with various characteristics in social, cultural, psychological, and academic terms. In other words, it means that each of them might have multiple backgrounds, habits, hobbies, behaviors, beliefs, and values. Despite all these differences, the organization is the structure that combine these people together for a specific purpose and let them be in a constant interaction with each other to achieve the common objectives of the organization (Keyton, 2005, p. 10).

In recent years, various specialists have studied the structure of the organization from different perspectives realize how the organization achieves these purposes and they have elaborated conceptual frameworks and models that have different or common points in their approaches to the subject.

Culture has been associated with the organization by researchers and the concept of organizational culture has been revealed. So, by examining the organizational culture of organizations, shared values, and basic principles, researchers have made conclusions in areas needed for analysis, development, change and management of organizational culture (Şişman, 2015, p. 163). According to the aim of the researches, the organizational culture has been studied in order to provide different benefits in areas of the organization, such as the determination of the necessary changes for the efficiency of the organization, determining the changes necessary for the efficiency of the organization and the organization in the environment where the organization is located (Bolman ve Deal, 2017, p. 10).

1.2 Organizational Culture in Universities

Universities are one of the few institutions that have almost never changed from the Middle Ages to the present in terms of their structure and functioning. The main purpose of higher education institutions is the creation and dissemination of knowledge. While the organizational focus is science, organizational units are departments in the university. The source of the identity perception they have for the academic staff is the scientific and professional communities they belong to with the science they are interested in rather than their corporate membership in the institution they work for (Sanyal, 1996, p. 4). In the twenty-first century, universities have a structure that serves wider, more complex, diverse students and chase wider targets than in the past (Scott, 2013, p. 15). The universities, which have a continuous and rapid change in social, technological, economic and political aspects, are obliged to adapt to these changes. In the pressure environment caused by this rapid change at both global and international levels, universities accelerate academic reforms such as the creation of common markets, the mobility of students and staff, free movement of services and products (Beytekin et al., 2010, p. 2).

Each university has its own culture. Everything from the university's name, logo, colors, mission, and history to the university's campus, architecture, the method of business management, graduates, community and clubs is a part of this culture. Each university has both an institutional culture with its goals, beliefs, and traditions evolved from its history, as well as subcultures shared between administrators, faculties, faculty, and students. Universities are governed by a structure consisting of faculty boards, faculty members and administrative managers rather than by one-handed CEOs, as in the business World (Min, 2017, pp. 27–32).

The organizational culture of the university is a special phenomenon due to the fact that the education departments rely on a self-organized system based on the principles of knowledge and learning.

University culture: within the scope of internal relations, functions as a platform in which academic and administrative managers, academic and administrative staff and students, public and private sector executives, alumni and parents of them, employers and partners from other educational institutions, competitors, and non-governmental organizations build various relationships (Vasyakin et al., 2016, p. 2). As can be seen, the university sees itself as an organizational actor, which constitutes a subjective strategy in the socioeconomic strife of contemporary society, that is, it has an important role in the formation of the information infrastructure and broadens the area of common values and beliefs (Serdenciuc, 2015, p. 5).

1.3 The Importance of Detecting Culture in Universities

All these structural features and functions of the universities have an effective role in their culture. Therefore, studying the cultural features of the universities will provide convenience to academicians, administrative staff, managers in strategy development, and decision-making processes for all stakeholders of the university. In this study, organizational culture is handled in terms of universities with higher education institutions. In this research carried out through the university, the type of organizational culture that academic staff perceived regarding their institutions was analyzed by using Competitive Values Framework model developed by Cameron and Quinn (2006).

1. What are the current levels of organizational culture types perceived by the university staff in terms of the organizational culture types included in the Competing Values Framework Model (Clan, Adhocracy, Hierarchy, Market) and which one is closer to be the dominant culture?

2 Method

This research was designed in the questionnaire model. The universe of the study consists of 185 academicians (Professor, Associate Professor, Assistant Professor, Assistant) and administrative personnel from Rectors to technical staff) working in various public and private universities in Georgia.

The questionnaires were sent via e-mail and social networks to 1000 staff who were working in the faculties and were holding various positions which can be reached during the research process. The reason for the low rate is that the study has been carried out with Academic and administrative staff that is a professional group having a high workload.

2.1 Data Collection Instrument

In this study, the questionnaire elaborated by Christopher P. Neck, Jeffery D. Houghton, Emma L. Murray in their Book titled: "Organizational Behavior A Skill-Building Approach" (2nd Ed.), modified and adjusted to Georgian respondents was applied through using Competing Values Framework (CVF) developed by Kim Kameron and Robert Quinn. In the questionnaire, the CVF there are 16 items related to four types of organizations: clan, adhocracy, hierarchy and Market culture. By answering questions provided in Table 1 (and lately modified) it was possible to reveal which type of organizational culture is dominant in Georgian private and state universities.

2.2 Data Analysis

The purpose of this chapter is to analyze the data obtained as a result of the research. In particular, revealing and comparing the existing organizational culture in private and public universities in Georgia; drawing conclusions and developing recommendations for elaborating organizational culture model that best fit to their institutions.

As mentioned above empirical research was conducted in Georgian private and public higher educational institutions utilizing a quantitative research method, in particular, an electronic Google self-assessment questionnaire was used to assess organizational culture, which included research questions on demographic characteristics and organizational culture. The questionnaire encompassed 16 questions, from which the respondents (academic and administrative staff had to mark the answer preferable to them on a five-point likert scale, mainly: 1 = completely disagree; 2 = I do not agree; 3 = I agree more or less; 4 = I agree; 5 = I completely agree.

demographic questions included the followings:

Table 1 Self-assessment questionnaire

	Not at all appealing	Somewhat appealing	A little appealing	Very appealing	Extremely appealing
1. Strict command of command	1	2	3	4	5
2. Outward looking	1	2	3	4	5
3. Flexibility	1	2	3	4	5
4. Independence	1	2	3	4	5
5. Respect for power and position	1	2	3	4	5
6. Bargaining and decision making	1	2	3	4	5
7. Vision and shared goals	1	2	3	4	5
8. Speed and Adaptability	1	2	3	4	5
9. Well-defined policies	1	2	3	4	5
10. Results oriented	1	2	3	4	5
11. Autonomy	1	2	3	4	5
12. Experimentation	1	2	3	4	5
13. Coordination and organization	1	2	3	4	5
14. Hard-driving competition	1	2	3	4	5
15. Facilitative and supportive	1	2	3	4	5
16. Innovation	1	2	3	4	5

Source "Organizational Behavior A Skill-Building Approach" (2nd Ed.), Authors: Christopher P. Neck, Jeffery D. Houghton, Emma L. Murray

University—Private—public **gender**—a woman—man; **Status at the university**—Administrative staff—Academic staff; **Administrative position held at the university; Length of stay in an administrative position** (service)—0–6 months—6–12 months—1–3 years—More than 3 years **Information about academic staff; Academic position held at the university**—Professor—Associate Professor—assistant professor—Assistant; **Length of stay at an academic position (tenure)**—0–6 months—6–12 months—1–3 years—More than 3 years.

Modified self-assessment Questionnaire included the following questions:

(1) I prefer a strict management style in the university (hierarchy). (2) I have a tendency to establish business relations outside the university (market). (3) I have a tendency to change (clan). (4) I am independent in performing work and adhocratic in making decisions). (5) I respect the position and power of others (hierarchy). (6) I make decisions based on negotiations (market). (7) I have mastered the vision and goals of the university (clan). (8) I can easily adapt to changes (adhocracy). (9) I prefer clearly defined university policies and processes (hierarchy). (10) I am always result-oriented (market). (11) I will spare no effort to introduce leadership (adhocracy). (12) I prefer a harmonious and harmonious working environment (hierarchy). (13) I am inclined (I feel comfortable) to act actively in the conditions of competition (market). (14) I have the ability to help others as needed (clan). (15) I have a tendency towards innovation, newness and innovativeness (adhocracy). (16) I prefer individual decision-making and autonomy of action.

3 Findings

This chapter presents the findings of the statistical analysis of the data obtained by the questionnaire applied to the participants. The tables and graphs of the research findings are given below.

The questionnaire results were calculated in the Ms. Excel file in accordance with the calculation method performed in the aforementioned manual.

From randomly selected universities A total of 185 respondents filled out the questionnaire, out of which 73 respondents were representatives of private universities, and 112 were from public universities (see Bar 1) 104 of the respondents were academic staff, and 81 administrative staff (see Bar 2 in percentage).

As for the positions held by the respondents in the universities, the answers are diverse and include employees from executives to technical staff.

The length of the position held by the administrative personnel (see Bar 3) is as follows: 54 person work for more than 3 years, 15 persons for 1–3 years, 10 persons for 6–12 months and 2 persons for 0–6 months.

If we consider the data of the academic staff, 65 of the respondents were associate professors, 24 professors, 11 assistant professors and 4 assistants (see Bar 4).

The seniority of the position held by the academic staff is as follows: 88 people work for more than 3 years, 10 people for 1–3 years, 4 people for 6–12 months and 2 people for 0–6 months (see Pie bar 5).

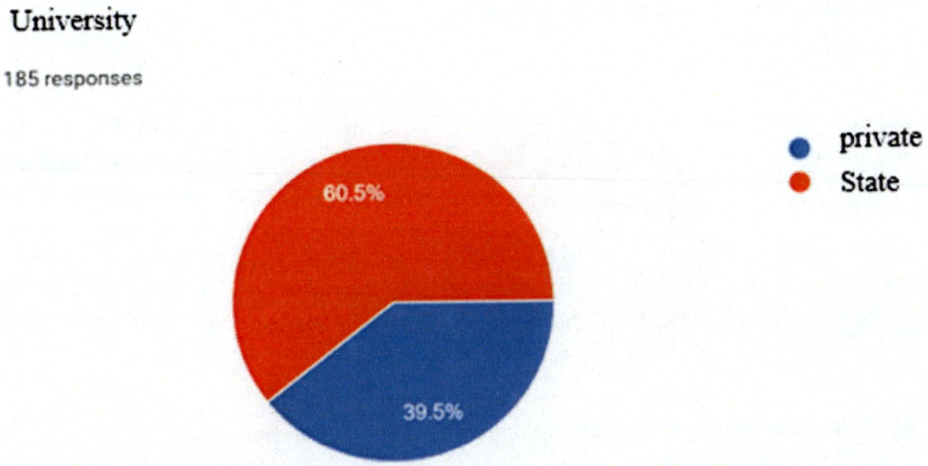

Bar 1 Total number of universities'respodents in percentage

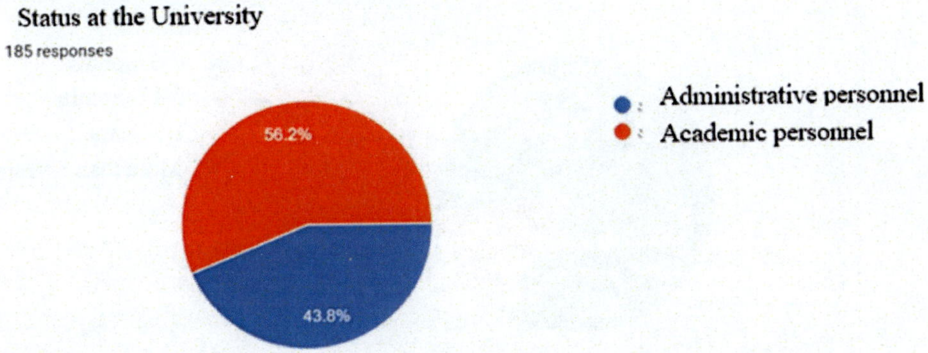

Bar 2 Distribution in terms of Academic and Administrative personnel in percentage

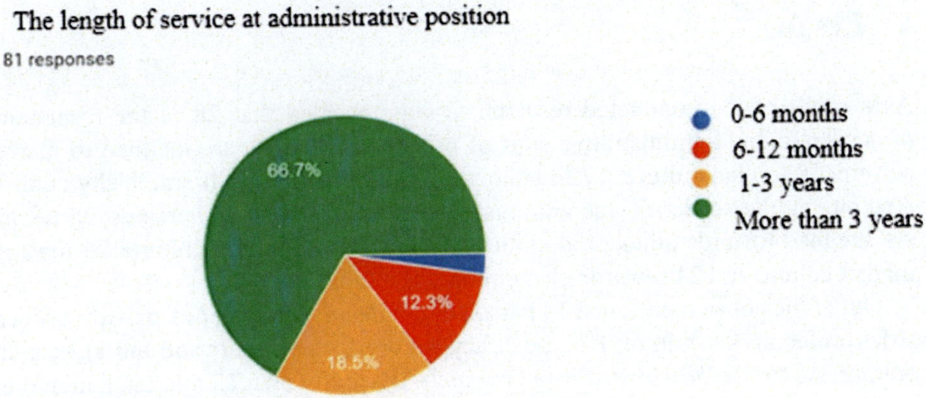

Bar 3 The length of the service at academic position

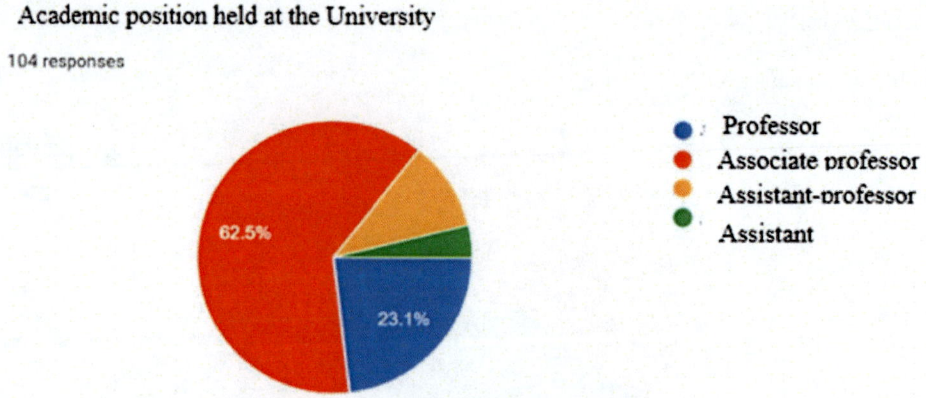

Bar 4 The time span of holding the position by the academic personnel

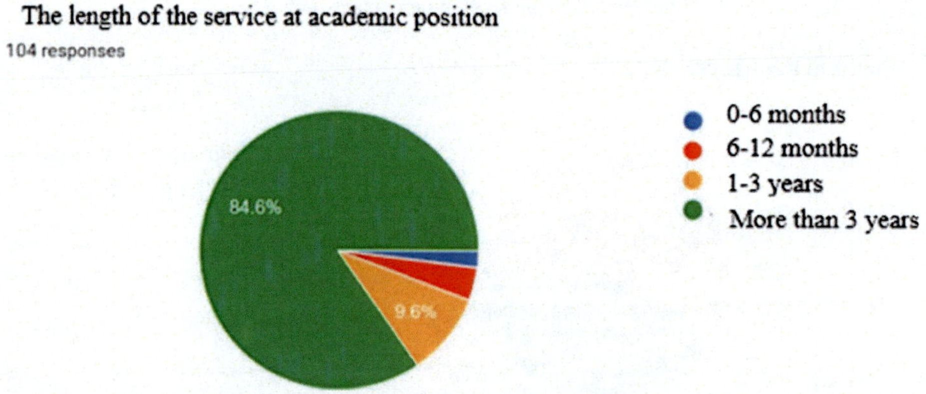

Pie bar 5 Academic position held at the University

4 Results

As a result of the conducted research, it was revealed that 28 of the respodents of academic and administrative staff of private universities are inclined to market culture, 18 to clan culture, 17 to adhocracy culture and 10 to hierarchichy culture. And among the academic and administrative staff of public universities, 35 people are inclined towards adhocratic culture, 31 towards hierarchy culture, 25 towards market culture and 21 towards clan culture (see Table 2).

Out of the above mentioned 14 person of *academic personnel* of **private universities** prefer market culture; 10 adhochracy culture, 9 clan culture and and 4 hierarchy culture; As for the *administrative personnel*—13 prefer clan,13 market, 8 hierarchy and 2 adhocratic cultures (see Chart 1).

Data of the **state universities** is the following: 25 person of academic personnel prefer clan, 20 adhocracy, 11–11 hierarchy and market cultures. From *administrative*

Table 2 Findings on the dominant organizational culture at Georgian universities

	Hierarchy	Market	Clan	Adhocracy
Total sum	41	53	39	52
Private university	10	28	18	17
State university	31	25	21	35

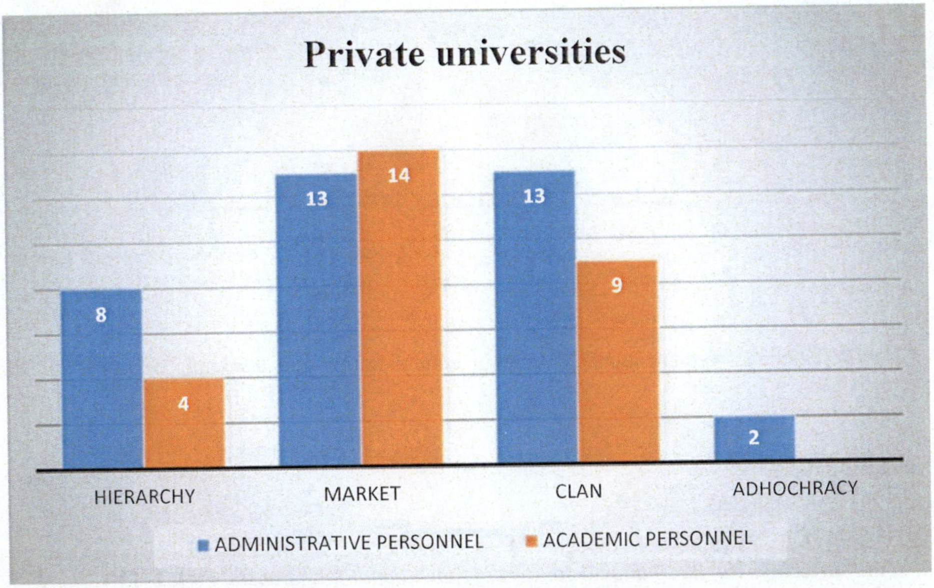

Chart 1 Dominant organizational culture in administrative and academic personnel of private universities

personnel 20 person prefer hierarchy, 13 clan, 7 market and adhocratic cultures. (see Chart 2).

5 Recommendations

The first phase of the research was to find out the dominant organizational culture at Georgian private and State Universities and what type of culture was preferable for academic and administrative staff. the further phase would be recommended to conduct quantitative research (interview) with the executives of the relevant entities to investigate their position regarding the first phase's research results and reveal their attitudes toward the way to developing innovative organizational culture model that fits to all of the representatives of the HIEs in order to increase its productivity and performance.

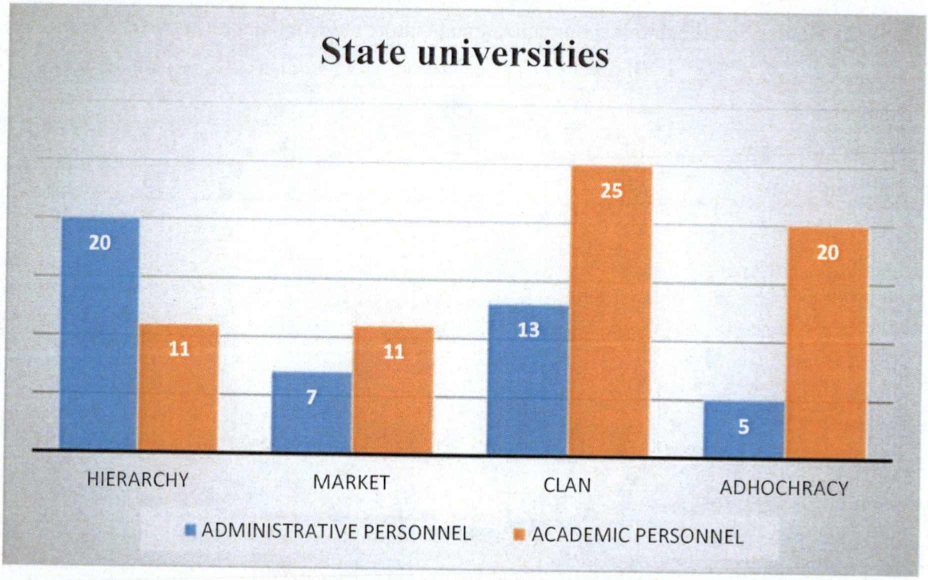

Chart 2 Dominant organizational culture in administrative and academic personnel of state universities

References

Beytekin, O. F., Yalçınkaya, M., Doğan, M., & Karakoç, N. (2010). The organizational culture at the university. *The International Journey of Educational Researchers, 2*(1), 1–13.

Bolman, L. G., & Deal, T. E. (2017). *Reframing organizations: artistry, choice, and leadership.* (Altıncı Baskı). Jossey-Bass. https://doi.org/10.1002/9781119281856

Cameron, K. S., & Quınn, R. E. (2006). Diagnosing and changing organizational culture: based on the competing values framework. (Üçüncü Baskı). Jossey Bass A Wiley Imprint.

Keyton, J. (2005). *Communication and organizational culture: A key to understanding work experiences.* Sage.

Min, J. (2017). Mergers in higher education: A case study of organizational culture, communication, and conflict management strategies in the university system of Georgia. Doctor of International Conflict Management Dissertations. http://digitalcommons.kennesaw.edu/incmdoc_etd/11/adresindenerisilmistir

Sanyal, B. C. (1996). Issues, trends, and international experiences. Institutional management in higher education: A training course for planners and managers of higher education institutions içinde (pp. 127–128). International Institute for Educational Planning, and UNESCO.

Scott, W. R. (2013). Organization theory and higher education. *Journal of Organizational Theory in Education, 1*(1), 1–24.

Serdenciuc, N. (2015). A reflection on organizational culture in higher education. *International Journal of Social and Educational Innovation—IJSEIro*, Forthcoming. https://ssrn.com/abstract=2795912

Şişman, M. (2007). *Organizations and cultures* (pp. 80–163). Ankara: Pegem Publishing.

Vasyakin, B., Berezhnaya, M., Pozharskaya, E., & Deberdeeva, N. (2015). Adaptation of graduates and students of regions to education in higher education institutions of Russia by means of social-psychological training. *Review of European Studies, 7*(3), 88.

Peculiarities of Digital Transformation of Higher Educational Institutions in Georgia

Vasil Kikutadze, Davit Sikharulidze, and Tamta Lekishvili

Abstract Georgia joined the Bologna process in 2005 at the Bergen summit. In addition, the country signed the association agreement with Europe in 2014, where the country's commitment to developing digital infrastructure in the country was outlined. In this regard, according to the 2021–2027 agenda of the association agreement between the European Union and Georgia, the importance of stimulating the digital economy and innovation in the country, promoting the development of e-governance and digital services, along with the development of digital skills and e-literacy of the broad strata of the population, was specified. Consequently, the reforms in the Georgian educational sector were actively launched, and the need for the digital transformation of educational institutions, including higher education institutions, was on the agenda. Taking into account the recent Covid pandemic, on June 12, 2020, amendments were made to the Law of Georgia on "Higher Education," where 47^7 articles specified the essence of distance learning and the features of its implementation. In particular, paragraphs 3 and 4 of this article define the obligation to select and properly use a distance learning application/platform for higher educational institutions, develop instructions/video guide for the use of the selected distance learning application/platform, and introduce it to students and staff of higher education institutions. Based on the abovementioned changes, the higher educational institutions operating in Georgia (in the 2021–2022 academic year, 19 state and 45 private higher educational institutions are operating in Georgia.) have actively started to take care of meeting the existing requirements. In particular, first of all, to conduct educational processes interactively, higher education institutions purchased electronic online training programs. The choice was mainly made on such software as zoom, jitsi, google meet, and Microsoft Teams. In addition, the e-learning

V. Kikutadze (✉) · D. Sikharulidze · T. Lekishvili
East European University, Tbilisi, Georgia
e-mail: v.kikutadze@eeu.edu.ge

D. Sikharulidze
e-mail: d.sikharulidze@eeu.edu.ge

T. Lekishvili
e-mail: t.lekishvili@eeu.edu.ge

R. C. Geibel and S. Machavariani (eds.), *Chances and Challenges of Digital Management*, Springer Proceedings in Business and Economics,
https://doi.org/10.1007/978-3-031-45601-5_21

programs for internal use owned by the universities were activated and functionally improved; the book fund was updated/supplemented with digital resources, the digitization of student services and management processes of higher education institutions became the top priorities, etc. It is worth noting that, along with the implementation of the mentioned processes, the problems accompanying the digitization process appeared consequently, in particular, the lack of digital skills, both among students and among the staff of higher educational institutions, less willingness to observe the norms of academic integrity in the process of online education; problems of infrastructural provision of universities and students, access to an unlimited Internet, etc. With these mentioned problems in view, higher education institutions actively started working on developing and implementing digital development strategies and action plans, which are clearly not a one-time process and require constant development. In this paper, we will discuss distinctive characteristics of the digital transformation implementation process that has taken place in HEIs in Georgia.

Keywords Digital transformation · Digitalization · University · Higher education institutions · Georgia

1 Introduction

The global process of transition to the digital economy and digital society leads to the irreversible process of the digital transformation of the educational process.[1] Digital transformation has become a topical issue in education since the second half of the twenty-first century.[2] It is a fundamental requirement for higher education institutions that consider themselves leaders in a very competitive environment.[3]

The digital economy is registered and legalized at the international level agreement on a new economic order. This is particularly relevant to the 2016 Ministerial Conference, June 22–23 meeting in Cancun (Mexico) attended by ministers of the Organization for Economic Cooperation and Development (OECD), the European Union, and many other countries (Ronzhina et al., 2021). The conference is considered a benchmark for the contemporary, deliberate movement toward the digital transformation of modern society (Sukhomlin & Zubareva, 2020).

Digitalization means the transformation process of an organization by introducing digital technology (Sebastian et al., 2017). Digitalization, a robust area that embraces multiple work and everyday components and demonstrates continuity, has been one of the major trends transforming society and sectors of society, especially in the last

[1] 2021–2027 agenda of the association agreement between the European Union and Georgia, Article 4, Recommendation N 1/2022.

[2] Law of Georgia on "Higher Education," Article 477, Tbilisi, December 21, 2004 (as of 2022).

[3] National Statistics Office of Georgia, indicators of higher educational institutions in 2021/2022 academic years.

decade. This trend is forcing nearly every industry to seize technological opportunities, and society faces the challenge of developing the necessary knowledge to keep up with its developments. One of the fundamental areas affected by digitization is higher education, where the teaching and learning process will be affected more than ever. In this context, digitization offers universities both opportunities and challenges. Higher education institutions (HEI) need to learn how to compete, poor working styles combined with new technologies, adoption of new technologies at undesirable levels, and skeptical attitudes towards digital reliability and continuity for various reasons (Kurnaz & Nafoussi, 2022). Higher Education Institutions need to keep up with the development of digital technology. Services and cloud technologies with traditional technical infrastructure and technical support teams ignorant of new technologies, rigid institutional policies, etc. (McCusker et al., 2018). With this in view, the study aims to investigate the digitalization in HEIs, the issue that gained particular importance during the recent pandemic of COVID-19. The study focuses on the analysis of the global tendencies and narrow downs on the peculiarities of the Georgian Higher Education System.

2 Literature Review

While discussing the digitalization process, various definitions of this phenomenon are provided by different experts and authors of publications. Among them, Tim Berners-Lee, one of the inventors of the World Wide Web, considers this transition a historical turning point in education (Stuart, 2014). One of the leading countries in this regard is the United Kingdom, where software engineering and information technologies have been compulsory modules for schoolchildren since 2015 (Machekhina, 2017).

Digitalization of education is often associated with the concept of open education, which is becoming unprecedentedly crucial in the European higher education system as the main driver of the modernization of education (Santos, EU Science Hub, 2022).

Digital transformation is transforming societies and economies, impacting everyday life more deeply than ever before and highlighting the need to increase the digital capabilities of education and training systems and institutions.

Digitization exists in all areas of the economy, including education. It affects not only university facilities but also the way of teaching. Most universities have been following new trends in recent years, but the ongoing pandemic is accelerating this trend. At the same time, digitization provided a solution to the unexpected closure of universities and the unavailability of physical space for the studying process (Hou et al., 2022). This process has substantially challenged the existing ways and classical approaches of teaching methods, as well as the content of the teaching programs (Chasanidou et al., 2014).

Digital technologies, mostly innovative hardware, can support the functioning of universities; however, HEIs cannot employ the full potential of digital technologies for many reasons. One of the most dominant reasons is that students, academics,

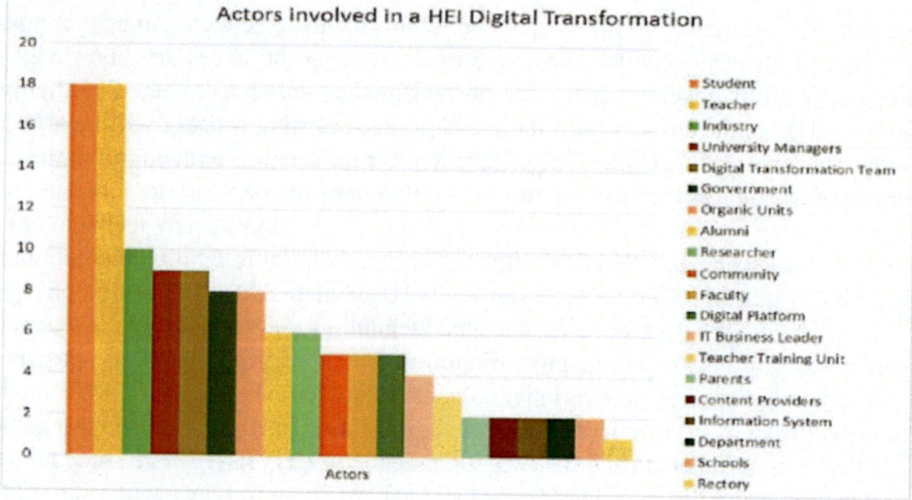

Fig. 1 Actors involved in a DT at a HEI. *Source* https://www.researchgate.net/figure/Actors-involved-in-a-DT-at-a-HEI_fig8_342052514

and other university staff face difficulty adapting to new technologies. To reach the maximum efficiency of modern digital technologies, all university stakeholders must undergo significant preparation and training in the digital transformation process (Fig. 1).

Horizon scanning of pre-and post-COVID-19 (Fűzi et al., 2022) universities are forced to focus on students, teachers, and internal processes to continue delivering education in the new digital context. Students play a crucial role in this process. Students' digital skills and perceptions of this transformation process can directly indicate their success. Teachers and students had to adapt to new teaching methods, and many were not ready (Maican & Cocorada, 2021). Some teachers were unfamiliar with information and communication technologies. Some students did not have enough resources to keep up with online classes and struggled to concentrate and adapt to this teaching method (Rehman et al., 2021).

As in other sectors, "the COVID-19 pandemic has highlighted global connectivity, vulnerability, and inequality" (Nkengasong, 2021). Education has changed dramatically with the massive increase in online learning, where classes are delivered remotely on digital platforms. A review of existing literature indicates that school closures due to COVID-19 affected 1,198,530,172 students in 186 countries (UNESCO, 2020). According to the 2nd International Association of Universities (IAU), a global survey report, higher education institutions have shown resilience; however, there are significant financial concerns, lowered research activities, overtime working staff, and a decline in student numbers (Jensen et al., 2022). Universities have had to develop strategies for rapid digitalization and elaborate plans for improving their employees' digital literacy and skills to meet the needs of global digitalization (Webb et al., 2021) (Fig. 2).

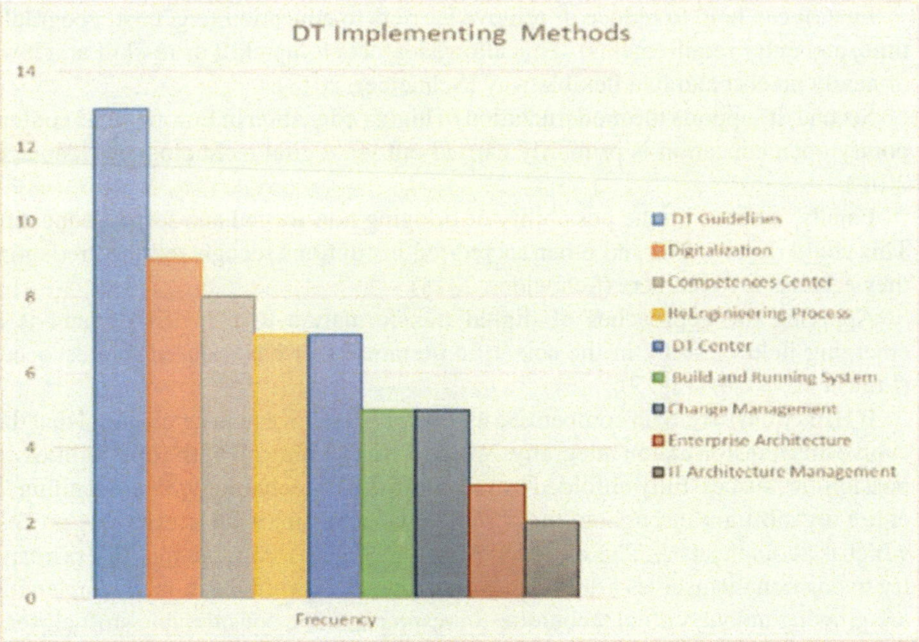

Fig. 2 Implementing methods of DT at a HEI. *Source* https://www.researchgate.net/figure/Implementing-methods-of-DT-at-a-HEI_fig9_342052514

Digitization can expand learning spaces and improve access to knowledge and education as a part of social welfare. Open Education and Open Educational Resources are critical factors in this process, among other factors (Ifenthaler et al., 2021).

Some researchers argue that the digitalization of education is at a very early stage of its development—despite the active use of digital tools by faculty to innovate and differentiate ways of teaching, student learning method has not changed significantly (Thoring et al., 2017). Technology has the potential to link university competencies in teaching and administration. Higher education institutions operate in an increasingly competitive environment and must look for efficient processes (Adler & Harzing, 2017).

Opening up education is an essential item on the European policy agenda for many reasons (Santos & Punie, EU Science Hub, 2022). The primary reason is to reduce barriers like costs, geographical location, time, enrollment requirements, etc. Another reason is supporting the modernization of higher education institutions in terms of using digital technologies. Finally, it allows formal and non-formal education (Santos & Punie, EU Science Hub, 2022). In this regard, the EU has elaborated the Digital Education Action Plan 2021–2027, which is a policy initiative defining the shared vision of high-quality, inclusive, and accessible digital education in Europe, and aims to support the adaptation of the education and training systems of Member States to the digital age (EU, 2020).

First, it can help to reduce or remove barriers to education (e.g. cost, geography, time, and entry requirements). This allows learners to up-skill or re-skill at a lower or nearly no cost and in a flexible way (Schneider, 2018).

Second, it supports the modernization of higher education in Europe since contemporary open education is primarily carried out via digital technologies (Schneider, 2018).

Finally, it opens up the possibility of bridging non-formal and formal education. This could occur if HE and other accredited institutions recognized the credentials they each issue to learners (Schneider, 2018).

Applying the approaches of digital transformation to the HEI domain is an emerging field of study in the scientific literature that has aroused interest recent (Lina et al., 2020) (Fig. 3).

If HEIs want to remain competitive and stay on the stage, it is far essential that they evolve this transformation integrally. Moreover, exploiting all of the possibilities and possibilities successfully unfolded by means of virtual technology, and redefining the entire organization throughout the complete value chain, is an irreversible process, which is a complex task. This assignment is more urgent for institutions that primarily try to position themselves firmly in a global market. Nevertheless, many universities are growing unique virtual techniques in response to the considerable shift closer to new technology usage. However, they need more imaginative, prescient capability and dedication to enacting them effectively. In this sense, it is far crucial to have an unlimited imagination and prescient of the entire Digital Transformation (DT) in HEIs, so one can acquire a top-level view of the modern-day nation of the artwork in

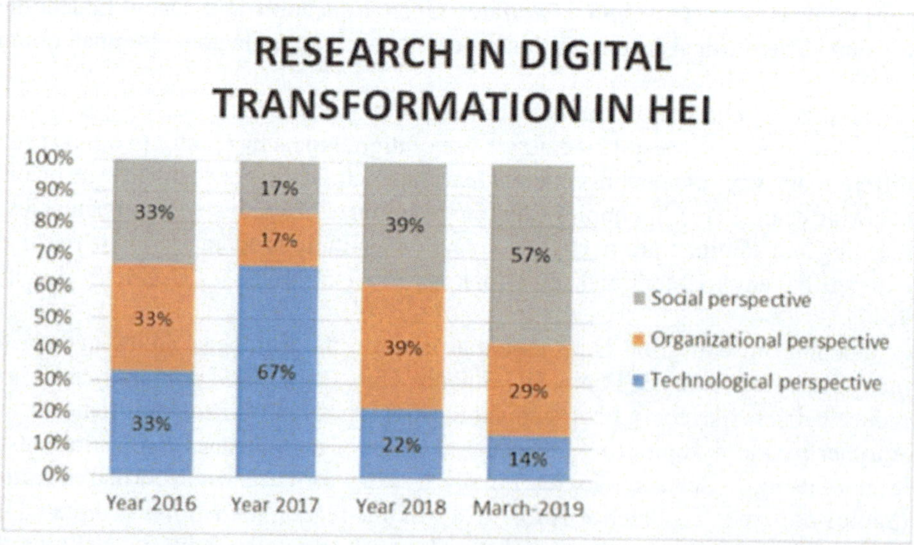

Fig. 3 Research in digital transformation in HEIs. *Source* https://www.researchgate.net/figure/Research-in-digital-transformation-in-HEIs_fig2_342052514

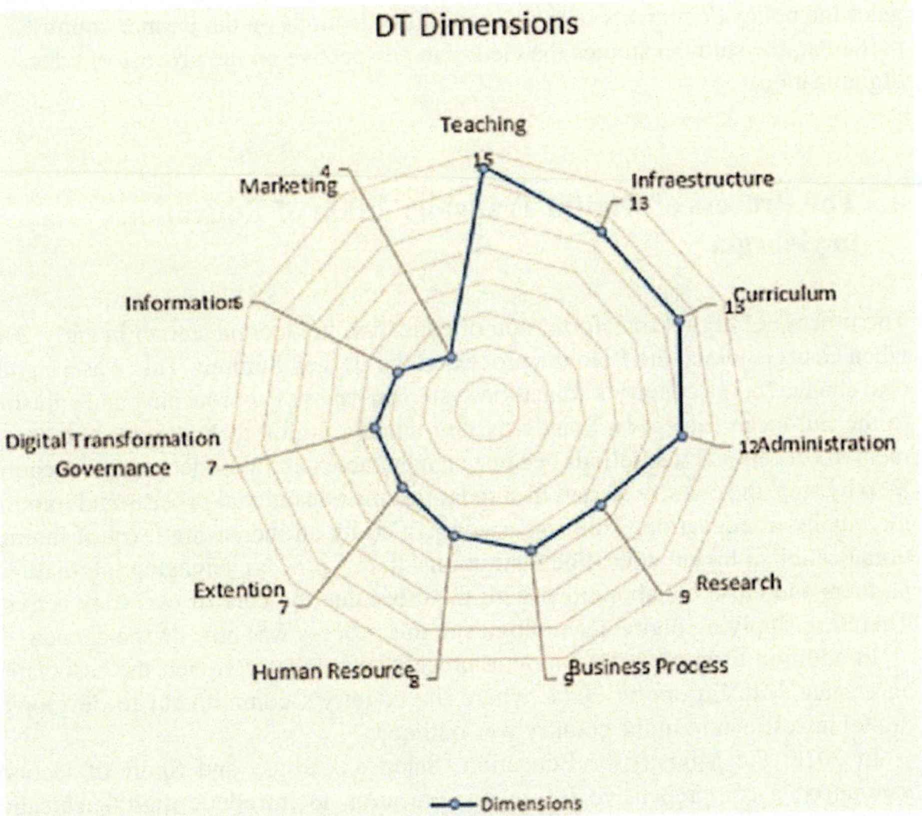

Fig. 4 Radar of the dimensions of the DT in HEIs. *Source* https://www.researchgate.net/figure/Radar-of-the-dimensions-of-the-DT-in-HEIs_fig3_342052514

DT in HEIs, and decide its exceptional traits as dimensions, actors and implementations, that have taken area withinside the system of virtual transformation inside HEIs (Fig. 4).

3 Research Methods

The study employed a qualitative research method. In particular content analysis and case study was used. Theoretical and empirical research methods in the framework of comparative analysis and interpretation of research findings were applied. The research is focused on searching for an innovative approach in the process of digitalizing higher education institutions. On one side, the study presents an extensive literature review on this topical issue and highlights the challenges and trends of HEI's digitalization from a global perspective. On the other side , the paper investigates the policy documents of the EU and its reflections on the partner countries; in particular, the study examines the Georgian perspective on the process of education digitalization.

4 The Process of Digital Transformation of Education in Georgia

The process of digital transformation of education in Georgia started in early 2005 when Georgia joined the Bologna process at the Bergen Summit. This was a significant change for the country's education system in terms of approaching and adjusting to the European Education Standards. Introducing digital technologies and equipment to educational institutions became an inevitable part of modernizing education. Step by step, the country started to standardize the educational process and improve the quality of education. This was accompanied by an increasing level of internationalization of higher education institutions. In this process, engaging international partners and close collaborations with them became the core of everyday activity. Therefore, applying digital technologies in this process was now on the agenda.

In addition to joining the Bologna process, the country signed the association agreement with Europe in 2014, where the country's commitment to developing digital infrastructure in the country was outlined.

In 2018, the Ministry of Education, Science, Culture and Sport of Georgia announced a comprehensive reform of education to introduce digital education to all public schools in the country. The Ministry of Education worked closely with Microsoft and the government's Education Management Information System, EMIS, to implement Microsoft 365 and digitally overhaul the education environment (Microsoft, 2020). A series of training and workshops were conducted through a network of EMIS specialists and Microsoft engineers to facilitate teachers' understanding. Localizing its user interface in Microsoft Teams and all online courses in Georgian and making them available to everyone increased its daily active users from 750 to nearly 300,000 in 3 months (MES.GOV.GE, Ministry of Education, Science, Culture, and Sport of Georgia, 2020) (Fig. 5).

According to the Ministry of Education interview, in the twenty-first century, digital technologies have particular importance in human activity. In order for students to receive a well-rounded education and at the same time be competitive upon graduation, they need access to electronic resources. Interactive online materials, online courses, collaborative study groups, digital libraries, and game-based lessons are all essential components of the modern learning experience (MES.GOV.GE, Georgian Ministry of Education Embraces the Future, Making Digital Laerning a Reality, 2020).

Alongside equipping educational institutions with modern information technologies, the ministry of education in Georgia stated that the reform should transform the philosophy behind how subjects are taught. It should always foster curiosity,

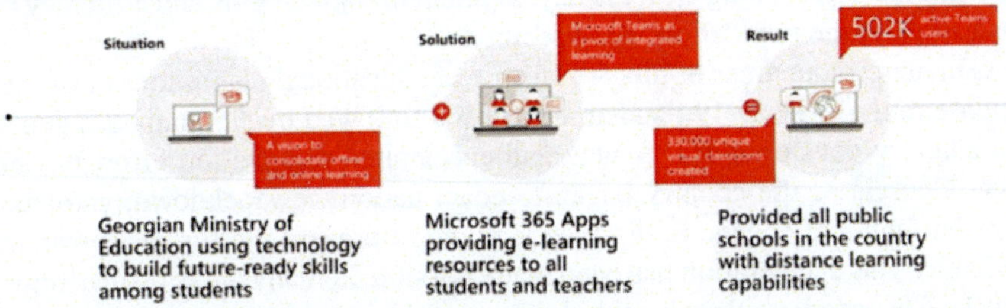

Fig. 5 Radar of the dimensions of the DT in HEIs. *Source* https://www.researchgate.net/figure/Radar-of-the-dimensions-of-the-DT-in-HEIs_fig3_342052514

and this is where the technologies can contribute largely. To this end, several solutions are integrated into Microsoft 365 apps, including libraries with digital learning content and chatbots that support Teams users and answer topic-specific questions. In addition, a Minecraft Education Edition pilot program was launched in 150 schools to develop game-based lessons and encourage student creativity, collaboration, and engagement (Microsoft, 2020).

Digitalization of Education remains among the European Commission's core mission priorities. In 2018, the European Commission launched the "Communication from the commission to the European Parliament, the council, the European economic and social Committee, and the committee of the regions" On the Digital Education Action Plan (EU, 2020), which is a detailed plan for the countries to foster the process of digitalization in Education. Besides the strategic plan, this document describes the challenges and opportunities of digital transformation for education. It highlights the importance of cooperating countries' contribution to the process (EuropeanCommission, Communication from the commission to the european parliament, the council, the european economic and social committee and the committee of the regions, 2018).

Communication from the commission to the European parliament, the council, the European economic and social committee, and the committee of the regions (EU, 2020).

The Digital Education Action Plan (2021–2027) aims to set a shared vision for quality, inclusive, and accessible digital education in Europe and to help Member States adapt their education and training systems to the digital age through updated European Union (EU) policy initiatives. The Action Plan, adopted on September 30, 2020, calls for action at the European level in the field of digital education to address the challenges and opportunities of the COVID-19 pandemic and to identify opportunities for teaching and training (teachers, students). It seeks to strengthen cooperation between policymakers, academia, national, EU, and international researchers (European Commission, Digital Education Action Plan (2021–2027), 2020).

In this regard, according to the 2021–2027 agenda of the association agreement between the European Union and Georgia, the importance of stimulating the digital economy and innovation in the country, promoting the development of e-governance and digital services, along with the development of digital skills and e-literacy of the broad strata of the population, was specified.

As in many other areas of life, the closure of educational institutions in Georgia in response to the COVID-19 pandemic has been followed by simultaneous and often contradictory developments. A new and accelerated digitization effort has begun across Georgia as the country began to enact nationwide lockdown, and students were sent home to engage in distance learning to prevent the further spread of the pandemic. This acceleration has been made possible in many areas by platforms and services developed by global technology companies. At the same time, this process promoted cooperation between the public, private sector, and educational institutions.

Consequently, the reforms in the Georgian educational sector were actively launched, and the need for the digital transformation of educational institutions, including higher education institutions, was on the agenda.

The COVID-19 pandemic has further accelerated the existing trend toward online and hybrid learning. It uncovered new and innovative ways for students and educators to organize teaching and learning activities and interact online in a more personal and flexible way. In parallel, adopting digital technologies for education has revealed challenges and inequalities between those who have access to digital technologies and those who do not (including those from disadvantaged backgrounds) (EU, 2020). It also raised difficulties related to the digital competencies of education and training institutions, teacher education, and overall levels of digital skills and competencies.

Information technology has become an essential tool for the higher education system in the conditions of COVID-19. In March 2020, 2,000 Georgian schools closed in response to the pandemic, and 600,000 students transitioned to online learning (Burduli, 2021). Many schools were closed for the entire academic year. While the impact of COVID-19 on business, politics, and human rights is actively debated, the impact on the education system is often overlooked; and this is happening even though, according to Georgians, education suffers the most (after the economy) of all areas of Georgian life (Burduli, 2021). This process has deepened the inequalities among the different members of society. The particular difficulties in access to education are faced by the population of rural areas and disadvantaged families. Access to the non-stop Internet still remains an issue in Georgia's regions.

The primary challenge for the government and the Ministry of Education, Science, Culture and Sport of Georgia was that no legal frameworks and regulations were dealing with and recognizing online education. Changing the teaching format worldwide has given the government and the ministry no chance to start the gradual transition to this format. Still, it was inevitably essential to act instantly—permitting HEIs to operate in a distance mode (Lekishvili & Kikutadze, 2022).

The activities of higher education institutions in Georgia and general can be conventionally considered in two main directions: management of the study process and administrative issues.

Accordingly, taking into account the current reality, higher education institutions had an inevitable need to digitize the mentioned processes, which clearly highlighted the need for the existence of normative regulations necessary for the functioning of the distance learning model, namely:

- Elaborating on the necessary regulations to ensure the implementation of distance learning at the country level was on the agenda. First of all, it was necessary to make appropriate changes to the Law of Georgia "On Higher Education," where in fact, the distance learning model was not regulated before this situation;
- The problem of providing the country with the Internet appeared because continuous Internet is still not available in some regions of the country;
- The need to develop appropriate guides and video instructions was identified in higher educational institutions in Georgia;
- The need for appropriate electronic portals for distance learning for higher education institutions was highlighted;
- The issue of providing computer equipment and Internet for students of HEIs was on the agenda;
- Higher education institutions needed online services for students; therefore, the issues of digitalization of university services were activated, including the part of student services;
- It became necessary to digitize university library resources and provide them electronically to students;

The process of digital transformation took the country to face many challenges. It should be noted that as of 2018, according to the data of the International Telecommunications Union (ITU), among the countries of the Eastern Partnership (Moldova 76%, Belarus 79%, Turkey 71%, Armenia 65%, Azerbaijan 80%, Ukraine 60%), Georgia was in one of the last places in terms of access to the Internet. by 63% (ITU, 2018).

In the process of transition to the distance education model of higher education institutions, providing the students and, in some cases, the academic staff with the necessary technical means and Internet resources turned out to be particularly problematic.

In the first case, most private universities provided their students with laptops for temporary use; in the second case, they offered free internet packages.

Following the financing of the mentioned measures, the inclusion of students in the online learning process has become relatively more manageable; however, providing students with continuous Internet access in the regions of the country remains a big problem, as it is known that the process of internalization in the country has not yet been completed and certain settlements are not accessible with access to the Internet.

5 Conclusion

Higher Education Institutions are more than ever affected by digital technologies in the study process and administrative activities. For the efficient functioning of the universities and, in many cases, to "survive," it becomes mandatory to apply digital technologies, not only at physical and infrastructural levels (by equipping buildings) but also to adjust the teaching and working methods to this new reality. One of the most challenging aspects of the digital transformation of education in Georgia is the readiness of all stakeholders, including students, academics, and the administration. Increasing awareness of the university's digital transformation process and developing their digital skills is the key to success in this process. As long as digitalization is not a one-time action but a constant process of development, it requires corresponding support for the stakeholders in terms of training and coaching to ensure effective implementation and a positive impact on quality education.

References

Adler, N. J., & Harzing, A.-W. (2017). When knowledge wins: Transcending the sense and nonsense of academic rankings. *Academy of Management Learning and Education, 8*(1), 72–95.

Burduli, T. (2021, April 29). *The digital divide: How the pandemic has exposed inequalities in the georgian education system.* Retrieved from Civil Georgia. https://civil.ge/archives/416960

Chasanidou, D., Gasparini, A., & Lee, E. (2014). Design thinking methods and tools for innovation in multidisciplinary teams (pp. 27–30).

EU. (2020). *Digital education action plan.* Retrieved from European Education Area. https://education.ec.europa.eu/focus-topics/digital-education/action-plan

EuropeanCommission. (2018). *Communication from the commission to the european parliament, the council, the european economic and social committee and the committee of the regions.* European Commission.

European Commission. (2020). *Digital education action plan (2021–2027).* European Commission.

Fűzi, B., Gering, Z., & Szendrei-Pál, E. (2022). Changing expectations related to digitalisation and socialisation in higher education. Horizon scanning of pre-and post-COVID-19 discourses. *Educational Review*, 484–516.

Hou, A. Y., Lu, I.-J.G., & Hill, C. (2022). What has been the impact of COVID-19 on driving digitalization, innovation and crisis management of higher education and quality assurance?—A Taiwan case study in alignment with the INQAAHE virtual review. *Nature Public Health Emergency Collection, 35*(3), 568–590.

Ifenthaler, D., Hofhues, S., Egloffstein, M., & Helbig, C. (2021). *Digital transformation of learning organizations.* Springer.

ITU. (2018). *ITU, Committed to connecting the world.* Retrieved from ITU, Committed to connecting the world. https://www.itu.int/en/Pages/default.aspx

Jensen, T., Marinoni, G., & Land, H. v. (2022). *Higher Education One Year into the COVID-19 Pandemic; Second IAU Global Survey Report.* International Association of Universities .

Kurnaz, S. Ç., & Nafoussi, G. (2022). Digitalization in higher education institutions: The case of Selcuk University. *Journal of Economics and Social Research*, 99–119.

Lekishvili, T., & Kikutadze, V. (2022). *Decision-making process transformation in post-COVID19 world in higher education institutions.* Springer Publishing.

Lina, M., Castro, B., Johnny, A., & Tamayo, A. (2020). Digital transformation in higher education institutions: A systematic literature review. *Sensors.*

Machekhina, O. N. (2017). Digitalization of education as a trend of its modernization and reforming. *Education, 38*(40), 26.

Maican, A., & Cocorada, E. (2021). Online foreign language learning in higher education and its correlates during the COVID-19 pandemic. *Sustainability, 13*(2), 781.

McCusker, C., Baskerville, R., & Cameron, J. (2018). *The 2018 university—Making the right choices, making it happen.* PwC.

MES.GOV.GE. (2020a). *Georgian ministry of education embraces the future, making digital learning a reality.* mes.gov.ge.

MES.GOV.GE. (2020b, August 21). *Ministry of Education, Science, Culture, and Sport of Georgia.* Retrieved from MES.GOV.GE. https://customers.microsoft.com/en-us/story/836788-ministry-emis-national-government-azure-en-georgia

Microsoft. (2020). *Georgian Ministry of Education embraces the future, making digital learning a reality.* Microsoft.

Nkengasong, J. N. (2021). COVID-19: Unprecedented but expected. *Nature Medicine, 27*(3), 364.

Rehman, I., Sobnath, D., Nasralla, M. M., Winnett, M., Anwar, A., Asif, W., & Sherazi, H. (2021). Features of mobile apps for people with autism in a post COVID-19 scenario: Current status and recommendations for apps using AI. *Diagnostics, 11*(10), 1923.

Ronzhina, N., Kondyurina, I., Voronina, A., Igishev, K., & Loginova., N. (2021). Digitalization of modern education: Problems. *International Journal of Emerging Technologies in Learning, 16*(4), 122–135.

Santos, A. I. (2022, February 2). *EU Science Hub.* https://joint-research-centre.ec.europa.eu/what-open-education_en

Santos, A. I., & Punie, Y. (2022, February 2). *EU Science Hub.* Retrieved from European Commission. https://joint-research-centre.ec.europa.eu/what-open-education_en#:~:text=Opening%20up%20education%20is%20an,and%20in%20a%20flexible%20way

Schneider, J. (2018). *Fostering digitization and industry 4.0 in vocational education—The fifteen core results of the project DigI-VET.* European Commission.

Sebastian, I., Moloney, K., & Ross, J. (2017). How big old companies navigate digital transformation. *MIS Quarterly Executive, 16*(3), 197–213.

Stuart, K. (2014, October 31). *Guardian.* Retrieved from theguardian.com. https://www.theguardian.com/technology/2014/jun/02/parents-guide-video-games-playstation-xbox-wii-apps-children

Sukhomlin, V., & Zubareva., E. (2020). Analytical review of the current curriculum standards in information technologies. In *Modern Information Technology and IT Education* (pp. 3–41).

Thoring, A., Rudolph, D., & Vogl, R. (2017). Digitalization of higher education from a student's point of view. In: *EUNIS 2017—Shaping the digital future of universities* (pp. 279–288). EUNIS.

UNESCO. (2020). *UNESCO.* https://www.unesco.org/. https://www.unesco.org/en/covid-19/education-response/initiatives

Webb, A., McQuaid, R. W., & Webster, C. W. (2021). Moving learning online and the COVID-19 pandemic: A university response. *World Journal of Science.*

The Application of Chatbots in Private Universities—A Critical Analysis of Economic Potentials and Challenges

Tobias Oskar Lassmann

1 Introduction

Current figures from the German Federal Statistical Office point to significant growth in the number of students enrolled at private universities in Germany since 1995. According to these figures, only approximately 16,000 students were enrolled at private universities in the winter semester of 1995, while approximately 270,000 students were recorded at private universities in the winter semester of 2019 (Statistisches Bundesamt, 2019, p. 8). At the same time, the number of private universities in Germany at which the designated students are enrolled is also increasing. According to a study by the "Stifterverband für die Deutsche Wissenschaft" in cooperation with McKinsey & Company, Germany, there has been a wave of new private universities being founded, particularly between 2000 and 2010 (Frank et al., 2010, p. 10).

The reasons that favor private education from the perspective of students are many and varied. However, scant research on the benefits of private education has been done to date. Since private universities can operate under conditions that differ from those that apply to non-private universities, there is a gap in the research on private higher education (Sperlich, 2007, p. 20).

The challenges that face private universities from an economic perspective are as diverse as those that face state universities. Private universities receive little or no state funding, which is why dependence on tuition fees, third-party funding, and grants are central competitive factors. Changing socio-political conditions, the ongoing internationalization of the higher education landscape, increased student expectations, and intensified competition with state universities pose further challenges for private universities. In this context, private higher education institutions run the risk of losing competitive advantages—especially with regard to internationalization and

T. O. Lassmann (✉)
E-Commerce Institut, Cologne, Germany
e-mail: tobias.oskar.lassmann@gmail.com

R. C. Geibel and S. Machavariani (eds.), *Chances and Challenges of Digital Management*, Springer Proceedings in Business and Economics,
https://doi.org/10.1007/978-3-031-45601-5_22

service orientation—due to the deregulation of the state higher education system, study reform, and new competitive financing formats (Frank et al., 2010, p. 7 f.).

Ongoing digitalization is also having an increasing impact on the German higher education landscape. In this context, a study on the German innovation system reveals that the requirements in terms of visions, strategies, and implementation concepts are growing in the direction of "digital universities". However, the respective strategic and organizational anchors in the overall concept of the universities differ considerably, and the degrees of implementation sought or already achieved in different areas also diverge significantly (Gilch et al., 2019, p. 10). At the same time, digitalization has already proved its disruptive potential in some sectors of the economy in recent decades. Highly profitable tech companies of considerable size grew out of "garage startups" within a few years, while listed corporations sank into insignificance because the potential of digitalization was underestimated, misjudged, or ignored. Although the underlying conditions of the markets in which educational institutions such as private universities operate are different, they also must compete with increasing numbers of market participants for resources and students. It can therefore also be assumed that those universities that manage to successfully implement digital innovations will create competitive advantages over their rivals.

2 Theoretical Background

The use of new digital technologies offers more possibilities in communication and information processing with customers, as well as internal cost reduction and differentiation characteristics in the marketplace. Communicating with customers via live chat interfaces has become an increasingly popular means of providing customers with real-time service. Chatbots demonstrate great potential in human-to-computer communication and have enjoyed increasing interest over the past decade with contributions from international companies such as IBM, Google, Android, and Apple (Abdul-Kader, 2015, p. 72).

Chatbots are computer programs that process natural language input from a user and generate suitable responses. These responses are based on predetermined scripts in combination with machine and deep learning. The technology behind chatbots is similar to that used in language-based assistants. All language-based systems have the added complexity of converting speech to text that any computer application can work with. Processing texts from a chatbot and a language-based system is done in a similar way (Khan & Das, 2018, p. 2).

This technology enables new user touch points, improve convenience, reduce service, sales, and support costs, and permit both one-to-one marketing and new data collection. Customers can obtain information and answers anywhere and at any time by using chatbots. For companies, the use of chatbots offers potential in terms of process optimization, expansion of customer acquisition, and cost reduction. On the one hand, target groups are offered a digital contact point that can deal with several requests simultaneously at any time and place. On the other hand, service and support solutions are made possible, which represent potential cost savings in terms of personnel as well as information and communication processing. In particular, the automation of recurring processes can be promoted through the correct use of chatbots.

However, the use of chatbots also poses several challenges. In this context, it is important to keep in mind that employees and users often approach digitalization projects with a certain amount of skepticism. Moreover, in practice, it is hardly possible to provide an accurate assessment of the results of digitalization projects or to consider them in isolation, as they are typically carried out in a combination of several actions and are dependent on other measures. Furthermore, data protection is also a challenge that significantly influences the success or failure of a chatbot project.

This paper, therefore, aims to investigate which economic potentials and challenges for private universities must be considered when implementing chatbots. The aim is to illustrate the extent to which chatbots could influence the value creation process of private universities in such a way that processes are optimized and communication with the target group improved. The central research question of the thesis is therefore: How can the use of chatbots offer private universities a competitive advantage?

3 Research Method

To answer the research question, the paper provides a theoretical background on the topics relevant to this thesis on the basis of scientific literature. In this context, chatbots and private universities, as central objects of investigation of this thesis, are put into context, delimited, and defined. For the purposes of this paper, the author programmed a chatbot prototype for private universities in order to investigate the research question as close to practice as possible. This was done with the assistance of the IBM Watson Assistant, a conversational Artificial Intelligence platform provided by IBM (2021, n.p.). Therefore, the functionality of the IBM Watson Assistant is also explained in more detail.

For this purpose, models and concepts based on economic literature are used to enable a systematic analysis. The chatbot prototype is utilized to present identified application examples. In addition, the challenges that private universities have to overcome when implementing chatbots are also listed. Taking into account the identified potentials and challenges, the paper presents an economic evaluation of the use of chatbots at private universities on two levels. On the one hand, the strategic level is considered in an evaluation of the use of chatbots that takes the competitive strategies of cost leadership and differentiation into account. Furthermore, on an operational level, there is an evaluation of the extent to which chatbots could provide an increase in efficiency (from an internal perspective) as well as additional customer value (from an external perspective) for the three areas of private universities under consideration.

A total of seven experts were interviewed with the assistance of an interview guide. Four of the experts interviewed have practical skills and experience with chatbots and were therefore asked specific questions about the general technological and business aspects of chatbots. In addition, three employees of the Fresenius University of Applied Sciences were interviewed, each of whom has special professional experience in the three thematic application areas of chatbots at private universities. The interview guide, which was created specifically for the qualitative study, was accordingly divided into questions directed at the chatbot experts and questions specifically for the experts in the application areas of private universities.

4 Case Study

Based on the theoretical background, the case study examines the potentials that the use of a chatbot presents for private universities in Germany. To illustrate this, Porter's model for examining competitive advantages along the value chain of organizations will be adopted as a basis. The three primary value creation activities "Marketing", "Applicant Management" and "Service" are identified as those activities that indicate a significant economic potential for the use of chatbots at private universities. For each of the three mentioned application areas, potentials are identified and illustrated using the chatbot prototype as an example. In addition, a model is derived and presented that serves as a proposal for a framework for the implementation and development of a chatbot project at private universities. The challenges that should be considered when using chatbots at private universities are also explained.

5 Conclusion

While digitalization is steadily gaining ground in many areas of society and the economy, the education sector should keep pace with changes in this field or even anticipate them. In Germany, private universities are under increasing competitive pressure to adopt innovative approaches in order to set themselves apart from the state universities that dominate the market. The aim is to offer the target group added value that distinguishes private universities from the others.

While private universities have been able to create competitive advantages in the past, particularly through intensive support for prospective and current students, the potential of digitalization should also be considered. In this context, chatbots provide the potential to combine the aspects of service and digitalization that are relevant for private universities. An AI-supported digital communication medium could create added value that goes beyond simple service optimization. At this point, in the author's opinion, the image enhancement that private universities could create through the use of innovative technologies should not be underestimated either. However, these effects are very difficult to grasp or measure. It can be assumed that the labor market, which increasingly demands skills relating to digitalization-relevant topics, has a major influence on the target group of private universities. When choosing what to study, potential students embarking on higher education generally set their priorities with a focus on the advantages they expect to gain in the labor market as a result. In this context, the author believes it would be unsurprising if the innovative digital presence of a private university were to positively influence the decision-making of the target group.

The active involvement of students would enable private universities to leverage three potentials in particular. First, it could be advertised that students could actively learn skills that are in great demand in the job market by working on practice-relevant projects with innovative technologies as part of their course of study. Second, the continuous development of the chatbot could be carried out at least partially by students at a lower cost than by external parties. In addition, this would imply a customer centricity, since the student—as a user of the chatbot—would actively participate in its development, and thus their requirements and desires would be included.

However, it is recommended that private universities should develop an initial prototype as professionally as possible and with the involvement of experts. In this context, it will be crucial to integrate such a prototype into the existing IT infrastructure as far as possible. The initial investment should ensure that a solid technical basis is created that imposes as few limitations as possible on future ideas. In the author's opinion, it will be problematic in the context of such a digitalization project to bundle all influencing energies in the same direction. It can be assumed that employees in particular—whose daily work would potentially be strongly influenced or even replaced by a chatbot—will initially be very critical of the project. Prospective applicants and students could also turn against the chatbot after only a few negative experiences. If a chatbot repeatedly presents wrong, insufficient, or irrelevant answers to a prospective applicant or student, it is not unlikely that this user will stop using the chatbot in the future.

The issue of data privacy should also be mentioned as an important challenge. It should be noted that young people, in particular, are becoming increasingly skeptical about algorithms that process a large amount of personal data. However, the capabilities of the machine and deep learning models integrated and linked in chatbots are based on the quantity and quality of the data collected. On the one hand, this also results in benefits for users. For example, the captured data allow the chatbot to train its algorithms on its own, optimizing future interactions for users, or enable university Marketing to capture valuable data that is helpful in communicating with target groups. However, negative examples from the past have made the topic of data protection extremely sensitive. It is important to ensure that data are handled responsibly from the very outset.

Overall, if the challenges referred to above are successfully overcome, the use of chatbots can create digital added value that promises competitive advantages, especially for those universities that identify potential fields of application early on—as "first-movers". Human–computer interaction and communication have already made impressive progress, and chatbots offer economically relevant potential that should also be taken into account by private universities.

References

Abdul-Kader, S. A. (2015) Survey on chatbot design techniques in speech conversation systems. *International Journal of Advanced Computer Science and Applications, 6*(7), 72–80. Essex Colchester.

Frank, A., Hieronimus, S., Killius, N., & Meyer-Guckel, V. (2010). *Rolle und Zukunft privater Hochschulen in Deutschland*. Stifterverband für die Deutsche Wissenschaft.

Gilch, H., Beise, A.S., Krempkow, R., Müller, M., Stratmann, F. & Wannemacher, K. (2019) *Digitalisierung der Hochschulen: Ergebnisse einer Schwerpunktstudie für die Expertenkommission Forschung und Innovation*. Expertenkommission Forschung und Innovation (EFI), Berlin.

IBM. (2021). *Watson Assistant*. IBM Cloud. Retrieved November 14, 2020, from https://www.ibm.com/cloud/watson-assistant

Khan, R. & Das, A. (2018). *Build better chatbots—A complete guide to getting started with chatbots*. Bangalore.

Sperlich, A. (2007). *Theorie und Praxis erfolgreichen Managements privater Hochschulen in Deutschland*. Fakultät für Betriebswirtschaftslehre der Universität Mannheim.

Statistisches Bundesamt. (2019). *Bildung und Kultur. Private Hochschulen*.

Statistisches Bundesamt—Destatis. (2019). Retrieved November 24, 2020, from https://www.destatis.de/DE/Themen/Gesellschaft-Umwelt/Bildung-Forschung-Kultur/Hochschulen/Publikationen/Downloads-Hochschulen/private-hochschulen-5213105197004.pdf?__blob=publicationFile